Iron Man vs. Captain America
and Philosophy

Popular Culture and Philosophy® Series Editor: George A. Reisch

For full details of all Popular Culture and Philosophy® books, visit www.opencourtbooks.com.

Popular Culture and Philosophy®

Iron Man vs. Captain America and Philosophy

Give Me Liberty or Keep Me Safe

Edited by
NICOLAS MICHAUD AND
JESSICA WATKINS

OPEN COURT
Chicago

Volume 115 in the series, Popular Culture and Philosophy ®, edited by George A. Reisch

To find out more about Open Court books, visit our website at www.opencourtbooks.com.

Open Court Publishing Company is a division of Carus Publishing Company, dba Cricket Media.

Printed and bound in the United States of America.

Iron Man vs. Captain America and Philosophy: Give Me Liberty or Keep Me Safe

This book has not been prepared, authorized, or endorsed by the creators or producers of the Iron Man or Captain America stories.

ISBN: 978-0-8126-9976-0

Library of Congress Control Number: 2018943330

This book is also available as an e-book (978-0-8126-9982-1).

For Family, everywhere.

We fight, probably too much.
But where there's love, there's always
a way to come back together.

Contents

A House Divided . . .

Marvel's *Civil War* was a glorious moment. Even before the movie, the epic clash of so many heroes was huge. What was really important, though, wasn't the awesomeness of seeing the good guys try to beat each other silly, it was seeing the matchup of two titans: Captain America and Iron Man. And we were all motivated to read on, not just because we wanted to know which one would kick the most ass, but because we wanted to know who was *right*! And that's what this book is all about . . .

The book you have in your hands is a little unusual. Often, philosophy and popular culture books explore many aspects of a pop culture phenomenon. This book focuses on one specific question, "Who is better?" You might think that there isn't much to say on this issue, and we're sure you have your own opinion already, but comparing Captain America and Iron Man brings out a lot of questions and problems we don't normally think about.

The reason why these two men in *philosophical* competition with each other is so important and terrifying isn't just because they are the good guys, but because they are both *our* good guys. Let's be honest, Iron man isn't exactly a Communist superhero, and Captain America is well *Captain America*.

Tony Stark is the poster boy for capitalism. In fact, Stan Lee created him specifically to see if he could make people love a ragingly selfish capitalist. Captain America was created originally as a kind of propaganda to support our war effort . . . his first issue shows him punching Hitler! BOTH represent key aspects of the United States: Our economic, social philosophy "competition makes things better" and the ideas of patriotism, liberty, and *just doing the right thing.*

When these heroes fight, they're revealing something we know at the core of our being is both a tremendous strength and a tremendous danger in our society . . . *We are at intellectual war with ourselves!* And we don't just mean liberals and conservatives, religious and non-religious, Ford and Chevy. We mean each of us living here in the States embodies a fight between these two men and their philosophies . . . the unsolvable problem of safety vs. freedom.

So, let's get to it . . .

Ding! Ding!

I

Iron Man Wins

1
How to Fail at Almost Everything and Still Be a Hero

Daniel Malloy

One thing Steve Rogers and Tony Stark have in common is that they're both failures. Rogers failed repeatedly in his attempts to enlist to fight in World War II, before finally being recruited for the Super-Soldier program. He's had his fair share of failures since then, too.

But Captain America's failures pale in comparison to Iron Man's. While Captain America has failed to complete missions and occasionally let people down, he's never failed to be every inch the hero. Iron Man, on the other hand, has.

Even setting aside his borderline tyrannical behavior in Marvel's *Civil War*, Tony Stark has proven himself time and time again to be arrogant, self-centered, and narcissistic to the point of sociopathy. He's killed in cold-blood and fallen into alcoholism. Even his origin is a story of selfishness rather than sacrifice. Steve Rogers became Captain America to save his country; Tony Stark became Iron Man to save himself.

Ultimately, though, it's Tony's failures that make him the better hero. Or, rather, it's the fact that Tony perseveres in spite of his failures that make him the better hero.

To Make a Hero

Let's begin at the beginning. In terms of character, Steve Rogers was born a hero. The scrappy kid from Brooklyn stood up to bullies, defended others, and gladly faced overwhelming odds long before he donned his cowl and hefted his shield.

Being a hero came naturally to Captain America—all he needed was a realistic shot at succeeding. Once he got it, thanks to the super-soldier serum and the vita-ray, he just kept doing what he'd done his whole life. He's just better equipped to do it now.

Tony Stark, on the other hand, wasn't born a hero. He was born a spoiled, selfish, arrogant playboy whose only concern for others consisted entirely in wondering what he could get from them. It took the trauma of being kidnapped and held hostage to make him even consider the fact that his actions have consequences. He didn't become a hero when he first donned the Iron Man armor. In some ways, Tony still isn't a hero. He's learning, and stumbling all along the way.

As any teacher can tell you, the fact that someone struggles to do something and puts a lot of effort into it doesn't necessarily mean they'll do it well. It doesn't automatically make the outcomes of their efforts good or better than someone who didn't struggle. We can see this when we compare Captain America and Iron Man. Cap doesn't struggle with what to do as a hero. He has his principles, and he stands by them. Doubt is rarely something he experiences. Doing the right thing comes as easily to him as breathing. In terms of their actions, there's no doubt that Captain America is the better of the two at being a hero.

But the fact that Iron Man struggles actually makes him the better hero. Tony struggles with broader issues—not just what a hero should do in this case, but also what it means to be a hero overall. His thinking on the latter shifts from time to time, which is why he stumbles in doing what a hero should. Should heroes strive only to keep people safe? Or should they also try to improve their lives? Which is more important: for people to be safe or for them to be free? Shellhead waivers on these questions, unlike the Sentinel of Liberty. That doesn't reveal any defect in Iron Man's heroics. Rather, it indicates an appreciation of the complexity of these issues.

The Value of Failure

In order to fail, you have to try. Tony Stark, as both an inventor and a businessman, tries things. Who is the bigger hero: the person who tries to keep things as they are, or the person who tries to make them better? I contend that it's the latter, regardless of how successful or unsuccessful the attempts are.

Captain America is, at the end of the day, a firefighter. He makes some efforts to prevent fires in the future, but fundamentally he's useless until something is actually on fire. Without a Red Skull or a Baron Zemo out there making trouble, Captain America has nothing to do and no real reason for being. Running around in his star-spangled suit, slinging his shield, and giving inspiring speeches serve no purpose in the absence of the kind of enemy you can punch.

Iron Man, on the other hand, is looking out for future fires and trying to prevent them from happening in the first place. The trouble for him is that global crises and supervillains' world domination plots are far less predictable than fires. So, Tony is trying to head-off problems before they start, but since those problems are unpredictable, he has to try a wide variety of different techniques.

Take, for instance, the *Armor Wars* storyline. Iron Man wanted to prevent his technology from being used in villainous ways, so he developed a new defense. He created a device that would shut down any Starktech he encountered. On the face of it, this is brilliant. Imagine going to war knowing you had a weapon that could render all of your opponent's weapons useless before the first battle even started. It's an unbeatable defense. Unfortunately, it's a defense that had unforeseen and unintended consequences—like the death of Titanium Man.

Or, in an even clearer example, Tony throws his weight behind the Super-Human Registration Act precisely because it's a pre-emptive strike against future deaths caused by superhuman battles. He knows the risks involved as well as Captain America does. He knows the principles Cap is fighting for in *Civil War*—if anything, he understands them better than Cap does. Cap has never really had a secret identity.

Tony, on the other hand, spent years peddling the fiction that Iron Man was his bodyguard. But Tony also appreciates the potential rewards of the Super Hero Registration Act (SHRA) more than Steve. He's seen the harm that can come to civilians as a result of unchecked super-power. Indeed, he's inflicted some himself. If everyone with superpowers were like Captain America, the SHRA wouldn't be necessary. But most people with superpowers are not like Captain America. Aside from the outright villains, there are far too many superhumans like Tony himself, who may have good intentions but often use their powers recklessly.

There's another reason Tony throws in with the forces behind the Super-Human Registration Act. Where Cap sees a fight based on principles that he can win—Cap never sees a fight he can't win, after all—Iron Man sees a fight that the superhero community is going to lose. The Super-Human Registration Act, or something like it, will pass at some point. The damage done by unchecked super-humans is simply too great and too frequent for governments to ignore it forever. By joining up and offering his support, Tony figures he can act as a balancing force, and help to preserve the principles Cap is fighting for. Captain America plans for victory, while Iron Man hopes for victory, but also prepares for defeat.

Ways to Fail

Optimists sometimes say that if you think about what you're going to do if you lose, you're setting yourself up for failure. The only way to succeed, they claim, is to make a plan and put it in action, assured that it will work. Never mind that your opponent may be doing the same thing, and that one of you will inevitably be proven wrong.

So, between Cap and Iron Man, these folks prefer Cap's approach to things. Which is not to say that Cap is like them. Cap's a strategist, after all. Any good strategist knows that things will go awry in your plan for victory. What matters is securing the victory, not preserving the plan. But while Cap prepares for the battle going differently than he thinks it will and for some parts of his plan to fall short, he always plans for success in the end. He doesn't prepare himself for utter failure. That makes his vision limited.

Tony, on the other hand, has learned through harsh experience that he has to prepare for utter failure. Set aside his career as a superhero—which is spotted with numerous false steps and bad judgments—and think for a second about his personal and professional lives. On the personal side, Tony's a recovering alcoholic who has relapsed in the past. Professionally, Tony Stark has been at the helm of numerous businesses with his name attached to them that have subsequently gone down in flames—sometimes literally. The list is truly impressive: Stark Industries, Stark International, Stark Enterprises, Stark-Fujikawa, Stark Solutions, Stark Enterprises (again), Stark Resilient, and Stark Industries (again). The history of these various companies is convoluted to say the least, but several of them represent failures on Tony's part.

Tony's personal and professional failures represent another sort of distinction in failure, one that our optimistic friends ignore. Some failures are internal, while others are external. What I mean is that some failures are things we bring on ourselves, such as Tony's alcoholism, while others are caused by circumstances beyond our control, such as Tony's loss of Stark International. The latter was caused primarily by Tony's rival Obadiah Stane who schemed to undermine Stark International and Tony's leadership in various ways that eventually led to the company being sold off. Our optimist friends would insist that all failures are of the internal variety, but that's simply false. No one—no matter how smart, brave, or confident—can control or account for every circumstance. Tony's living proof of that.

The Virtue of Giving Up

Iron Man is a better hero than Captain America because he knows when he's beaten. That seems odd, sure, but it's true. It isn't heroic or moral to continue fighting or striving in the face of overwhelming odds. It's just foolish. Take a famous and quite inspiring moment in Captain America's history: his battle with Thanos in *Infinity Gauntlet*. In the best circumstances, Cap would stand very little chance against the Mad Titan. In this case, Thanos has the added advantage of possessing all of the Infinity Gems, making him, for all intents and purposes, God. He could end Captain America with a thought. Nevertheless, the Sentinel of Liberty takes the fight to Thanos.

That seems admirable, but it really isn't. It's not as if Cap is going to make a difference in the final outcome through this fight. At best, he's ensuring that he dies a noble death. At worst, he's throwing away a valuable resource in any future battle with Thanos. In Cap's case, the virtue of perseverance is pushed too far and becomes the vice of stubbornness.

This is one of the secrets of heroics that make Iron Man better at it than Captain America. Shellhead knows how to accept failure and retreat from the battlefield when the battle is lost. You can see this in the number of times he's walked away from the superhero lifestyle altogether, or in his repeated decisions to turn over the operations of one of his businesses to someone else.

Aristotle (384–322 B.C.E.) was the first to outline this odd quirk of virtues: too little or too much is not enough. Where the Star-Spangled Avenger has too much perseverance, the Golden Avenger has just enough. Cap lives and dies by his principles; Iron Man is more flexible. He can yield for greater good, or give up on the battle to win the war. Or even give up the war. Sometimes, victory is not within your grasp, and nothing is served by continuing to fight. This thought is not inspirational, and it may even sound defeatist, but it's not. Realistically assessing your chances for success or failure is the first step to avoiding catastrophic failure—the kind you can't come back from.

The Perversity of Perseverance

Although I've been praising Iron Man as a hero, there's nothing inherently heroic in the pattern of behavior I've described so far. Looked at a little abstractly, I could just as easily be describing the actions of your run-of-the-mill, world-conquering supervillain. The Red Skull makes big plans, fails, goes away, and comes back for more with an entirely new plan. So what makes Iron Man's perseverance different from the Red Skull's, or Dr. Doom's, or Magneto's, or Apocalypse's, or any number of other would-be world conquerors? What makes Iron Man's perseverance virtuous, while theirs is vicious? Broadly speaking, there are two sorts of answers to this question. One says that there is no difference, the other says there is.

Those who maintain that Iron Man's ability to keep going in spite of his failures is the same as Dr. Doom's call perseverance an instrumental virtue. It's a good trait for a person to have, in that it helps them to achieve their goals. But it isn't inherently good, because it attaches with equal ease to good and bad goals. The firefighter who runs into a burning building to save a baby is brave, but by this thinking, so is the thief who runs into the same burning building to steal an expensive painting. The virtue in question—bravery, in these cases—has no built-in connection to good or bad goals. It's a tool in your toolkit, to be used when appropriate.

More traditional virtue ethicists, on the other hand, argue that while Iron Man's perseverance is virtuous, Dr. Doom's is vicious. Now, this gets tricky. The same pattern of behavior can't be virtuous in one case and vicious in another. There has to be some notable difference between the two patterns, beyond just their distinct goals. The difference has to be internal to the pattern of behavior itself. This is where the traditional virtue ethicists play their hand. They argue that the goals of the pattern of behavior are not external to the behaviors themselves. Goals are connected, after all, to our motivations, and we wouldn't act at all without those. So, in order to get at what makes Shellhead's perseverance different from Doom's, we have to look at what their motivations are and how they tie in to their patterns of behavior.

The Golden Avenger is motivated by a few things. Like all heroes, he wants to keep people safe. He'd also like to go a bit further and actually make their lives better. There are also some other, less noble motives mixed in there. Tony can be self-aggrandizing and a bit of a show-off, and those tendencies play into being a hero, too. For all the comparisons that are made between them, Tony Stark and Bruce Wayne are very different characters. Tony wouldn't be a hero at all if he couldn't wear his shiny suit and do it in broad daylight. Lurking around at night dressed up like a bat, beating up low-level criminals wouldn't feed his ego enough. There's also a somewhat darker, more fundamental drive to show others and himself that his life is actually worthwhile. But the things that really push Tony to don the Iron Man armor time and time again are the motives of a hero. He wants to help people.

The fact that he spent many years denying that he was Iron Man shows that his more selfish motives were at least held in check. Now, that would mean that Tony's perseverance is virtuous because it can't be separated from the heroic drive to help people. This is difficult to show, but you can see it in the times when Tony gives up. Often, the reason Tony abandons a project or course of action is because it's doing more harm than good or he could help people more by doing something else. When he's walked away from being Iron Man, for instance, it's usually because he made a massive error as Iron Man and didn't want to risk repeating it.

Victor von Doom is not so nobly motivated. To give the man credit, those who live under his rule are fairly well taken care of.

Latveria is prosperous and a technological powerhouse on the world stage. The citizens of Latveria have nothing in the way of freedoms or human rights, but they are protected and provided for. If Doom achieved his plans to conquer the world, presumably everyone else would be subject to the same sort of treatment. But helping people or improving their lives isn't what motivates Doom. He's driven solely to subject everyone and everything to his will. If Doom ever did manage to conquer Earth, he still wouldn't be content. He'd be pushed to conquer elsewhere—taking on the Kree or Shi'ar, perhaps. He takes every instance of someone or something not bowing before his will as a personal affront. Like Tony, Doom is a self-aggrandizer. Unlike Tony, Doom's ego isn't tempered by any sort of empathy or selflessness.

How this difference in motives makes Doom's perseverance different from Tony's is best displayed by how they both handle defeat. Tony genuinely examines what led to his failure, so he can improve and do better next time. Doom, on the other hand, looks for someone to blame. It's inconceivable to Doom that he could possibly fail, so he never really accepts that he has. Instead, he draws the conclusion that his plans didn't succeed because of someone else's incompetence or treachery.

So, Iron Man's tendency to get up, brush himself off, and come back for more after a failure is internally different from Doom's. Goals make a difference. Tony, for all his tendencies to be arrogant, self-centered, and vain, remains virtuous—or at least, that's what he's trying to be. He doesn't always succeed. He sometimes gives up too easily and sometimes doesn't give up when he should. *Civil War* saw instances of both. Arguably, he caved too quickly in agreeing to the Super-Human Registration Act. Likewise, he maybe held out too long when he realized where Captain America stood on the issue. It isn't always true, but many times someone like Cap can serve as an excellent moral exemplar—if he's on one side of an issue, and you're on the other, you're on the wrong side. But that's because heroism comes easily to Cap. It doesn't to Tony, which is all the more reason he deserves praise for his perseverance. Go, Iron Man, go!

Mistakes Make the Iron Man

Tony Stark is a massive failure, and a true hero. He isn't a failure just because he fails a lot. He's a failure because he approaches each new challenge in the full awareness that he may fail—he expects and plans for it. The fact that he often fails doesn't prevent him from trying. Indeed, it almost seems to drive him to try again, and try bigger next time. He wasn't great as a solo superhero, so he founded the Avengers. When the Avengers (and all the other superteams) failed to stop the accident that triggered the *Civil War*, he tried again and tried bigger: not just organizing Earth's mightiest heroes, but organizing them all. When he fails, he assesses why he failed, and tries to improve.

Sometimes improving means trying again. Sometimes it means giving up and walking away. The trick to persevering is knowing which is which. Old Shellhead hasn't quite mastered that one yet, but he's getting there.

2

Just Not the Hero Type (Not!)

TRIP MCCROSSIN

"You're a hero," Private Lorraine says to Steve Rogers, in *Captain America: The First Avenger*, having just read of his recent exploits in that day's edition of *The Stars and Stripes*. She holds up the headline, "400 HUNDRED PRISONERS LIBERATED." Rogers, technologically enhanced "super-soldier," had single-handedly freed the survivors of the 107th, caught behind enemy lines after the battle at Azzano, including his childhood friend James "Bucky" Barnes. Still, he resists the moniker. "That depends," he insists, flustered, "on the definition of it really."

He appears to be almost as uncomfortable with being called a hero as he was before the super-soldierly and ostensibly heroic rescue. "For the longest time I dreamed about coming overseas and being on the front lines, serving my country," he confesses to Peggy, assigned to taking the stage to sell war bonds, and "I finally get everything I wanted, and I'm wearing tights."

He eventually becomes one, however, unquestionably, by popular acclaim. "A hero to the world," we hear from a display narration in the Smithsonian, in *Winter Soldier*. As for his superheroism, while this would come as a surprise to Superman and Batman, who'd already come to us (June of 1938 and May of 1939 respectively) by the time Captain America did (March of 1941), and might seem a bit picky to Wonder Woman, who came to us only a few months later (October of 1941), Agent Phil Coulsen tells Rogers, in *The Avengers*, that he's "the first superhero."

Tony Stark, on the other hand, different as he is—glib boy wonder, say, to Rogers's earnest boy scout—shares with Rogers his aversion to the *hero* and *superhero* monikers. "My father helped defeat the Nazis: he worked on the Manhattan Project. A lot of people," he says early in *Iron Man*, "would call that being a hero." About himself, however, in the movie's concluding press conference, he betrays a reticence similar to Rogers's. To "insinuate that I'm a superhero," he insists, "would be outlandish and fantastic." "I'm just not the hero type," he continues, "clearly, with this laundry list of character defects, all the mistakes I've made, largely public." He can't be a superhero because he's not heroic, that is, and he's not heroic because he's flawed—and worse, publicly so. "The truth is," however, he goes on to confess, even while insisting that he's neither heroic, nor superheroic, "I *am* Iron Man."

Rogers and Stark share an ambivalence about their heroism. Even so, they're clearly different, which means that how they each define their underlying heroisms may differ as well. And the differences, whatever they may be, presumably become most pronounced in the context of their *Civil War* struggle.

What's a Superhero? What's a Hero?

What makes a superhero a superhero? We might reasonably begin, in attempting an answer, with a bit of parsing. They're *super heroes*, we might think. As such, then, they presumably share at least some of the attributes conventionally associated with their less super counterparts. Consider the following four.

- First, and most generally, heroes act to safeguard others. What would it mean to be a hero who doesn't, who stands by in the face of other people's jeopardy? Granted, the scope of their safeguarding may vary, as is clear from the history of superheroism. While their patriotic rhetoric, not to mention some of their apparel, is originally and persistently nationalistic, as Avengers, their mandate is broader. "The world owes the Avengers an unpayable debt," US Secretary of State Thaddeus Ross admits, in *Civil War*, for having "fought for us, protected us." Locally or globally, you're not much of a hero if you're not doing the basic safekeeping thing.

- Secondly, heroes safeguard those around them, near or far, in a manner that's *moral*. Granted, heroic actions may not be immediately recognized and appreciated as such, given the collateral damage involved, all the worse if cumulative. Iron Man's and Captain America's storylines, intertwined with the Avengers' storyline, are increasingly preoccupied with this worry—most recently in the movie adaptation of *Civil War*.

- Thirdly, heroes safeguard those around them, near or far, in manner not only moral in general, but more specifically *altruistic*. Heroes may benefit in this or that way by acting heroically, but the goal of their action is restricted to moral and beneficial safeguarding. In saving the survivors of the 107th, he was, Cap insists to Private Lorraine, "just doing what needed to be done." He would never have orchestrated the defeat at Azzano, that is, so that he could act the hero.

- Fourthly, heroes safeguard those around them, near or far, in a manner that's generally moral, specifically altruistic, and also *atypical*—in ways that the unheroic are unwilling, though not necessarily unable, to act. If a hero's actions weren't atypical, then heroism would simply be too widespread a phenomenon to be any longer very meaningful.

What makes heroes "super"? What makes them so is the conventional exaggeration of the first and the fourth attributes. On the one hand, heroes act to safeguard others not in a one-off or even occasional manner, but *systematically*. Rogers/Captain America has been doing his super boy scout thing, Stark/Iron Man his super boy genius thing, more or less continuously since 1941 and 1963 respectively. On the other hand, they act in a manner not just atypical, but *radically* so. "Was he wearing a parachute?" one of the STRIKE agents asks in *Winter Soldier*, as Captain America jumps from the plane. "No," Brock Rumlow answers, smiling incredulously, "No, he wasn't." Similarly, when Loki throws Stark out of a window, many stories up, in *The Avengers*, he's saved, with Jarvis's help of course, by summoning his suit.

While Captain America and Iron Man are similar in these respects, as presumptive heroes, there're two additional, less conventional attributes of heroism to consider.

(Super)Heroes as (Super)Samaritans

In addition to heroic acts consisting of the generally moral, specifically altruistic, atypical safekeeping of others (the acts of their "super" counterparts being systemic and radically atypical), don't we also want them to be *supererogatory*—performed, that is, without obligation? In other words, if a Good Samaritan is someone who acts to promote another's welfare, *on purpose*, but *not out of obligation*, then we can think of a hero in the same spirit, and not as just a *Good* Samaritan, but as an *Extraordinary* Samaritan. Heroism is a function not only of acts, but also of actors. So perhaps being supererogatory is our fifth attribute. To get at this idea, let's compare the following two cases.

On the one hand, we've Wesley Autrey. On January 2nd, 2007, Mr. Autrey jumped into the subway tracks at the 137th Street station in Harlem to save a young man, Cameron Hollopeter. Mr. Hollopeter had fallen in as a result of a seizure, and Autrey laid himself over him in between the tracks as the oncoming subway rolled over them. For this, Autrey was dubbed the "Hero of Harlem." When asked what motivated him to act as he did, however, he resisted the language of heroism. "I don't feel like I did something spectacular," he tells us— nicely echoing what Rogers tells Private Lorraine, "I just saw someone who needed help and did what I felt was right."

On the other hand, we've Captain Chesley "Sully" Sullenberger. On January 15th, 2009, Captain Sullenberger piloted US Airways flight 1549 to a remarkable emergency water landing on the Hudson River. The plane had been disabled shortly after taking off, and his actions saved the lives of all aboard, and those who would have been injured or killed if the plane had crashed almost anywhere else in the vicinity. For this, Sullenberger was dubbed the "Hero of the Hudson." Interestingly, though, while then Mayor Bloomberg was surely right that he'd done "a masterful job of landing the plane in the river and then making sure everybody got out," why did he not say more? In the midst of the "Great Recession," when he would have been delighted to have a new hero on hand, why did he not take advantage of the occasion? Presumably, for the same reason Sullenberger himself admits. Reflecting as laudable a modesty as Autrey's, and again Rogers's, he felt that his actions were simply "what we're trained to do."

Both Autrey and Sullenberger are surely to be admired for their modesty in resisting being called heroes. Still, there's reason to resist such resistance for one of them, which in turn sheds light on Iron Man's and Captain America's respective heroisms. To train to sit in a captain's chair, that is, and eventually sit there, is to accept certain obligations toward one's passengers, but simply to stand on a subway platform is to accept few, if any such obligations toward your fellow commuters.

Because Sullenberger's training compelled him to act and his position obligated him to do so, while his actions were certainly commendable, they're not those of a Good Samaritan. Autrey, by contrast, was not obligated to act as Sullenberger was, so his acts were as a good Samaritan—an *extraordinary* Samaritan. It's not for nothing that he's more widely known as the "Subway Samaritan," and for precisely this reason he's also the "Hero of Harlem."

Let's take care not to find ourselves on a slippery slope, however, where the idea of Samaritanism as a characteristic of heroism leads not only to questioning Sullenberger's heroism, but also that of police officers, fire fighters, and military personnel, who, while routinely called heroes, are so also by virtue of doing well what they're "trained to do." In other words, let's distinguish the *act* of *becoming* a hero, by accepting an extraordinary duty to serve the public, from the subsequent *behavior* of *being* one, by fulfilling their duty on a regular, routine basis.

Even if we're reluctant to attribute heroism to them simply for doing their jobs, we needn't extend such reluctance to the fact that they *chose* such dutiful, dangerous jobs in the first place. Also, *certain* acts they complete to fulfill their duty might still be properly heroic, being relatively conspicuously "above and beyond the call." Routinely rescuing the Joneses from fire, burglary, or the ravages of war might not be all that heroic, except perhaps if involving extraordinary peril.

With the distinction between Autrey and Sullenberger still in place, then, how do Iron Man and Captain America measure up—how relatively heroic are they as superheroes? Consider the phenomenon of superhero retirement.

In *Civil War*, Stark's and Rogers's tête-à-tête in the wake of the attack on the Sokovia Accords ceremony related them interestingly in this respect. Rogers is detained, for acting to help his fugitive friend, Bucky, who, as the Winter Soldier, is accused of perpetrating the attack. Stark extends an "olive branch," as he says. It's an uncommonly personal gesture, which leads Rogers to ask after Pepper Potts, Stark's companion since *Iron Man*, in response to which he confesses that and why they're "taking a break." The scene stands out, precisely because it's uncommonly personal, but also because it tells us something about their respective heroisms.

"A few years ago," Stark confesses, "I almost lost her," Pepper that is, "so I trashed all my suits, then we had to mop up HYDRA, and then Ultron (my fault), and then, and then, and then, I never stopped." "Because the truth is," he adds, "I don't want to stop." "I don't want to lose her," he adds, "I thought the Accords could split the difference," essentially taking the "and then, and then, and then," out of the Avengers' hands, and so out of his. He'd also already said that "taking a break" is "nobody's fault," and so not his, because, at the end of the day, it's not so much that he doesn't want to stop, but that he can't, of his own accord at least. And Rogers is sympathetic, because, in this respect at least, he's the same.

"I see a situation pointed South" he confesses, "I can't ignore it." "Sometimes I wish I could," he adds, which Stark rejects. "No you don't," he insists. "No," Rogers responds, grinning, his benevolent insincerity revealed, "I don't." It seems he's not able to follow Stark and others in signing on to the Accords, not only because he finds the idea of superhero supervision politically problematic—the risk of Avengers being tasked with something they don't agree with, or forbidden from something they do—but because even if he did, he couldn't abide by them. It's not in his nature, any more than Pepper would testify it's in Stark's.

In terms of our fifth heroism-as-supererogatory attribute, where do Stark and Rogers stand? Like fellow Avenger Clint Barton, a.k.a. Hawkeye, who we learn has retired since *Age of Ultron*, but who comes out of retirement in *Infinity War*, Stark is compelled to be Iron Man, but less irrevocably than Rogers is compelled to be Captain America. They're superheroes alright, but because of the shared compulsion, in current terms neither is the most heroic of the bunch, even while, mirroring Autrey's and Sullenberger's relative heroisms, Stark is still more heroic than Rogers.

(Super)Hero Reproduction

In addition to heroic acts consisting of the generally moral, specifically altruistic and supererogatory, and radically atypical safekeeping of others (again, the acts of their "super" counterparts being systemic and atypical), don't we also want them to be, finally, sixthly, *replicable*? Let's look again at Autrey, but let's give him now a superpower particularly helpful in safeguarding Hollopeter, and see how this may alter our sense of his heroism.

What if we were to learn, that is, that prior to helping Hollopeter, Autrey had acquired the ability to render himself immune from harm from the train passing over him, as he lay atop Hollepeter—by, say, surrounding the two of them in an impregnable force field, in the manner of The Fantastic Four's Sue Storm. This wouldn't have made it *easy* for Super Autrey to safeguard young Cameron, but would nonetheless have shielded him from harm. But if it'd been *he* who helped Hollopeter—Super Autrey as opposed to the real-world Autrey—we would naturally understand the manner of assistance as unavailable to us, making it difficult for us to imagine that we'd have acted as he did, or would in the future, should the occasion arise.

The question is this: however *super* Super Autrey would be, and however grateful young Cameron would surely still be, would *we* still think of *him* as a hero? Arguably, we wouldn't. Perhaps the Fantastic Four might happily become the Fantastic Five, but *we* are going to be neither happy nor relieved to learn that Autrey was really Super Autrey and so in no real danger. Part of the reason we value the *real-life* Autrey as a hero, and value heroes in general, is because we imagine that if *they* can do what they do, then *we* can as well.

In this spirit, Iron Man's actions, while extraordinary, are the result of Stark's abilities, which are refinements, however remarkable, of ones otherwise routinely human, and so replicable by the rest of us. Captain America's actions, by contrast, result from abilities that are out of reach of the rest of us, and so are not replicable, either in principle or in practice.

Granted, Captain America's abilities are not otherworldly. They result from being administered an experimental serum, of perfectly human origin, developed by the unfortunately moral Dr. Abraham Erskine, as part of a World War II super-solider development program. But the formula for the original serum was lost with Erskine's death, and subsequent attempts to recreate it have failed, and those stolen by HYDRA at the outset of *Civil War* have been used, and by the end of the film the resulting subjects are all deceased. In effect, then, there is, and can be only one Captain America, which, on the current analysis, makes him no less a superhero, but somewhat less heroic.

Iron Man and Captain America are both superheroes, who work for and among us, but only the former is fundamentally *of us*. We can be grateful to both of them, yes, but on different bases. While we can aspire to be like Iron Man, however unrealistically, we can't reasonably aspire to be like Captain America.

Superheroes and Super Heroes

The Golden Age of comics created superheroes who reflect our shared goal of developing and using, as William Moulton Marston wrote, "great power, when we get it, to protect innocent, peace-loving people from destructive, ruthless evil" (quoted in Jill Lepore's *The Secret History of Wonder Woman*, p. 185). Captain America came to us in the spring of 1939, during the run-up to World War Two, when humanity was seriously in need of superheroes. In the same spirit, Iron Man comes to us in the spring of 1963, at the height of the Cold War, when we were again in serious—arguably even more serious—need of superheroes.

Our ever-expanding cohort of superheroes undoubtedly means many things. Among them, it seems, is a sort of bafflement. How can it be, we can't help but wonder in dismay, that as we move farther and farther away temporally from these twentieth-century cataclysms, we seem *not* to be moving farther and farther away behaviorally? We are as beset as ever, in other words, by the problem of evil—asking ourselves no less frequently and urgently how we can make sense of the seemingly incomprehensible, which is, to paraphrase Marston, that "innocent, peace-loving people suffer from destructive, ruthless evil." We not only feel powerless to defend against "destructive, ruthless evil," but to understand it in the first place. So we turn to superheroes.

After all, when threatened with the incomprehensibly bad, who better to turn to than incomprehensible saviors? Captain America fits the bill, obviously. But we also look to more comprehensible *super heroes*, such as Iron Man. Why?

Our long struggle with the problem of evil, so awfully conspicuous in twentieth-century atrocities, evolved during the Enlightenment in two important ways, Susan Neiman has proposed. On the one hand, it evolved to include, in addition to its theological rendition—how to reconcile God's perfection with human suffering—a secular one, which we see Marston channeling above. On the other hand, in response to both versions of the problem, primarily two competing perspectives arose, which are with us still today—one insisting that "morality demands that we make evil intelligible," the other that "morality demands that we don't" (*Evil in Modern Thought*).

We include *super heroes* in our ever-expanding cohort of superheroes as an intelligibility-making gesture. We hold on to the hope, in other words, that there may be a few brave souls still, not just in our midst, but *in our ranks*, who will help lead us out of our peril, and in the process inspire others to do the same. Likely it'll take *super heroes* still to save us from unintelligible evil, at least initially, but they'll be super versions of *us*, so *we*'ll be inspired to save *ourselves*, at least eventually.

Back to Collateral Damage

The worry over "collateral damage," has long been a staple worry in the ethics of warfare. The phrase itself, however, now solidly part of the common lexicon, appears to be a more recent development, coined in the early 1960s, in between our two Avengers' arrivals. All the more interestingly, it's become an increasingly regular staple of superhero storylines.

Civil War came to us in the comics in 2006 and 2007. A subcohort, the New Warriors, consisting of a teenage and young-adult band of (as it were) junior Avengers, hatches a plan to gain more prominence. They sign on to an unnamed reality-television show, in order to boost their profile, and as they prepare to confront a handful of supervillains in Stamford, Connecticut, they look forward to, as Speedball goes on to say to Microbe, what "could be the best episode of the entire second season." It all goes horribly wrong, though, resulting in one of the supervillains causing "eight or nine hundred casualties," many of them children. "This is the straw that broke the camel's back," Goliath, a.k.a. Bill Foster, says to Ms. Marvel during the aftermath, "the start of witch hunts." He's then pictured wondering to himself, more poignantly, "Who the hell can justify this?"

In the next panel, we see an unnamed official pronouncing on *Larry King Live* that banning superheroes "in a world with thousands of super-villains is obviously impossible," but, "training them up and making them carry badges . . . sounds like a reasonable response." Her self-proclaimed reasonableness is bolstered in the following panel by a religious figure speaking from a pulpit overlooking a congregation, which we soon learn includes Stark. "We ask you, Lord, for your mercy," he implores, "not only for the souls of the children who perished, but for the super-people whose carelessness caused this tragedy." The Superhuman Registration Act is what's in play here, which would register superheroes as "weapons of mass destruction," reveal their underlying identities, and enlist them as government operatives. The centerpiece of the storyline is the divide—the "civil war"—between superheroes who accept it, led by Stark, and others who resist it, led by Rogers.

In the *Civil War* movie, US Senator Ross confronts the Avengers, in the wake of their recent activities, qualifying the Avengers' heroism as "dangerous." Hence the United Nations' call, which he's come to them to communicate, for international supervision. The "Sokovia Accords," stand in for the earlier Superhuman Registration Act, according to which the Avengers would "no longer be a private organization," but "operate under the supervision of a United Nations panel, only when and if that panel deems it necessary."

"What would you call a group of US-based, enhanced individuals," Ross asks, clearly rhetorically, "who routinely ignore sovereign borders, and inflict their will wherever they choose and who, frankly, seem unconcerned about what they leave behind?" After this, he projects scenes of startling collateral damage in New York City, Washington D.C., Sokovia, and Lagos. This is poignantly emphasized by the example of Charlie Spencer. "You murdered him," his mother tells Stark. He was "building sustainable housing for the poor," he later reports to his fellow Avengers, assembled to decide whether or not to accept supervision under the Sokovia Accords. "We dropped a building on him while we were kicking ass," he adds, in anger and frustration. "There's no decision-making process here . . . We need to be put in check," he concludes, by the Sokovia

Accords in particular, because "if we can't accept limitations, if we're boundary-less, we're no better than the bad guys."

"If we sign the Accords," Rogers replies, "we surrender our right to choose" to ignore this limitation, cross that boundary. "What if this panel sends us somewhere we don't think we should go," he worries, "or if there is somewhere we need to go, and they don't let us? . . . We may not be perfect," he concludes, "but the safest hands are still our own." He makes the claim that in signing the Accords, the Avengers would not be taking responsibility for their own actions because the "document just shifts the blame" to the United Nations, presumably for whatever collateral damage may still occur. He is particularly concerned because it, like any other organization, is "run by people with agendas, and agendas change." "That's dangerously arrogant," James Rhodes (a.k.a. War Machine) responds, seeming to speak for Stark, pinpointing the worry with Rogers's worry.

One kind of humility is Rogers's "just doing what needed to be done" retort to Private Lorraine's admiration, with its echoes in Autrey's "I just saw someone who needed help and did what I felt was right," and also in, albeit with added nuance, Sullenberger's "just doing what we're trained to do." It seems that what Rhodes is calling for is different, however, and also more evident in Stark than in Rogers. As we find the former more heroic than the latter, on heroism-as-replicable grounds, we can't help but ask whether this, too, differentiates their heroisms.

Another sort of humility is accepting that there are others who do, or at least may, know better than we do about what's best in this or that situation. It's hard to imagine Autrey not acting as he did on that fateful January day in 2007—unless perhaps there'd been some organization recognized for its moral authority, which offered a morally compelling argument to the contrary. In that case, were he to act, and we shared his recognition of the moral authority of the organization in question, he might seem to us less heroic, if heroic at all.

It's also not out of the question that even if the hypothetical were the case, and he were directed not to attempt to save young Hollopeter, that he would have done so anyway. Indeed, he might have believed himself—as we might also believe him—to be right to resist, even if the compelling moral argument in question were enshrined in law, and disobeying meant punishment. He might have disobeyed, were he morally compelled to do so. After all, anything less would mean that we leave no place for the heroism of civil disobedience.

"What if this panel sends us somewhere we don't think we should go," Rogers worries, or "if there is somewhere we need to go, and they don't let us?" The proper answer is that if you discern a morally compelling reason or set of reasons why you should not go where "you don't think you should go," do what you "don't think you should" do, then, whatever the threat of punishment, once you've made your case to those who would impose it you should hope to have the moral courage to refuse. Likewise, if your moral compass compels you to go somewhere you're prevented from going, or do something you're prevented from doing, then, again, keeping in mind the above caveats, you should hope to have the moral courage to persevere.

"We may not be perfect," Rogers insists, "but the safest hands are still our own." He's talking about the Avengers, of course, but he could easily have been talking more generally. While such hands may, indeed, appear safest to those who wield them, however, they're not the most righteous if little or no attempt is made to imagine that their perspective may be ill-advised or limited. Stark, whose conspicuous lack of humility is part of his charm, is nonetheless, in this respect, more humble than Rogers, and in being so is more heroic. After all, as we recall from the second of its proposed attributes, heroism without righteousness is no heroism at all.[1]

---

[1] Some of the ideas presented here I began to explore in earlier essays, in *Adventure Time and Philosophy, Girls and Philosophy, Batman, Superman, and Philosophy,* and *Wonder Woman and Philosophy.* I'm grateful to their editors, Nicolas Michaud in the first and third instances, Richard Greene and Rachel Robison-Greene in the second, and Jacob Held in the fourth, for their encouragement and assistance on these occasions. I'm also grateful to Susan Neiman for my interest in, and understanding of the related problems of heroism and evil, to whose work I owe the Wesley Autrey example in particular. I'm grateful as well to Erin Carlston and Carisa Showden for the case of Sully Sullenberger, and what I believe is the helpful contrast it provides to Wesley Autrey's, and for their patience and assistance in helping me to sort this out. I'm additionally grateful to the folks in my enlightenment and problem of evil classes, generally speaking, and the summer of 2015 cohort in particular, for raising the worry involving police officers, fire fighters, and military personnel. Naturally, none of the above are responsible for what I've done with their insights and encouragement. Finally, I'm no less grateful to the current volume's editors for patience and assistance far above and beyond the call.

3
Will the Real American Hero Please Stand Up!

HEIDI SAMUELSON

He's the star-spangled man with a plan! Surely Captain America bleeds red, white, and blue. He fought for America in the war to end all wars. He has knocked out Adolf Hitler over two hundred times. He has fought against neo-Nazis, fascists, and anarchists. He always says he's protecting the American dream, and he even once considered running for president.

Meanwhile, Tony Stark works for himself. His relationship with the US military and government is more out of self-interest and profit than patriotism. Look at his track record: he sells weapons, he stops selling weapons, he gives the Variable Threat Response Battle Suit to his friend James Rhodes (a.k.a. War Machine), he instigates the Superhuman Registration Act, he destroys the Registration records, he builds and tinkers with Iron Man suits that surely violate the United Nations Convention on Certain Conventional Weapons. So, which of one these men is the true American hero?

The answer to this question depends on what we think American values are. The Declaration of Independence opens with the phrase "life, liberty, and the pursuit of happiness," but what do these American ideals that Cap says he's protecting really mean? If we look back in history, part of the answer can be found across the pond in the work of two British philosophers—John Locke (1632–1704) and Adam Smith (1723–1790). These two men gave us ideas like liberty, private property, representative democracy, and capitalism, and their work was important to the founders of the United States. The spirit of their ideas still exists in neoliberalism and global democracy today.

Current American values support neoliberalism, which is a form of capitalism where individuals pursue their own interests without a lot of government interference. This includes things like privatization, free trade, and reducing government spending so the private sector—including weapons manufacturers like Stark Industries—have a bigger role in the economy. The idea is that if people do what is good for themselves, then their actions will end up helping others and the prosperity of the wealthy will eventually benefit everyone. Some argue that the spread of neoliberal economic policies also promotes democracy around the globe, which allows more individuals to have a say in their government and to pursue their interests. Neoliberalism has its critics, claiming the US government might have sacrificed some of its early ideals like liberty in favor of imperialism. Really what this means is that today's ideal American might not be a champion of liberty like Captain America, but a genius, billionaire, playboy, philanthropist instead.

Real American Values

Marvel creator Stan Lee has said that Tony Stark was written to be the "quintessential capitalist." Though capitalism didn't fully develop in America until the early twentieth century, the ideas of a global free market started forming in the seventeenth and eighteenth centuries in the philosophies of Locke and Smith. These ideas were adopted by early Americans and continue to be at the heart of American democracy, and Tony is the perfect example of these ideologies.

Locke is sometimes called the father of classical liberalism, where neoliberalism gets its basic principles. Classical liberalism starts in Locke's *Two Treatises of Government* with the idea that man is naturally free, autonomous, and equal in the use of his rational agency. Locke's understanding of this "natural law" is that no one should harm the life, health, liberty, or possessions of someone else.

Thomas Jefferson read Locke's work, and the idea of natural law, or "natural rights," was put into the Declaration of Independence: "We hold these truths to be self-evident, that all men are created equal, that they are endowed by their Creator with certain unalienable Rights, that among these are Life, Liberty and the pursuit of Happiness."

These ideals have been carried over to the internationally used concept of human rights, including the organization Worldwatch, headed by Tony's best friend James Rhodes (*War Machine* 1, #6). But Locke didn't stop at natural rights. He also had the idea that you own your labor. So if you put your labor into working land or natural resources that no one else occupies, then that makes that land or resources your private property. Locke thought people needed to protect their property from being taken over by the government, and that's why they agree to form governments in the first place. So, if a man uses his own resources to build Iron Man suits, then it is well within that man's natural rights, and the government cannot claim to own the suits.

Though he was an Englishman, Locke supported expanding into North America. Even before the United States was a country, the wealthy and the elite had sway and power in the original colonies. The history of the American economy also has its roots in Smith's theory of capitalism that he wrote in *The Wealth of Nations*.

Like Locke, Smith thought individuals should be allowed to live without a lot of government interference. Smith encouraged free trade instead of government tariffs and gold-hoarding. Smith said that in a stable economic system, people will be more likely to pursue their own interests and specialize in production. Smith added that when people have shared interests, their competition will end up—with the help of an "invisible hand"—benefiting society by giving people more options while keeping prices low. Tony Stark's industriousness and his rivalry with fellow weapons' manufacturer Justin Hammer is a great example of Smith's vision.

But Smith's theory was more than economics. In *A Theory of Moral Sentiments*, Smith writes that we make good, moral judgments because we develop a natural sympathy for other people when we see ourselves in others. Today we call this "empathy," which some theorists argue is necessary for democracy and is a social "gain from trade." Smith seems to think that this is needed for the economic side of his theory to work. He argues that if we become sympathetic out of habit, then it would function as an invisible hand—the same invisible hand in his economic theory—and everyone would benefit socially and morally. We see this with Tony, who often thinks that he is doing what is best for other people, and that his actions will help others.

Tony is without a doubt an American neoliberal who came out of the tradition of Locke and Smith. Stark Industries is part of the military-industrial complex that supports the US military. When he stops selling munitions and changes the company to Stark International, Tony continues to be a leader in the technology sector and maintains his alliance with the US government.

Sometimes capitalists get a bad rap, but Tony also exemplifies the sometimes ignored side of Smith's theory—he shows sympathy toward other people. Sometimes he seems self-absorbed and paternalistic, like when he interfered in Sokovia in *Age of Ultron*, but he genuinely seems to care about other people in spite of his ego. As a co-founder of the Avengers and a member of the Illuminati, he frequently puts his life on the line to protect people.

So far it seems like Tony Stark is the ideal American. But this is only one side of the history of American values.

Vs. the Myth of the American Rebel

Another take on American values comes from the story that the United States was established by an army of rebel fighters who no longer wanted to pay taxes to the British government, which didn't provide them adequate representation. Rebels dumped tea into Boston Harbor and started forming shadow governments, convening with the First Continental Congress in 1774. Locke argued very clearly for the right of revolution when the people are no longer being represented by their legislature. His ideas were influential in the American Revolution. So, the founding of America would be what Steve Rogers might call standing up to a bully.

But this is only part of the story. America was previously occupied when English and other European settlers arrived. Philosophers like Locke, who valued property—as the mixing of labor and land—considered a large land mass like North America to be an opportunity for the English settlers to use their own labor (as well as slave labor). For Locke, man had a natural right to exploit land and resources, and the indigenous people were not using it to its best advantage. Using the land often involved removing, sometimes brutally, these indigenous people from the land. Steve Rogers might also call this a pretty severe case of bullying, putting him in conflict with this side of American values.

Today, the United States is considered a "superpower," which means it has influence all over the globe. A superpower exercises its power through technological, cultural, military, and economic influence. Being a superpower is also usually associated with the possibility of destroying the world. Instead of the spread of liberty and encouraging people to pursue their interests to the benefit of all, in practice, it looks a lot like the US pushing itself onto others to benefit the US—or private investors like Stark Industries. American values can be twisted to turn the US into a bully, as when market interests are pursued without considering the sympathy required for Smith's invisible hand, and Steve Rogers knows it.

In the Marvel cinematic universe, Steve says, "I don't want to kill anyone. I don't like bullies. I don't care where they're from"—to explain why he wants to fight in World War II. Although he believes the US is on the right side of the war, his sense of duty isn't really patriotic. He doesn't want to sell war bonds or collect scrap metal or do safer things that would also help the country's war effort. He does not simply want to support America or the US military—he wants to fight against bad people who take away the liberty of others.

Captain America is a symbol against fascism and hatred. Captain America was an intentionally political character, created by two Jewish men—Joe Simon and Jack Kirby—in 1940 during World War II. In the first issue of the comic book, Captain America punched Adolf Hitler. Cap continued to fight Nazis and the Japanese in World War II (and later neo-Nazis like Crossbones and Doctor Faustus). But when Captain America fought in World War II, it had less to do with American values and more to do with it simply being the right thing to do. The American thing to do isn't always the right thing to do, and Steve doesn't lose sight of this.

Captain America entering World War II to stand up to a bully wasn't because of taxation without representation or to support free trade or because of a strong sense of duty to the US government and military. It was because a bad man was committing massive human rights violations. Though human rights are routed in the natural rights that Locke argued for, we cannot ignore the limitations of Locke's ideas. Locke really only meant his *Two Treatises of Government* to apply to Englishmen. He personally profited from the African slave trade and thought people could sell themselves into servitude.

When his and others' ideals were put into the governing documents of the United States of America, the only people who were considered free citizens were white, male property owners. Oftentimes, as history has shown, "free citizens" can end up being the bullies. Captain America might represent a portion of American ideals—like Smith's sympathy—but the US hasn't always lived up to them.

In *Captain America* #268, Steve says. "I represent the American dream! A dream that has precious little to do with borders, boundaries, and the kind of blind hatred your ilk espouses!" With statements like this, he stands up for everyone—including people who weren't always considered American citizens. He explicitly states in the "Capmania" miniseries that his battle is "against injustice . . . against cynicism . . . against intolerance" (*Captain America* #471). Instead of living according to the liberal ideal of freely pursuing your interests that Locke and Smith intended and that Tony lives by, Steve embodies an even wider ideal, beyond the individual and beyond American borders.

Declaring Yourself a Superhero

Tony Stark clearly embodies neoliberal American values, but is he a hero? He often claims to be looking out for himself, but he routinely bears the burden for the entire world. As one of the co-founders of The Avengers, he turns himself into superhero in spite of the fact that he has no super powers.

Most superheroes have a secret identity that few people know, and they try very hard to keep secret. While Tony does try to separate himself from the Iron Man identity in the comic books, in *Iron Man* (Volume 3) #55, he discloses his identity to the public. In the first *Iron Man* movie, Tony reveals his identity at a press conference without much hesitation. By having people know that he is Iron Man, he puts even more of a burden on himself to do the right thing, both in and out of the suit.

And, perhaps because of his role in the arms industry, he often works with the US government to help.

In the infamous "Civil War" story line, he proposes the Superhuman Registration Act, which was designed to have all super-powered individuals in the US register with the federal government and act as licensed agents. The intention was for inexperienced superhumans to get the right training needed to use their abilities. Of course, this causes Iron Man's infamous feud with Captain America, and the end result is that Tony is appointed the Director of SHIELD and sets up a team of government-sanctioned Avengers.

Tony doesn't only work with SHIELD. Once he makes his Iron Man identity public, he runs into the problem that the military can now replicate his technology. After a defect in the armor nearly causes a disaster, Tony takes a position as the US Secretary of Defense so he can keep an eye on the government's use of his armor. Although it's short-lived, this is an example of Tony recognizing that a hero can, and sometimes should, work with the government ("Best Defense," *Iron Man* Volume 3, #73–78).

This is echoed in the *Civil War* movie, where Tony, still reeling from the guilt over the harm he caused with the Ultron disaster, agrees to sign Sokovia Accords—a global agreement that would put enhanced individuals under the supervision of a United Nations panel.

By recognizing that sometimes individual interests need to be kept in check in civil society, a value found in both Locke and Smith, Tony sees that good can be done by working with the US government.

Vs. Giving Up the Shield

While Tony embraces roles of power within the government, Steve frequently opposes it, giving up his iconic shield and ditching the Captain America identity more than once. Even though he was meant to be a patriotic character, after World War II it was hard to maintain that image. He stands for ideals, for "the dream," and that dream isn't always supported by the US government. In *Captain America* #250, Steve refuses to run for office because holding office means compromising his ideals for the sake of politics.

In 1974, when Marvel comics dealt with their version of Nixon's Watergate scandal, Steve finds out that high in the ranks of the US government are members of the terrorist organization "the Secret Empire" (*Captain America* #180). He takes up the moniker Nomad, meaning "man without a country," and loses the red, white, and blue uniform. He recognizes that he cannot support a US government that is corrupt and engaged in secret terrorist actions. If he was truly embracing the American spirit of rebellion of the nation's founders, then he might take up arms against the government. Instead, he still fights for the greater good, telling an army general that he is not loyal to anything, "except the Dream."

In *Captain America* #312, he also goes up against Flag-Smasher, an anti-nationalist supervillain who believes that the idea of nationality needs to be destroyed. He uses terrorist techniques to spread his message, destroys national symbols, and demands the surrender of Captain America. Although Captain America helps SHIELD take down Flag-Smasher, it wasn't in defense of the patriotic symbols. It is the anarchist ideals of Flag-Smasher that Steve really opposes. Once again, this points to Steve's loyalty not to American values or the US, but to his opposition to anyone causing harm.

In another comic run, Steve goes up against a man known as "Nuke"—a mentally unstable supersoldier with an American flag tattooed on his face (*Daredevil* #233). Steve is ordered to work directly for the US government, but they were the ones who created Nuke in the first place. He is so troubled by their actions and corruption that he resigns and drops "America" from his title, instead going by "The Captain."

Not only is Steve's loyalty to America shaky, he is not the only person to hold the Captain America moniker. Instead of being attached to the identity, he willingly gives the shield to Bucky Barnes even after he is brought back to life (*Captain America: Who Will Wield the Shield?* Volume 1). In a later comic run, after his serum is neutralized and he rapidly ages, he appoints Sam Wilson to be Captain America (*All-New Captain America*, Volume 1). What this shows is that Steve Rogers sees himself as a defender of an ideal, but that isn't tied with a country, the shield, or the title of Captain America.

You could argue that standing up to the government and being self-critical is part of American ideology, but Steve is too often willing to separate himself from the country in order to uphold his ideals. The "dream" he upholds is one of freedom and equality, which morphed out of Locke's natural law theory and was mostly meant to protect private property from being taken by a king. Steve's values aren't exactly un-American, but they are values that America hasn't upheld, and Steve is the first one to point that out by abandoning his Captain America identity. The righteousness of Captain America has little to do with America and seems to come from Steve Rogers himself.

The Final Showdown

In the "Civil War" story line where Steve and Tony face off, Tony sides with the US government. He has been the Director of SHIELD and the US Secretary of Defense, key roles in helping protect the American people. Though he never served in the military, he is a strong supporter of the military, first with Stark Industries weapons and then with technology.

Iron Man is undoubtedly also a hero who feels the need to protect humanity, just like Captain America, but he does so in a truly American way. He embraces the full gamut of American values, knowing when to act on his own and when to play the system in order to suit his interests and in the interest of protecting others. He doesn't try to uphold liberty and justice in an ideological way—he personally lives freely and with sympathy. Instead of demanding the government uphold ideals, he tries to fix things himself, ultimately going along with the government because it's practical to.

Captain America is a ranked military veteran. He gave his body to the US military, let them conduct an experiment that permanently altered his physical makeup, and he fought in World War II. There is no question that he served the United States. But even with the red, white, and blue, Steve Rogers has a love-hate relationship with America. He has fought against Nazism, neo-Nazism, fascism, anarchism, and terrorism, but the ideals he stands up for are not strictly American ideals. Steve Rogers stands up to bullies, stands up against fascism, and he stands up for human rights and the dream of equality. And when it comes down to it, the official actions of the United States do not always support those ideals even in the Marvel universe, with actions like registering free citizens, unjust military intervention, and developing unconventional weapons. Marvel has had numerous Captain America runs that reflect this conflict when Steve Rogers challenges the US government.

So who's the real American hero?

Captain America stands up for the little guy. He is an icon for the disenfranchised, the bullied, and those fighting for liberty and equality. This definitely makes him a hero, but not strictly an American hero.

Meanwhile, Iron Man follows American ideals from their origins in Locke and Smith into the neoliberalism of the twenty-first century. He is a more practical hero, an industrialist who sees the value of working with the government to achieve a greater good, and it is these hard-working, practical values that make him the real American hero.

4

He's a Hero in a Bottle, Baby

STEVE INSOOKS

Okay, seriously: this is bullshit.

Take one look at the table of contents of this book and you can see it is clearly crap! Why are there more chapters saying that Captain America is better than Iron Man? I'll tell you why . . . Because Captain America is a spandex-wearing, situps-obsessed loser who wouldn't be shit without a shield that is way more super than he is! Okay, okay, maybe I'm being a bit harsh, but I have good reason for my argument here. I'm saying that the simple fact that Captain Pearly-Whites has more "philosophers" supporting him is proof that he isn't the winner.

In fact, I think there is a whole lot of lying to ourselves going on here. And so let's clear the air. If you really get down to brass tacks, there are a few reasons you hear over and over why people might think that Captain "Look Both Ways Before You Cross the Street" is more "heroic". . . "Steve is more relatable." "Steve has super powers: Stark doesn't." "Steve is humbler, nicer, willing to help the little guy, blah blah blah." So let's take a look at some of those "reasons" and bust some blue-spandex-wearing butt.

Will the Real Superhero Please Stand Up?

Okay, so first off, Cap is more relatable, right? He is more liked, as is proven by more authors writing to support him. But, your honor, I object! The fact that more people like him is proof that he *isn't* the winner! I realize I might be losing you here. It seems obvious to anyone that the true winner would be the guy who has the most people in his corner, right?

Wrong. In fact, I'd like to argue that the more liked a guy is, the higher chance that he is really not that impressive at all. We like likeable people, right? I mean to say we like people whom we can relate to. People like us. So if more people like Mr. "Eat a Healthy Breakfast, Kids," then doesn't that mean he must be *less* of a hero? After all, if *regular* people relate to a superhero, then how super can that hero really be?

I realize this sounds harsh. And I certainly don't mean to alienate you, my dear reader. But we can't all be playboy, philanthropist billionaire with fabulous hair, can we? I mean, someone has to be the ordinary guy! If there are no ordinary guys, then we don't need heroes, right? And so my point is this: if part of the argument is that Captain Too-Tight Pants is better because he's more relatable, he is someone *like* the ordinary guy, then he really isn't that impressive of a hero.

A superhero has to be super. Period. And that means excelling where other people fail. If Captain "Does His Daily Squats" is so relatable, then he can't be all that super. What is it that Rogers excels at, anyway? He isn't that strong (and don't get your underoos in a bunch; I'll get to that in a minute). He isn't that smart (Last time I checked, cellphones were still basically powered by magic to him). What does he do that well? True, he seems like a really nice guy. And true, he is pretty willing to sacrifice himself. But that makes him a hero, not a superhero. All the people out there willing to sacrifice themselves for others or for a greater good are certainly heroes, but we don't call them superheroes. Think about it like this: in a planet filled with Hulks (Imagine the insurance premiums!), the Hulk isn't very super—he's normal. *Our* Hulk could still be a hero on that planet (for however long that planet lasts), he could do heroic things, but the fact that he's not significantly different from the rest would prevent him from being thought of as a "*super*hero."

Power Corrupts but It's Nice to Have When Flying a Nuke into Space and Saving the World (Remember That???)

Maybe a "normal" person *can* be a superhero . . . no powers necessary. But to do that would require going wayyyy above and beyond what our average hero would do with the power you have. So let's talk about powers for a moment and how they are used. The truth is, as far as superpowers go, Steve needs to eat more Wheaties. True, my pal Tony doesn't have any powers, but I want to argue that that is part of what makes him *better* (And don't worry, I'll get to that). Tony does have a super intellect, though. After all, if Steve went toe-to-toe with Banner, he would be a messy bit of star-spangled paste. Who can go up against Hulk? Iron Man. So if it is the powers themselves, then Steve isn't much better off than Tony is, but who *does more with what he has???* That's right: Tony "Watch Yourself, Ladies: I'm About to Smile" Stark!

On one hand, we might want to say that having powers is key to being a superhero, but we also know that can't quite be right because someone can have powers and be a villain. So the powers aren't enough, what you do with those powers counts. And we know you have to go above and beyond, you have to be special in some way, to fall into the category "super." And super is, if we are honest, about *what you do with what you have.* Someone being super goes above and beyond. Of our two contenders, who does more with what he has? Tony. *and* notice that even though Tony starts with less power, *he can do more than Rogers can.* So Tony starts with less and, even so, ends up more "super."

Humility Is for Monks and Car Salesmen

And that brings me to an important point here. This idea that heroes need to be humble and nice, and generally sweet people is troublesome. True, our heroes do have to save the day. Otherwise, they are villains—or, well, just sitting on their butts with lots of power—so, basically politicians. But nowhere in the superhero rule book does it say that they have to be humble, and all "Let Me Pretend that I Don't Know I Have Buns of Steel." In fact, I think that this humility is just more bullshit. It isn't legit. If you are humble because you know you are awesome, then really you are just lying to people. You know you are super, but you let all the not super people believe that you don't think you are super. But why would a superhero not admit that he's super? If the point of being a role model is to inspire people to be like you, then you have to a) be awesome and b) *admit that you are awesome.* If you don't believe you are awesome, then why would you make obnoxious (and poorly

acted) public service announcements encouraging impression-
able kids to be like you? Stop lying to us all, Cap!

Obviously, a hero needs to believe in himself (yes, yes: or
*her*self). If the hero doesn't believe, then what's the point? You
run around accidentally saving people? If you're going to go up
against Dr. Doom, or Loki, or Thanos, you better believe you can
cut the mustard. Now you and I both know Captain Credit-Me-
Not doesn't run from a fight. But every time he pretends that he
is still that poor sick kid from Brooklyn, he is insulting *actually
sick kids*. Look, seriously: There are sick people, people with
physical struggles, people with far fewer abilities than Rogers
and they get out there and make themselves heroes! In fact, I'd
claim that a few of them push themselves so hard, and do such
amazing work that they count as *super*heroes, and they never
took a super-serum! In other words, even with whatever ails
them, they are out their saving lives and doing good. Rogers, on
the other hand, pretends like he is one of those heroes. Like he's
some poor sick kid overcoming the odds. When, really, he's a lab
procedure gone luckily right. So what right does he have to act
like he isn't all that, when he has so many advantages that
other people don't have? If he were as honest as he seemed, he
would acknowledge his "superness" and show respect for people
who actually have to struggle to do super-hero work!

Again, I realize I may seem like I'm being a bit harsh. But isn't
there something to be said for the self-made man? (And before you
go all crazy on me, I'm not saying this in some "Good Ole' Boy, Yay
Capitalism" way. Obviously, Stark had funds to start him.) Rogers
came out of a bottle, but Stark has to work for every invention he
has. I'll never understand why we would pick the guy who was
basically just gifted his superness over the guy who *had to build
it*. Rogers is basically as good as he is ever going to get. But every
day, Tony Stark is working to improve Iron Man. And while
Captain "Look How I can Bounce Quarters on my Abs" might
improve his 50-mile run by a third of a second, Tony will find a
way to build a suit that can take down Thanos. So Stark isn't just
more powerful than Rogers, *he will become increasingly so.*

Nice Guys Are Just Bad Boys Who Lie

Okay. So far, we know that Stark had to come from farther
behind and do it himself to become super. We know that Stark

has gone far beyond Rogers's super powers. We know that Rogers is basically lying when he acts humble, and that his "relatability" really just seems to go to show that he isn't that super. And I would like to add to the argument that Rogers is actually holding people back, while Tony is giving us reason to go forward. I think I've shown, that particularly in Rogers's case, that his brand of humility is a bit disrespectful to people who really have to struggle. And, now I want to argue that this humility is something that also helps hold people back. When we pretend that we are not awesome, we not only hold ourselves back, but we are also suggesting to other people that they don't really need to be awesome, either. After all, like I said before, to be a good role model you have to acknowledge that you are someone worth modeling after.

One thinker who captures this idea pretty well was Friedrich Nietzsche (1844–1900). Now, true—some of his work was supposedly used by Nazis, but we are going to ignore that fact, because, well . . . it's a bit inconvenient. The stuff that I really want to look at is Nietzsche's worry that when someone is awesome, our social tendency is to try to hold them back. As evidence, look at pop stars: we love to make them heroes, but isn't it even more fun when they go nuts, shave their heads and start holding babies off of roof tops? If we are honest, we will admit that the reason why tabloids line checkout line shelves instead of bibles, books on physics, or *Moby-Dick* because we love to relish in the failure of others. So, we tend to get a bit pissy when a hero acts like he's all that. Some part of us wants him to fail. And if he doesn't fail, then we want him to at least to pretend that he isn't all that much better than us.

The idea that we don't need to be that awesome and that we resent it when other people are awesome is what Nietzsche called a "sheep morality" and I will call the "Steve Morality." The Steve Morality tells us that we need not to rub it in other people's faces when we do better. We shouldn't gloat when we win. And we should act like anyone can do what we do. But we wouldn't be *super*heroes if anyone could do what we do, AND some people who could, don't!

Look at Olympic athletes. They deserve respect. And they get some respect. But I remember when one famous Olympic swimmer got caught smoking the devil's lettuce. Well, not only was he in trouble for doing a drug, but it was like the whole of society turned on him. People were calling for him to give up his medals, endorsements were pulled, and he was forced to apologize. But what was it that he was really apologizing for? He wasn't endorsing smoking. He did it privately, where no one was supposed to see. It was between him and his Thor.

But instead, society acted like that athlete needed to be taken down a peg, and he held a conference humbly apologizing for how he let everyone down. But how should a hero act in that situation? We assume humble. But I suggest to you that the heroic action would be, not humble, but honest. Imagine if, instead, that swimmer had come out and said, "You are just jealous! You are all just jealous because while I'm out there practicing every day, twelve hours a day, you are sitting on your couch *watching* me be awesome. You're just jealous because what I do best, I am the best at in the world. And whatever it is that *you* do best . . . well, you are just mediocre." And, of course, everyone would freak out and chastise him and say what an awful guy he was. But wouldn't what he was saying also be true? Why did we enjoy his fall so much? And people like Captain "Oh Look at Me I'm Just Like You . . . If You'd Just Submit Yourself to a Super-Secret Science Experiment That Gives You Super Powers" just encourage the idea that heroes shouldn't acknowledge they are heroic, for fear that they will piss off the sheeple.

Who Are You Gonna Be?

Well, maybe you think it's bad, but I think that real hero inspires people to go above and beyond. Nietzsche wrote about how a superman was the kind of person who didn't let himself be held back by everyone else's mediocrity. If they want to be average, let them be, but don't let them make rules just to hold the heroes back. Rules like, "Pretend you aren't super to make us feel better about our soda-swilling, Dorito-stuffing, sofa-sitting lives." The sheep try to hold you back, but you press on and *make yourself the best version of yourself you can be.* A super-person, Nietzsche seems to be suggesting, isn't what happens when you try to be what everyone else thinks is best, it is when you try to be what *you* think is best. So every time Rogers kowtows to the masses and tries to be like them, not only is he insulting them, but he is failing to do what he could really do to be awesome—be the best version of himself, rather than be the hero everyone else wants.

So sure, that kind of attitude might seem arrogant. And Tony seems to have that in spades, along with money, looks, and ladies, but it is also a whole hell of a lot more honest. Because what's more inspiring... a hero who comes down to your level and says, "I'll be just like you" or a hero on the mountaintop who says, "What? You can't fly? . . . Well, then, build yourself a F*#&ing suit and get your lazy ass up here!?"

5
Why the Good Man Is a Great Leader

CLARA NISLEY

Morality provides the fundamental motivation for Captain America and Iron Man; as good guys, Cap and Iron Man think deeply about their actions. In *Captain America: Civil War*, they have to consider their moral and political obligations.

As members of the Avengers, they occupy different positions in the organization and are required to participate in decisions that will alter their roles in providing a secure world. The decision to accept or reject the Sokovia Accords will allow one superhero to become the leader of the Avengers. The ensuing battle between Cap and Iron Man leads the two Avengers to pick a side and their friends to choose between the two superheroes.

Their relationship as friends and as fellow members of the Avengers give them a shared responsibility to make the right choice. Their characters are called into question: who most has the attributes of a good man? We have two heroes, and while both are supposed to be good men, they disagree tremendously over which action is right. So in the end, we need to figure out who's actually right, and to figure that out, we need to figure out which of them really is a good man.

In the movie, *Captain America: Civil War* Iron Man believes that he and his fellow members should sign the Sokovia Accords because Tony Stark recognizes the harm he and his fellow superheroes have caused in Sokovia. He shows Steve and his fellow superheroes a picture of Charles Spencer, a computer engineering student who went to Sokovia to build sustainable housing for the poor. Aware that he and his fellow Avengers have caused the deaths of Charles Spencer and many other inhabitants of Sokovia by fighting Ultron, Tony decides to sign the Superhero Registration Act. He has chosen to side with Thaddeus Ross; the Avengers have to accept the Sokovia Accords as a means to an end—justice. Tony sees himself as a citizen with superhuman powers who plays an important part in keeping the world safe. After all, what is a superhero for? So, here we see Iron Man thinking about the idea of a good man. Iron Man believes that he ought to do justice by the people of the world, which means that imposing limitations on the Avengers is politically reasonable. Acting against the Accords would be an unjust act, if he believes in the teachings of the ancient philosopher Aristotle, who claimed that the state's purpose is to protect against injustices. He understands that a good man needs to practice temperance, and the destruction in Sokovia shows that he and his fellow Avengers used excessive force. Iron Man recognizes that he needs to employ his intellectual powers for good, and he needs to stop the recurring acts of injustice by signing the Sokovia Accords for the benefit of society.

We might believe that Cap should obey the rules of the United Nations and sign the Sokovia Accords, given that the Avengers are members of a group characterized by its relationship to the US government and the World Security Council, through SHIELD. But, the Avengers would have to submit to the Superhero Registration Act, which Steve believes would limit their powers to act. He thinks that he and his fellow Avengers have the right to and responsibility of self-governance. This is not unusual, given the dangers Cap confronted when he didn't conform to the political authority to endorse the Commission's rules, which was documented in *The Choice*.

Cap questions the oversight by the United Nations and refuses to sign the Accords because of his experiences in *The Choice*, early in Cap's membership in the Avengers. The Commission on Superhuman Activities asked him to become an informant so that the Commission could exercise power over superhuman activity in the government's interest. Rogers refused to inform the Commission, as this would require him to act against his fellow Avengers. This story of political alienation to some extent explains why the Cap challenges the Sokovia Accords. The Cap was not able to endorse its policy—

the Mutant Powers Act—which required that all mutants register with the Commission, and Steve Rogers, at least temporarily, abrogated his role as Captain America and resigned from the Commission on Superhuman Activities.

The stories in *The Choice* and *Civil War* are different but relevant to one another. The actions of Captain America are best understood when we understand his character. Steve goes to Bucharest to save Bucky and fight the German Special Forces. At the end of *Captain America: Civil War*, Steve writes a letter to Tony, stating, "I've been on my own since I was eighteen. I never really fit in anywhere, even in the army." We might have expected Cap's friendship with Iron Man to have survived their disagreement over the Sokovia Accords. When Captain America gave up his shield, along with his uniform; Tony Stark made him one of adamantium, only to have Cap return it. In *Civil War*, Cap uses his shield to hurt his fellow Avenger. Although Cap is a man who shows courage and does good, in *Civil War*, he has allowed his anger to take hold.

Let's turn to what Aristotle has to say about friendship. Aristotle states that men who hold power "are thought to need friends most of all." He claims that a true friendship is between men who are good. This raises the question whether Captain America is a good friend. Good men, Aristotle claims, are men who have the virtues of temperance and courage. The Cap's friendship with Iron Man is partly based on courage, which they both show, when confronted with supervillains, such as Loki.

But, Steve has not shown temperance in his vicious act against Tony Stark. He has been rash in his actions. Cap, according to his own statement, acted "like a sixteen-year-old kid" when he led the battle in Lagos. Steve Rogers should have developed proper ethical habits during his youth; he was born with the potential of becoming a good man, and this should have been his goal after becoming an enhanced human. Was he indifferent to the deaths caused by his rash actions in Lagos, in his attempt to save Bucky? His primary concern was to protect his childhood friend and fellow soldier, Bucky, who Steve saved and recruited to the "Howling Commandos" to fight HYDRA.

As an Avenger, was it right to save Bucky? It was in the HYDRA facility where, under the direction of Zola, Barnes turns into the Winter Soldier. As the Winter Soldier, he attacked and killed Howard Stark and his wife and attempted to kill Nick Fury. Steve Rogers does not know that Tony's parents died at the hands of Bucky in *Captain America: Winter Soldier*, but he's made that assumption: If Bucky "was good, and he becomes bad . . . must I still love him?" In Lagos, Cap begins asking Brock Rumlow questions about who the person was behind the attempt to steal a biological weapon; he learns that it was his old friend Bucky Barnes. Cap admits that he "should have clapped the bomb." It was his decision to go to Lagos and his decision was for the good of society. And,

> insofar as a man of moral strength chooses the good and follows the guidance of reason, his character resembles that of the morally virtuous. But, as his passions are in opposition to his will, and consequently he is in a state of ceaseless struggle from not possessing a fixed and permanent disposition, to that degree his character is not that of virtue.

This "ceaseless struggle" exists in Steve: even if he disagrees with the Sokovia Accords, his obligation arises from providing the Avengers with assurance to a co-operative arrangement. They are his comrades and are like brothers and sisters. But, as we see, Steve Rogers's friendship with Tony Stark and the Avengers is incidental. He puts his fellow Avengers in danger in his mission to save Bucky and is arrested, along with Black Panther and Falcon. As friends and superheroes, they should have "like feelings and character." But, the Cap's refusal of the terms of the Sokovia Accords dissolves the Avengers. In choosing what is the most advantageous to him, Cap does not do what is the most noble.

We see that Bucky is not responsible for the King of Wakanda's death. But as the King of Wakanda—T'Chaka, Black Panther—states, "Victory at the expense of the innocent is no victory at all." If the Cap submits to his passions, how then, is he a good man? He wants to continue fighting supervillains without being accountable to anyone for his actions. War Machine tells him he's arrogant. He's been told by Vision that their "very strength invites challenge, . . . which invites conflict . . . which breeds catastrophe." Vision later warns Cap to surrender "for the collective good." It is not surprising that both end up on Iron Man's team.

We see the connection between friendship among the Avengers and that of enhanced individuals with the responsibility to use their superpowers for the good. What holds them together are not only their skills but what each contributes to the community of Avengers. They must, for the unity of the Avengers through their special relationship, come together. They have a common interest or common end, which, according to Vision (who seems to agree with Aristotle), should arouse cooperation toward their common goal. But, instead, Cap decides to tear a rift in his association with the Avengers. He not only causes a rift between himself and Iron Man, but is the cause of the Avengers taking sides. This raises the question whether Cap is a good man.

Cap lacks practical experience as well as the proper virtues to lead the Avengers. The Avengers have abilities to use their superpowers for the good, but they need a good man to lead them. The complex difficulties that virtuous superheroes have to exercise require a good man who understands his function within the Avengers. He is a fellow Avenger and is part of an association of superheroes—mostly enhanced humans—who rest on an agreement between them. Their function as enhanced humans is at least in part the same as humans who lead their lives virtuously.

As humans, we do not live by instincts but by choosing a "way of life." The Avengers, too, must come to choose their actions through their character. After all, the function of a good man relates to his choices, which involves him consulting with his friends in a process toward noble performances. He will pursue how he will live and the rational choices he makes. This leads us to the question: Are the new Avengers lead by a good man who is able to wield his power responsibly, or should he hand over his power to the UN? A good man shows us that it is possible for all autonomous superheroes to gain rational control over their non-rational desires.

Cap believes that he is more capable of ruling over the Avengers because he rules in accordance with what he thinks is best for them. His right to rule must be based on his virtuous aspirations. But, as Secretary of State Thaddeus Ross says, for the past four years the Avengers have "operated with unlimited power." Cap and his fellow associates share in the destruction of cities around the world, but he refuses to recognize any political obligations to the UN. He does not think that he should endorse the Sokovia Accords for the sake of a well-ordered world but has decided to operate by a set of rules that are above and apart from the good. But, the truly good man has to think of the good of others.

The value Cap places on the special skills and sacrifices of the Avengers determines whether he's fit to rule. If we follow Aristotle, the Avengers are dedicated to the virtue of justice, so as fellow Avengers, each should have a share in the decisions for the public interest. But, Cap refuses to deliberate and a good leader deliberates on his choice for the good of the team. Instead he chooses to leave and thinks only that the Accords have taken away his self-imposed right to rule, so Cap and his new team have decided to go into exile to avoid going to prison.

Captain America has picked a side, and so have his team members. The question we need to answer is whether Cap's team is on the side of justice. The condition of their old Avengers has been peace and order. But, now, political co-operation between team Cap no longer constitutes an alliance that benefits the safeguarding of the world. Cap has built a team that is neither for the good of the world nor for the good of the Avengers. They are no longer a community of superheroes who share in decisions over which invaders to fight. Instead, they are divided in two with Cap and his new team members as group of outlaws. The Avengers have split, and the world might not be safe with the two teams as odds with each other.

Cap does not have the bonds of trust to uphold the friendships needed to obtain justice. He considers the Sokovia Accords a surrender of their rights to choose. His new team and his obligations to them arise from the sacrifices they each make, rather than arising from a common interest in accordance with the principles of justice. Our superheroes are responsible for correcting the unfairness that threatens the citizens of the world, so their actions within the public sphere should be aimed at justice.

Aristotle refers to "an army whose good is found both in the order and in the leader, and more in the latter; for he does not depend on the order but it depends on him." When Cap leads his fellow Avengers against Crossbones, his team fails. Scarlet Witch's mistake when she deflects the bomb from Cap causes more destruction. It is under Cap's leadership that the team fails, even by his own admission. So here we say that Cap is not a good leader. A leader needs the virtues of a good man, which is neither excessive nor scarce in regard to his desires. Cap had to make sure that Lagos was safe, but in doing so his leadership was responsible for more civilian fatalities.

A virtuous leader—to be a good ruler—would and must possess practical wisdom, but the incident in Lagos was an act of injustice, so he has been unable to meet the virtues of ruling. As Black Panther, the new King of Wakanda states, Roger is both "warrior and King." His human soul, just like the new association of Avengers, has an order, with each part performing a different function. Part of his function as a ruler is to find a mean between the continuum of destruction and complete boundless actions. And just as his soul should be ruled by the reason and not by his appetites, so the highest good for the whole society requires observance of the rule of law. Yet, he believes the way in which the Avengers should be managed is not through political coercion by the UN, which he believes is the end goal of the Sokovia Accords. This raises two questions: Can Captain America rule as an unimpeded ruler? Can he, unconfined by the U.S. government and UN regulations, rule the new Avengers with moderation and justice? He would have to lead by a well-ordered soul, and so far he hasn't.

It would take a man of intellectual skill to keep these superhumans in check, as the temperate man is the one who leads rationally. Thus, Iron Man is a better leader because he has the intellectual power to make critical decisions and clearly recognize the strength of his fellow Avengers. He understands that the Avengers must live their lives through the use of reason and justice and by following laws that allow enhanced individuals to live virtuous lives. For our superheroes, the virtue of justice requires a bond among the Avengers "for the administration of justice."

Iron Man believes that the threat to the people requires that the government have oversight of the Avengers. The oversight will prompt the Avengers to deliberate on possible injustices where their superhuman powers may cause civilian deaths and destruction. It would require that the Avengers be regulated by the United Nations panel. Whether the UN panel is the proper authority to rule is a matter for Iron Man and the Avengers to consider. But, Iron Man's team would rather choose being ruled with the idea that they have some say in the rulings. And Iron Man would rather have the whole team together, because it would be large enough to defend itself from the bad guys, including those with superhuman powers. Iron Man believes that the bonds that they have would enable them to perform just actions. Iron Man is concerned with being a good man and with the advantages of having the whole team together in times of war.

We don't normally think of courage in battle, but courage has a goal. The leader of the Avengers needs to consider the motivation behind his actions. He shouldn't be too bold; we have seen that boldness leads to destruction. Iron Man, a soldier in battle and the leader of the Avengers, must have "political courage," to estimate the force to carry out the attack on his enemies and avoid "disgrace" from reproaches he and his fellow Avengers have had to suffer.

Reason must direct a good man in his bravery against his enemies. Leading the Avengers requires the skill of a ruler who is governed by reason, temperance, and courage. Iron Man must consider the destruction of states and civilians when waging a successful war. He must direct the Avengers with their different skills in war, and all must be part of the team Iron Man. He knows that in ruling the Avengers, they must pursue war through maintaining courage and moderation in their activities. He understands that the Avengers must have the share in the deliberating and judging, and that they are a multitude of superhumans that must have limitations or otherwise be "no better than the boundless bad guys." So, if we are to take Aristotle's account of ruling, a good man must understand that he has the Avengers to run. He emphasizes that they must work together to preserve the Avengers, and each has a different task to perform based on their different superhuman powers. And by following the UN panel decisions, they will moderate their aggressions and their actions the way a brave person would.

The Avengers have been split by two men who think they can rule based on the superiority of their wisdom. But only one can be right. By signing the Sokovia Accords, Tony Stark comprehends that it attributes to the morally good man. Vision, now part of Iron Man's association, states that "oversight is not an idea that can be dismissed out of hand." Iron Man must keep in mind the good of society, which primarily resides in ordered actions. He reaches this conclusion because he recognizes that his creation, Ultron, is responsible for the destruction in the Battle of Sokovia.

The Avengers' actions to save the world are the reasons for the war and destruction, which now has to become integrated into Iron Man's decision and how it affects the collective lives of the other members of the Avengers. He understands that the Avengers are instrumental members of an association that fight for justice, which requires courage to face dangers and face whom they have wronged. The Avengers are engaged in supremely just actions by abiding not to harm people and to follow the rule of law. The Avengers are friends and their friendship is rooted in the establish laws of the UN Regulations to protect individuals from harm by monitoring their actions. The Avengers' duties not to do harm do bind them to the UN panel, because no particular action may be determined in order not to do harm. Iron Man has the capacity an individual needs to reason and make decisions. Individuals are able to make judgements that make these decisions choiceworthy.

In the past the Cap was able to bring Iron Man onto his side in the Helicarrier, SHIELD's mobile base. Iron Man "exerts himself for the good . . . and . . . wishes himself what is good . . . and . . . is related to his friend" who is a friend to those with the same qualities of character. If Captain America is a good man he must have the confirmation of Iron Man, to ground the Cap's actions as admirable.

In *Civil War*, Captain America is placed between his friendship with Barnes and his friendship with Iron Man. Cap's moral goodness is relative to his judgment. He must choose between his childhood friend Bucky and Iron Man. If he were a good man, he would wish the good of Iron Man and his fellow Avengers. The bond that characterizes the Avengers is based on cultivating their moral virtues. And, when Bucky was changed and Captain America "is unable to change him [back], he [must] give him up." Friendships allow an individual's virtues to thrive. And Bucky doesn't share the virtues of a good man and a superhero. Cap must then, look into his soul and determine where he stands. He must follow the part of his soul that governs, the rational part, which has the capacity to properly order his sentiments. This means that Captain America must live under the guidance of the virtues of justice and temperance, which can only take place in the Avengers. It also implies the ability to bring his friends together into a virtuous harmony. But, he hasn't. He has questioned his friendship with Tony and his allegiance to the Avengers. He has caused disunity among them by breaking up the Avengers.

In the end, Cap didn't do what was advantageous to the team. Given all the events in *Civil War*, we saw Cap do what was for the sake of self-indulgence and not for the sake of the Avengers. He created a team of lawless superheroes. We see the distinguishing characteristic of men of different character: one willing to place himself above the law and forego his friends, and the other who's wise and temperate. Cap believes himself a leader, but he has not been able to lead Iron Man and his fellow Avengers to work for the same end.

By choosing what he best knows to be good, he is a man of a certain character—a good man. But, when he makes the choice not to endorse the Mutant Powers Act and refuses to sign the Sokovia Accords, he is not simply reasoning as an ordinary citizen, but as a leader. He influences political decisions, based on his superhuman powers. He must make choices, which implies moral excellence based on his unique position, which is the role Steve Rogers voluntary assumed, as leader in the new Avengers. But, as Captain America, Steve Rogers has a connection with the Avengers that is particularly distinctive of enhanced humans and their capacities. As a member of the Avengers, his identity comes through an awareness of the history with the Avengers and the interest he takes in its future, which therefore, gives rise to the bonds he and Tony Stark have.

It's not easy to settle the disagreement between Captain America and Iron Man. One believes the UN is strong-arming them, whereas the other feels the need for a government authority to oversee the Avengers. But Cap may not truly be the good man, if he chooses to promote the life of a solitary soldier. At the end, we see him throw down his shield; a shield created by Tony's dad, and abandon the Avengers to leave with Bucky. At the end he writes Tony Stark a letter. "The Avengers are yours. Maybe yours more so than mine."

Through exercising his virtues, Iron Man ensures the safety of humanity and exercises the virtues that support the idea of justice. Is he better fitted for judging? Aristotle proposes that having the quality of wisdom is connected to choice. At the end of *Civil War*, Iron Man makes the choice. He considers and deliberates about actions that reflect not only his interests but the interests of the Avengers.

Aristotle says that our capacity for thought, if used to make good moral decisions is a quality that we admire in each other. In saving the planet from evil in *Avengers: Age of Ultron*, the Cap and Iron Man used their intellect, but in their attempt to destroy Ultron, they cause great destruction in the Eastern European country, Sokovia. It is the rational part of the soul that is concerned with choice. And for Iron Man, the rational choice lies in a mean between two extremes. He is better fitted for judging and sharing in deliberation. As such, he makes choices that unlike Cap are directed by practical wisdom. He considers and deliberates on actions that the US Secretary Ross presents, and he reflects not only on his interests but the interests of the Avengers. But Cap, as a leader of the new Avengers has not employed wisdom and has not shown that he has the qualities of a good leader. He has not shown that he has the moral disposition to do what is just. He's not concern for the common welfare of the Avengers. Cap has made decisions based on his emotional friendship with Bucky instead of his fellow Avengers. For instance, he has thrown away his shield, has abandoned the new Avengers, and betrayed Iron Man. He is presumably lacking intelligent deliberation to promote justice.

So now we see who the good man is. Iron Man believes that signing the Sokovia Accords is done for the sake of the Avengers. He regards the authority and the established rules of the Sokovia Accords. As members of the Avengers their familiarity with one another's characters has lead them to trust and regard each other as friends. Tony Stark has been given thirty-six hours to find Captain America, and after twenty-four hours Tony calls the Cap "brother."

Aristotle used the word "philia" to refer to affection among equals, and we could use this word to include the feelings that the Avengers have for each other. If we look at the type of friendship that the Avengers have, we can argue that they have a friendship based on virtue, and they become better because of their association in the Avengers. The fact that their friendship is based on their individual virtues means that they have a moral bond. Besides, the Avengers are a community of superheroes which contributes something distinctive to each of their lives.

Iron Man considers its members valuable by keeping the Avengers together to fully realize that they are virtuous super-heroes. His leadership obligates him to those who chose to risk their lives. He believes in the need for an authority that provides order and security, and he understands that through that authority, he and his fellow Avengers have a say in the decisions to save the world. Tony, in order to obtain a higher level of virtuous activity, has concern for his friends and for the common good of humanity.

Iron Man is truly the good man and the one who should lead the Avengers on their next quest.

6
Who's the Better Friend?

COLE BOWMAN

Captain America is a better friend to his comrades than Iron Man is. But don't take this to mean that he is better *for* his friends than Iron Man, because the way he treats his friends has staggeringly significant, negative repercussions that ripple through the Marvel universe. This is why, to truly understand which is the "better" man between the two superhero powerhouses, we must look at their friendships to measure their worth.

While at first it might not seem as provocative as some of their other characteristics, the nature of their friendships is the most important quality that either of these superheroes has. Friendship may not appear to be as pivotal as their ties to the military, the strength of their willpower, or even their intellectual acumen, but it is one of the defining traits of not just what makes a person, but what makes their relationship with the world at large. Friendships can signal political alliances, friendships can compromise morality, friendships can build virtue. The way that each of these men engages with his friends ultimately makes up who he is as a person, and especially who he is as a hero.

Both Iron Man and Captain America have long, sordid histories stretching back to the Golden Age of comics and beyond. Because of this, they have a snarled web of relationships that highlight who they are as people in a way that few other aspects of their histories can. By looking at these relationships, we can uncover which of them is the better leader, which of them has the best interest for humanity in mind and which one has an overall more positive impact upon the world around him. Whichever of them is the better friend is also the super-hero best suited to make choices for the good of us all.

O My Friends, There Is No Friend

The above title is the beginning of many of the criticisms of friendship in philosophy. As it was first attributed to Aristotle (384–322 B.C.E.) in his groundbreaking work *Nicomachean Ethics,* it is a natural inclusion in any discussion of friendship even the ones having to do with superheroes, because before we start to tear apart the very concept of superhero-related friendship, we must first know what friendship is.

We understand friendship to be an affiliation between two or more people that is mutually acknowledged. The problem is that there is no *one* definition of friendship in philosophy, but luckily many philosophers have attempted to define the parameters more specifically. Many great thinkers have defaulted to a more poetic stylization to describe the nature of friendship when pressed, which is probably because their friends read their works.

Cicero (106–43 B.C.E.) was famously quoted saying, "a true friend is one who is, as it were, a second self." So, like the time that Hydra put Johanne Schmidt's brain in a clone of Steve Rogers, making him Rogers's "second self?" Probably not.

One surprisingly useful definition came from Pythagoras (around 570–495 B.C.E.): "Friends are as companions on a journey, who ought to aid each other to persevere in the road to a happier life." So your friends are your companions and they are responsible for helping you achieve a happier life? That's vague, at best, so we should look further.

Aristotle, one of the greatest philosophers of all time, took on the task of discussing the nature of friendship nearly three thousand years ago. *Nicomachean Ethics* was Aristotle's answer to questions on the nature of all the relationships in our lives, especially friendship. He worked extensively on the subject, proposing a system of three categories that these types of relationships can be sorted into. These categories were:

friendships of pleasure,

friendships of utility,

and friendships of virtue.

According to Aristotle, the first and most common type of friendship is that of pleasure. This kind of friendship is literally defined by the fact that the people involved in it derive pleasure in the other's company, and thus find value in the other person. These kinds of friendships are what many people would consider shallow, but are sprinkled throughout our everyday lives. A friendship of pleasure is the kind of friendship that does not necessarily benefit either party, but is perpetuated out of habit and ease more than a desire for growth and aid. These friendships are founded on mutual interests, like watching movies or fishing, or running around the Washington Monument, as is the case for Steve Rogers and Sam Wilson in the Marvel Comic Universe.

In fact, another pertinent example of this kind of friendship comes straight from the pages of Captain America's life. While he has had a number of good friends and allies, he has also been folly to those people who seek out his friendship simply because of the pleasure that they gain from familiarity and conversation with a noted celebrity. We see this happen near the two hour mark of *Captain America: Civil War*, when Ant Man joins Cap's side against Iron Man. Ant Man doesn't join because he believes in the principles that Cap is standing beside or because he dislikes Iron Man's political opinions, but simply because he's a fan of Captain America. While this friendship of pleasure paradigm isn't necessarily true from Cap's standpoint, it is definitely the motivating factor behind Ant Man's involvement. This becomes immediately clear when Rogers asks Scott Lang (Ant Man) if he knows who they're fighting and he replies, still obviously stupefied by Cap's presence: "Something about some . . . psycho assassins?"

A friendship of utility, on the other hand, is equally suspect to modern folks because it doesn't necessarily have mutual benefit at its core. A friendship of utility is that kind of friendship that exists specifically because of its usefulness in the lives of the participants. While this is, according to Aristotle and many other later philosophers, preferable to the simple pleasure friendships, it is still a shallower form of friendship than the ideal. These kinds of friendships are characterized by the simple benefit that a friendship causes in one's life and not by a desire to see to another's well-being. It's a very selfish form of friendship, something Tony Stark can attest to from personal experience.

A friendship of utility is presented quite beautifully in the relationship between Obadiah Stane and Tony Stark. While the two had been acquainted for quite some time through Tony's father, Howard Stark (who was Obadiah's business partner), they developed a friendship of their own after Howard's death. As far as Obadiah was concerned, the role Tony played in his life was as a benefactor for his successes. Having Tony around provided him with wealth, opportunity and technology. From Tony's standpoint, Obadiah was someone he could shuffle responsibility off onto whenever he didn't feel like dealing with it. They were both useful to each other and pretty much nothing more. It's little surprise that the moment this dynamic changed, their relationship fell apart. While Stane's specific motivations are different in the movie and the comic versions of Iron Man's story, in both he decides that Tony Stark is no longer useful to him and he takes action to remove him from Stark Industries, ultimately leading to Obadiah becoming the super-suit-wearing villain Iron Monger. Like in the case of Stane and Stark, friendships of utility can become toxic to one or both parties in a short amount of time should their level of utility change.

Aristotle valued the third kind of friendship above the rest, asserting it as the "true" form of friendship. The third order of friendship, according to Aristotle, is that of virtue. A friendship of virtue is based out on a mutual interest in the betterment of the self. Not unlike the friendship of utility, this relationship serves to help each friend gain. Unlike the friendship of utility, however, this kind of friendship is almost certainly founded without the prospect of *material* gain. Rather, a friend of virtue will help to nurture your pursuit of becoming a more virtuous person and vice versa.

To be a friend of virtue, you must want the best for your counterpart and do whatever is in your power to help them achieve it. This is exemplified beautifully in the relationship between Bucky Barnes and Steve Rogers, with each of them at different points throughout their decades-long friendship showing up just to help the other one achieve the "right thing."

One important thing that distinguishes a virtuous friendship from the others is that it doesn't necessarily need to be reciprocal, according to Aristotle's *Eudemian Ethics*. In the foundation of such a friendship it is more important to be on the antecedent side of love or caring. It's more important to love than to be loved. While an equanimity is very important in the context of friendships of pleasure or friendships of utility, Aristotle believes virtuous friendship will thrive if at least one participant is actively giving care to the other, even if the other never reciprocates.

While this seems unfair or, in the very least unequal, it is important to remember that there is something of an ulterior motive to virtuous friendships. This motive is for person A to help person B achieve a more virtuous existence, from the perspective of virtue ethics. Therefore, when person A shows person B love, or teaches them a moral value, they are in turn nurturing their own moral self. This is probably why Aristotle believed it to be the definitive form of friendship. It's friendship's version of the HulkBuster suit. While sometimes unwieldy, it helps to protect the self while benefiting the other people around it.

Any conversation about friendship must almost necessarily involve a discussion of directionality as well. This is where Aristotle's orders of friendship meet the challenge of everyday life, because there is such a thing as a one-sided or an unevenly distributed friendship. Aristotle explores the concept a bit in his examination of friendship, asserting that the best kinds of friendship are those that are equal in their attention to one another. Very little can go more wrongly in a friendship (or, indeed, any other kind of relationship) than to have it be anything other than mutual. If your friend doesn't treat you with the same amount of love and respect as you treat them, you'll probably feel slighted and hurt. Now, the relationships between superheroes is no different. An entire subplot exists in the Iron Man franchise to illustrate the disconnect between Pepper Potts's devotion to her relationship with Tony Stark and his own ignorance of her needs and desires.

To tie this back into the previous Aristotelian orders of friendship, consider the impact if person A were engaging in a friendship of pleasure with person B, but person B was directing a friendship of utility to person A. The inequality between the two would necessarily sour the relationship. In *Nicomachean Ethics*, Aristotle states that no matter which level of friendship person A assigned to person B, they both benefitted should person B treat them as a virtuous friend.

This is where Aristotle's vision of friendship comes into conflict with later philosophers, some of whom we will explore a little later on. The major argument against this ideal of friendship is that it's untenable for a long period of time or across a network of more than a couple of friends. The Hulkbuster Suit of virtuous friendship can't run forever. Even worse, it can only protect so many people at a time.

To understand the practical challenges of a virtuous friendship, we need to look back at the friendship between Steve Rogers and Bucky Barnes. Specifically during the *Winter Soldier* story arc, Steve acts according to Aristotle's virtuous order of friendship, sacrificing a great deal to bring his friend to a more virtuous path. While Bucky is eventually redeemed by Steve's actions, it's also important to look at the ramifications of his redemption, because the sacrifices that Steve made were at the direct cost of the wellbeing and safety of others. It's easy to see that, despite the fact that he's on the antecedent end of this friendship of virtue, Captain America does not become a more virtuous person for helping the Winter Soldier because he put other people in harm's way to do so, not the least of which Tony Stark himself. This is the folly of Aristotle's orders of friendship: singularity versus universality. Steve Rogers favors Bucky over others, so other people are left in the wake of literal destruction caused by Steve's attempts to help him.

This is why equality in friendship is so important, despite Aristotle's assertion that virtuous friendships can do without it. The only way for Steve Rogers to also gain virtue from Bucky is for Bucky to treat him as a virtuous friend. Aristotle would likely disagree with this point, because he spared no time cultivating relationships that wouldn't help him to be a more virtuous person at the end of said relationship (virtue was kind of Aristotle's *thing* . . .). But most average people aren't looking at friendship in the same way that Aristotle was. From a more practical, everyday understanding of friendship, so long as each person is on the same level, that's what matters. Value assigned equals value acquired. Good work for everyone involved, if an only if each person is mutually invested.

If you look back to our old friends, the Avengers, you find inequality in most of the relationships that are taking place throughout their shared history. While it's never explicitly stated that they are each seeking friendship from either Stark or Rogers, the way the team is divided during Civil War mostly comes down to these *relationships* and not the ideologies that galvanized the two leaders into action.

Enemies, There Are No Enemies!

In his work *Human, All Too Human*, German philosopher Friedrich Nietzsche (1844–1900) plays with Aristotle's earlier assertion "'O my friends, there is no friend" with the phrase above. "Foes, there are no foes" (p. 149). he says, asserting the inverse of the Aristotelian quote and perhaps grounding out the true meaning of the nature of friendship by doing just so. In his work, Nietzsche announced this inversion as though it were a catastrophe—a strange thought when thinking of an enemy. It would be catastrophic to learn once and for all that your enemies (your foes) have not been so for the entirety of your relationship (for, indeed, enemies *are* a relationship). Imagine fighting a war and realizing at the end of it that the enemies that you have been pursuing have not been your enemies all along. I wonder how the Avengers would feel knowing this little fact right about now.

This brings us back to the ongoing war between Captain America and Iron Man. Their conflict arose originally as a result of a proposed Superhero Registration Act in the Marvel comics universe. In the Marvel cinematic universe, the Sokovia Accords, which call for hero registration and international oversight, press the schism between Cap and Iron Man. Though there had been some tension throughout their storied histories, it wasn't until these proposed legislations came in that their tenuous relationship hit heads. In both the cinematic universe and the comic universe, the heroes have the same view: Captain America believes in the individual freedom of each superhero, trusting their autonomy and ability to self-govern, while Iron Man believes that superheroes need to be held accountable by the world's governments and that they owe people without superpowers access to their identities.

This division between ideologies is an old one—the struggle between personal autonomy and social responsibility—but there is something potent about transposing it over the structures of a superhero story, because of the necessary ramifications of a schism between people with superpowers. If Nick

Fury and Agent Coulson were to have a bar fight, the toll *could* be traumatic, resulting in physical injury, property damage and probably some really hurt feelings. But that would be just about the scope of it, because both Fury and Coulson are regular, if remarkable, humans. If two superheroes have a bar fight, however, the toll is much more likely to involve collateral damage, destruction on a massive scale and scores of injured (or dead) bystanders. One of the core issues of a superhero-related existence is the matter of scale. Damage is orders of magnitude greater than it would be in a situation with just humans (withholding the fact, of course, that some humans have access to weapons of mass destruction). What comes of this idealistic difference between Cap and Iron Man is that the problem does not end with simple disagreement because of this scale. Superhero problems are greater (just like the rest of what they do). Because of this, superheroes have to be more careful about both their enemies *and* the friends. The city of Sokovia wouldn't have been destroyed if Ultron hadn't had the power he did and the people who were trying to stop him—The Avengers and their friends—hadn't had the same level of power.

The Politics of Friendship

Twentieth-century French philosopher Jacques Derrida (1930–2004) offered a significant new perspective in the philosophy of friendship in his work *The Politics of Friendship*. Derrida collected the ideas of many of his predecessors (Aristotle, Nietzsche, Montaigne, Cicero, and *many, many* others) and galvanized them into a forceful explication of the *consequences* of friendship, not just the means of friend-making, as had many of his predecessors. It's these consequences that we'll find the most relevant to our understanding of Cap and Iron Man. In this work, Derrida detailed the means by which much of the political discourse of the world could be boiled down into the simple articulations of the relationships between influential people.

Though the work itself is essentially a collection of essays on the topic of friendship, the central theme of the self within the scheme of friendship and politics is threaded throughout. Ultimately, Derrida suggests that an ideal paradigm of humanity instills the idea of fraternity or brotherhood in us all. While he acknowledges that the idea of *brother*hood is problematic, necessarily reinforcing the idea of androcentrism and eclipsing anyone who does not neatly fit into the *brother* role, he insists that its usefulness as a concept is worth the price. In fraternity, he finds the ideal of mutuality, individualism, and the acknowledgment of the self. In fraternity, there is equality and care. Derrida's fraternity, however, insists upon inclusion of daughters, inclusion of others unknown, and inclusion of those unequal in social status or income. Derrida's fraternity is the underpinning quality in a true democracy. And, indeed, he asserts that should people be able to rely upon fraternity as a social norm, democracy would be the only viable option for political discourse, because the value of all people would be level no matter where they come from. *Your* opinion would be just as valuable as Black Panther's, even though he is both a king and a superhero.

But what does this have to do with friendship? Put simply, Derrida built this entire thesis upon the principles of friendship that his philosophical predecessors put forward for him. Derrida's fraternity is an echo of Aristotle's virtuous friendship, in which each person invests value into one another, but with one important caveat. Derrida's friendship insists upon equality and mutuality. This simple change in emphasis solves the problem with Aristotle's version that we discussed before. By refocusing Aristotle's perspective of virtuous friendship in this way, Derrida makes the case that the kind of friendship that only benefits one party is not a friendship at all, but a device to benefit the self. For a true friendship, everyone must be valued at the same level. There is no room for "better" friends, because everyone falls into the same order. In that way, the ideal of friendship is democratic, just like fraternity. In a speech to the University of Essex, Derrida explains what friendship and democracy have to do with one another: "Democracy means, minimally, equality—and here you see why friendship is an important key, because in friendship, even in classical friendship, what is involved is reciprocity, equality, symmetry…"

And this is truly the heart of the matter of politics and friendship in the Marvel universe. If politics are, as Derrida suggests, the result of relationships, the way that Tony Stark and Steve Rogers treat their friends has global impact because of the scale of their influence. Stark is a billionaire in charge of one of the largest companies in the world with technology that is responsible for reshaping the face of warfare itself. Steve Rogers is an international celebrity, super soldier, and military commander who has become the face of what it means to be a superhero. The most significant relationships that these men have are formed are with other such remarkable people. When *their* friends have a bar fight, it's not just broken glass and hurt feelings, its entire cities left in ruin, global economies thrust into upheaval and scores of innocent people put in harm's way.

This is why it's important to examine the friendships that make up the Avengers. Despite all of their individual relationships with one another, the true testament of their worth comes down to how they treat mankind in general. Do they treat regular people democratically, as equals with reciprocal responsibility for each other's well being? While an individual would most likely want to chum around with Captain America because he's kind and charming, he gives priority for some people over all others as we see with his treatment of Bucky Barnes. His individualistic ideology is reflected in his individual attentions to his friends. He favors the other superheroes over the desires of regular humans by refusing the Sokovia Accords (or the Superhero Registration Act), and thus refuses the importance of Derrida's democratic friendship. He would rather have the superheroes regulate each other, reinforcing the idea that they are somehow *more* than the average human.

Tony, however, doesn't give priority to any other particular person. Tony isn't all that enjoyable and definitely forgets his friends' birthdays, but Tony doesn't put priority over one person's life rather than another's. Tony understands that it is a superhero's duty to submit to the will of the rest of mankind. A superhero might have greater power or more resources than a mother who works in human resources for the state department, but said superhero is not more inherently valuable than the mother. Steve Rogers, on the other hand, asserts through his actions time and time again that an individual is more important than the collective of humanity. This is why Tony Stark is better for his friends than Captain America.

Oh, my friends, there is no superhero friend. For in one friendship, you thrive as an individual at the cost of your place amongst all of mankind. And, in another friendship, you are never mutually acknowledged, but your place as a part of humanity is assured. Captain America is better *to* his friends, but Iron Man is better *for* his friends.

II

Cap Wins

7
How Captain America and Iron Man Embody America

JOHN ALTMANN

One of the things we commonly hear during election season is, "America is a land of opportunity." We make idols out of people like Steve Jobs, Oprah Winfrey, and Donald Trump, to serve as examples of the truth of America being such a land. These symbols of industry are the core of what America is about and so to love America and to feel a sense of patriotism, we should pull ourselves up by our bootstraps and follow in the path of these symbols. Right?

There's a contradiction here, and that contradiction is at its most defined when we look at the lives of Tony Stark and Steve Rogers. When we look at Tony Stark, what we see is the poster child of the American Dream. He's rich, at the forefront of innovative technology, and has used that technology and wealth to empower himself as Iron Man and become a protector of the world.

Tony Stark serves as a mirror to how America views itself as a nation. The problem is that while Tony Stark might be the epitome of the American dream, he's the furthest thing from patriotic. Because, rather than being motivated by a love of country, Tony Stark first and foremost has a love for himself and occasionally shows love for people in his orbit.

Stark is an individualist and even though he's a member of the Avengers, his decisions are always informed by things that see him at the center. The biggest example of this was his championing of the Sokovia Accords, which came about after Stark was confronted by a mother whose son was a casualty of Ultron in Sokovia and who blamed Stark for his death.

Now compare Tony Stark to Steve Rogers, a man who lived in the age of World War II America, a man who wanted to serve his country as a soldier against the Nazi threat. He was so desperate to serve, in his first movie we see him even agreeing to be a human test subject for the secret scientific project of a serum designed to make super soldiers. Rogers put himself at great personal risk to serve his country and for what? To become a mascot who sells war bonds.

Compare that with Tony Stark bragging at a congressional hearing in the second Iron Man movie that he has successfully privatized world peace. Comparing these two men provides us with a philosophical account of what patriotism is and what it is not. Iron Man may be a symbol of America. But Captain America, in his patriotism, is the embodiment of its very conscience.

There Is No Me in Patriotism

The English philosopher Roger Scruton defines patriotism in his book *The Meaning of Conservatism* as an understanding that we stand or fall together as citizens and that we work together to maintain the traditions and customs that define our nation. One word that could best frame Scruton's definition of patriotism is community. A nation is a kind of community and so in that sense, teamwork is the key to a healthy and strong nation.

No one person as an individual can maintain the integrity and well-being of a nation upon their own shoulders. Captain America understands the significance of teamwork and demonstrates that understanding in his first film. Iron Man, on the other hand? He thinks he can hold the whole world upon his shoulders well beyond the United States of America.

For the majority of the first two Iron Man movies, Tony Stark is a man who is very much into himself who believes far more in his own individual efforts than extending his hand in search of the help of others. In this light, Tony Stark can rightly be characterized as an individualist. We see this most prominently in *Iron Man 2* when Tony not only tells a senator at a congressional hearing that he cannot have his Iron Man suit, but then turns and faces the people attending the hearing, throws up two peace signs, and says that he has successfully privatized world peace. He's very resistant to the idea of teamwork, which he makes explicit in *Iron Man 2* when he tells Rhodes that he works alone.

Tony Stark only embraces the idea of teamwork when all other options are off the table and Stark finds himself at the end of his rope. It is clear that Tony Stark not only lacks the sense of community to be a patriot, but that Stark's very creation of the Iron Man suit is reflective not of a love of country or the world, but of a love of himself and a celebration of his technology and resources. It is this idea, that Tony Stark loves himself and believes himself to be the only one capable of defending America and the world, that makes Iron Man a poor symbol of patriotism, which calls for a love of neighbor as much as oneself. Neither a nation nor the world is made great by a sole pair of hands putting themselves into the soil to do the work. Even if the hands are part of a super-powered Iron Man suit.

Now compare Tony Stark's narcissism and his individualist approach to heroism with Steve Rogers, who, if we are to follow Scruton's definition of what makes a patriot, was a patriotic American from early on in his life. In the first Captain America movie *The First Avenger*, Steve Rogers is living in the era of World War II and all he dreams of doing, is serving in the military to combat the Nazi threat that is currently terrorizing the world. The problem is, he is very physically frail and has many times failed the physical exam to determine who can serve.

Rogers could quit, but he holds serving his country to such a degree of importance that he subjects his body to scientific experimentation whose end goal is the creation of a super soldier. Even then, however, Rogers will face adversity, as a Hydra agent had infiltrated the experiment and killed the head scientist Erskine and then himself. Despite such a tragic occurrence, Rogers will not quit on his dream or on his beliefs in community.

After Hydra's successful infiltration, Steve Rogers is more eager than ever to face Hydra and keep America safe. Senator Brandt won't permit this, however, because the Hydra attack results in the super soldier formula being lost. So instead, scientists continue to study Rogers to regain the formula while Rogers is touring the country promoting war bonds as Captain America. While doing so, he learns that his best friend Bucky Barnes has been captured and seeks the help of Peggy Carter and Howard Stark to fly him to where Barnes has been captured.

After Rogers rescues Barnes and releases other prisoners of Hydra, Rogers recruits Barnes and others to commit numerous assaults on Hydra's bases. Working as a team, they are able to do significant damage to Hydra even at the cost of Barnes's apparent death and Rogers freezing himself at the end of the struggle. Steve Rogers is a born team player and one who embodies better than Tony Stark ever could Scruton's model patriot: one who recognizes that we stand and fall together.

Thoughtful Patriotism versus Reckless Cosmopolitanism

One of the most common arguments against patriotism and being patriotic is that patriotism, which as we know is a sense of love and pride in one's country, may transform into nationalism, which is a sense that one's country is superior to all others. So if patriotism possesses this underlying danger, what is the alternative?

One approach known as cosmopolitanism, means being a citizen of the world. Having a world consciousness, the cosmopolitan argues, would mean caring about the suffering and struggles of people well beyond your borders, which would mean not supporting some things in your own nation, like greater military activity. Of course, cosmopolitanism can have its faults, just as patriotism can have its strengths; it's just all a matter of how you approach it. Nowhere is this more evident than the cosmopolitan Iron Man and the patriot Captain America.

Tony Stark has shown his cosmopolitan nature dating back to the first Iron Man movie, when he tests his Iron Man suit by liberating villagers in Afghanistan from the brutality of The Ten Rings, the same group that kidnapped Stark at the beginning of the film. He also exhibits his cosmopolitan mindset later in the movie when he fights against his former mentor Obadiah Stane, who sells the Stark Industry weapons the Ten Rings get ahold of, and who makes his own version of the Iron Man suit and powers it with Stark's reactor that Stane rips straight from his chest. Stane plans to mass-produce the suits for warfare and plans to take over Stark Industries, reverting it back into a military weapons company. Tony realizes how much destruction those weapons cause around the world and resolves to stop Stane which he ultimately does. For as narcissistic as Stark can be, the betterment of the world is never far from his thoughts.

But his cosmopolitan mindset is at its strongest after the first Avengers movie. Stark, upon learning of aliens, gods, and other worlds which he sees as potential grave threats to Earth, develops PTSD and drives himself to exhaustion and his relationships into the ground as he builds an army of Iron Man suits in *Iron Man 3*. Now while at the end of *Iron Man 3* Stark has those suits destroyed, he doesn't destroy his global defense system known as Ultron. In the second Avengers movie, Tony Stark activates Ultron and eventually it becomes sentient.

While Ultron was designed to serve as a global defense system against threats such as the aliens we see in the first Avengers movie, Ultron comes to the conclusion that humanity must be wiped out if the Earth is to be truly protected. Now while the Avengers do ultimately defeat Ultron, its existence shows that Tony's cosmopolitan mindset can ironically harm the Earth, if he tries approaching cosmopolitan solutions as an individualist and relying on his own capabilities. He has no sense of community except for the Avengers, whom he has put in danger multiple times, even though he defends them as well.

For Stark to strengthen his existing sense of cosmopolitanism, he needs to not just be a citizen of the world, but to listen to those in *his* world just as Captain America does. The creation of Ultron was a decision he took upon himself without consulting even those closest to him. Had he brought the matter before the Avengers, they could have discussed it as a team should and hearing the opinions of those like Captain America, might have convinced Tony that the creation of Ultron was not the best path to take to world peace.

Steve Rogers has always known how to be thoughtful with his patriotism. Having grown up in the era of World War II, and having fought against Hydra in his own time, he sees the terrors of nationalism and the threats that having an obsession over your country's power and standing in the world can pose, namely, government overreach. This is precisely the problem that Captain America faces in his third movie, *Civil War:* after the Avengers tried to apprehend Brock Lumlow (who stole a biological weapon from a lab in Lagos) and got into an altercation that saw Wakandan humanitarian workers lose their lives.

In response to this, the UN draws up the Sokovia Accords, named after the land of Sokovia which Ultron destroyed in *Avengers: Age of Ultron*, which would permit the UN greater oversight and control over the Avengers. The Accords would require superheroes to register in databases, and follow certain governmental guidelines. Tony Stark is for the Accords, because he feels that the Avengers should be supervised, so that the humans they constantly endanger will be able to have a stronger sense of trust in the Avengers.

Steve Rogers is against the Accords because he doesn't trust the government's judgment as much as his own and he recognizes that the government having this amount of control puts everyone at serious risk. We can see the conflict here. Stark is trying to make the Avengers a more effective superhero unit by having non-superpowered humans, the same people they are charged with protecting, be able to have a greater say in their lives. In Tony's mind, the powers of the Hulk are on a par with a Stark Industries missile. We know Stark has a disdain for weapons being used against innocent civilians because of the Ten Rings from the first *Iron Man* movie, and he recognizes that the Avengers have become the weapon.

Steve Rogers, on the other hand, because of his love of country and knowing what it means to be a part of a community, looks out for his teammates, his country, and because Hydra has targeted his country and Rogers has made that a priority, by him fighting Hydra it also benefits the world. This shows that thoughtful patriotism can be just as effective as cosmopolitanism. Because when you're able to focus on a land or people that you love, there's a better chance of that love changing the world than the detached and calculated approach that is meant to serve the whole world. Captain America believes that if they are constrained in their abilities as the Avengers, they will be less effective at protecting nations that need them and on the whole, less effective at protecting the world. You could say that Steve Rogers's belief boils down to: When you stop a villain terrorizing one nation, you spare the world that suffering.

Morality Comes from Community

The philosopher Alasdair MacIntyre believes that patriotism is necessary to lead a moral life. This is because our moral development is rooted in a particular community, with its own set of customs and its own history. So being a patriot in MacIntyre's view means following the morality of your particular community to lead a morally rich life.

Both Steve Rogers and Tony Stark grow up in unique communities. Steve's father suffers from alcoholism and so, he is primarily raised by his mother, who teaches him about bravery, love, and other values she wants him to carry with him throughout his life. Tony Stark, on the other hand, grows up with a father whom he is never close with, and both of his parents die in a car accident when he's very young. So we can see that Tony Stark and Steve Rogers come from two very different communities, both found in the same America and which are deeply reflected in their actions as both Iron Man and Captain America.

Because Tony loses his parents at a very young age, he's scared to grow close to anyone else for fear of losing them and so, because he sees no better way, he embraces the individualist mindset. When he builds an army of Iron Man suits, not a single person knows of his plans. When he engineers Ultron and activates it, no one can stop him because nobody knows he has to be stopped. But Tony only does these things because he wants to preserve the lives and relationships of others all across the world. That's why in the first *Iron Man*, Tony is determined to save fellow captive Yinsen, who has a wife and a child at home.

When Yinsen dies, Tony destroys the weapons of the Ten Rings, so that they lose a certain degree of capability to harm anyone else the way they harmed Yinsen. Tony knows the pain of losing a sense of community and has witnessed first hand others lose their sense of community too. When he aligns with the Sokovia Accords after he talks with a mother who tells him the Avengers killed her son, this makes him a great cosmopolitan, because you can say you truly care for the world when you acknowledge that you yourself are a threat to its welfare. It is the ultimate sign of Tony taking responsibility for his actions.

Steve Rogers has always been a team player. In his first movie we know when he becomes Captain America, he listens to his superiors at first and becomes a mascot to sell war bonds because it is a role that serves his team, despite it being personally unsatisfying. When Captain America knows the threat that Hydra poses around the world, he recruits Bucky Barnes and other heroes to take down Hydra's bases. In *Captain America: Winter Soldier*, there is a mole in SHIELD's ranks who is working for Hydra and is furthering Hydra's agenda of world domination. So Captain America teams with Black Widow and The Falcon to uncover the mole and to stop the Winter Soldier, who is a Hydra-serving assassin.

In that movie, it is revealed that the Winter Soldier is actually Bucky Barnes, who was taken by Hydra and brainwashed. Captain America refuses to give up on Bucky, because unlike Tony Stark who has more or less always felt alone, Captain America has been a man of community ever since he was the frail Steve Rogers training alongside Bucky Barnes to join the military. The community for Captain America has since become the United States as a whole, but the man under the suit, Steve Rogers, recognizes Bucky Barnes as not only a fellow American who shares his ideals despite the brainwashing, but also a member of the more personal community of those Steve Rogers cares for most. It is this sense of love combined with a strong sense of community, that makes Captain America's thoughtful patriotism so powerful.

Captain America continues to fight for his country and for his best friend Bucky in his third movie, *Civil War*. We already know Captain America's strong stand against the Sokovia Accords, because he feels that such an action is the government overstepping its boundaries and that the Sokovia Accords pose serious risks to fellow Avengers as well as to all other people with superpowers or abilities.

Iron Man supported the Sokovia Accords because he thinks the Avengers need to be held more accountable and he also wanted to ease the nagging of his own conscience because his machines are still hurting people in lands beyond his personal proximity. An even bigger disagreement between Captain America and Iron Man than the Sokovia Accords in *Civil War* though, is the fate of Bucky Barnes. As we learned in *Captain America: Winter Soldier*, Bucky was brainwashed by Hydra and hasn't been his true self. In *Civil War*, Tony Stark sees footage towards the end of the movie that Bucky was the reason his parents were killed in that car accident so many years ago. This is the last straw for Tony, he was already weary of Bucky because he works for Hydra and thus poses a threat to the entire world with his capabilities as an elite soldier, but knowing that Bucky killed his parents breaks him emotionally as he now knows it was Bucky who took Tony's community from him. Rogers on the other hand, knowing that Bucky isn't himself, sets out to protect Bucky and fights Stark so that he won't kill him.

Captain America wins the struggle but the greater war seems to permanently break the bond between Captain America and Iron Man. Tony Stark's anger at the perceived selfishness of Steve Rogers for putting Bucky's life above the lives of the world and Bucky's friendship above the friendship Steve has collectively with the Avengers, makes it so that he can't reach out to him in forgiveness. Rogers can and does, however; at the end of the movie he writes Tony a letter telling him that if Tony ever needs them, the Avengers will be there for him.

Captain America's sense of community, which he began nurturing as a young man training for the military, allows him to see the very best in everyone. To be a patriot, you must see the very best in your country even when it is at its lowest. Tony Stark's individualism, meanwhile, makes it so that he can't see beyond himself and all that entails. Iron Man could learn much from Captain America's patriotism and the truth is, we all can.

Can the Two Extremes Meet?

We know now that Iron Man is an individualist while simultaneously being of a cosmopolitan mindset. Individualism and cosmopolitanism contradict each other, and we see this conflict play out in all three of the Iron Man movies as well as both of the Avengers movies.

While Tony's heart is consistently in the right place, such as when he stopped the Ten Rings and liberated that Afghan village, Tony always initially tries to do these things alone and not involve his friends such as Rhodes because Tony feels involving them increases the risk of harming them. Captain America on the other hand, has been a lifelong patriot and a man who is all about the team. He loves his country, but is willing to stand against the decisions of its leaders if he believes them to be harmful, like the enacting of the Sokovia Accords. At times Captain America is too concerned with his own community—remember his determination to rescue

Barnes despite all of the wrongdoing he commits as a brain-washed agent of Hydra? Being too concerned with your own community can make you blind both to its faults and how they harm the world at large. This is how patriotism turns into nationalism, which can ultimately lead to the same fascism that Captain America has rejected since he first fought Red Skull and the Nazis.

So the question has to be raised: Since both of these men represent America in one form or another, can they meet in the middle? While I have made the case that Captain America's patriotism is morally preferable for America's future and something we can all learn from, that is not to say Iron Man's approach is completely without merit. Perhaps the answer is as political philosopher Martha Nussbaum once expressed; being a patriot first and growing into a cosmopolitan later. Nussbaum agrees with MacIntyre that we all begin our moral development with our family, friends, and country as a community, but she believes that we can use the morals we adopt from that community to extend our moral concerns beyond our borders.

It is here where we can look to Tony Stark. After the events of *The Avengers* where Loki attempts to be a conqueror with an alien army, Tony doesn't see just a threat to the United States but to the entire world. In response to this threat Tony created Ultron as a global defense system. While Ultron itself was disastrous, the sentiment behind its creation, that being a global protection system against extraterrestrial threats, was on point and could have taken a better direction if Stark had welcomed the opinions and the knowledge of his fellow Avengers, rather than relying solely on his own intellect.

So perhaps when we look at Iron Man and Captain America, we see two halves of the best possible American we are all capable of being: Iron Man is someone who recognizes that the world is worth protecting, and while Captain America also makes this recognition, he does so only in the sense that he sees it as a side effect of keeping his own community safe. Steve Rogers has less of a cosmopolitan mindset and more of a selfish desire to protect and strengthen his personal relationships, which happen to service the world at large.

While Rogers could benefit from Tony's open-mindedness about the world, Tony could learn from Steve about the value of deep and rich friendships that could have the power to change the world. In the end, maybe there's no need for a civil war at all between these two, just as there's no need for a civil war between any of us as neighbors in this nation and as neighbors of the largest community imaginable: the Earth itself.

8
Believing the Impossible in a World of Compromise

MATTHEW WILLIAM BRAKE

Steve Rogers is a man of faith. Various incarnations of the character show this to be the case. In the first Avengers movie, Cap quips to Black Widow, "There's only one God, Ma'am"—but Steve's faith isn't just reserved for divine beings. As he writes to Tony Stark in *Captain America: Civil War*, "My faith's in people . . . and I'm happy to say that, for the most part, they haven't let me down."

By contrast, Tony Stark is a man of reason. He's a brilliant thinker, but he lives in the "real world." While he believes that many things are possible, he doesn't have the faith to believe in the impossible, as Steve Rogers does.

In a cynical and technologically advanced age, "faith" can seem like an antiquated concept—kind of like Captain America. The problems of the modern world seem to demand a realist. A skeptic. A cynic (maybe that's why we love Tony Stark, besides Robert Downy, Jr.'s brilliant performance). But it's only by trusting in the impossible, like Cap, and acting accordingly that we can truly find heroic hope to face the problems in our world. We must never stop having faith that, as Captain America says, "There is always a way" (*House of M* #1).

Ethics vs. Religion

In *Captain America: Civil War*, the fallout from *Age of Ultron* combined with the death of a number of civilians in a fight with Crossbones leads the UN to propose establishing a council charged with oversight of the Avengers in a bill entitled the

"Sokovia Accords." While proposing that the Avengers sign the Accords, Secretary Thaddeus Ross says, "Compromise. Reassurance. That's how the world works."

Responding similarly to the way his character did in the comic book version of the story, Tony concurs with Ross and supports the Sokovia Accords; however, Steve maintains that the Avengers need to stand for something beyond what is dictated by social standards of morality, which are susceptible to the whims of the majority, with Steve arguing, "What if they tell us to go somewhere we shouldn't, or what if there's somewhere we should go, and they don't let us."

In many ways, Cap and Shellhead represent the distinction that philosopher Søren Kierkegaard (1813–1855) makes between the ethical and religious spheres of existence. In *Fear and Trembling*, the ethical is described as a domain of reason, in which "the whole of existence of the human race rounds itself off as a perfect, self-contained sphere, and then the ethical is that which limits and fills at one and the same time" (*Fear and Trembling*, p. 68). In other words, every moral decision can be understood according to universally accessible reason, and the universal accessibility of reason leads Kierkegaard to refer to the ethical as a "social morality."

In a merely ethical world, the idea of God or the need for faith is unnecessary. Kierkegaard describes God as a "vanishing point" in the ethical. Someone like Iron Man, a man of reason, can ultimately only hope to be a tragic hero in this kind of world, having to choose between the lesser of two evils in a world of uncomfortable, but understandable, choices. However, such a position still leaves us guilty, and ultimately in despair. While reason is capable of grasping all of the possible human options, the religious sphere encourages faith in more than is humanly possible. In making heroic choices, it is willing to hope for more than what reason or the "social morality" is capable of grasping. Like Cap, faith acknowledges the limits of the compromises and reassurances of the crowd or social majority and aims at something higher than a choice between the lesser of two evils.

Civil War (The Comic One . . .)

The comic-book version of *Civil War* kicks off when a group of amateur heroes called the New Warriors ambush a group of villains near a local elementary school in Stamford, Connecticut. The heroes are out of their league, and one of the villains, Nitro, sets off an explosion that not only kills most of the New Warriors, but many of the children at the school as well. In response, Congress enacts the Superhuman Registration Act, which, among other things, requires superheroes to divulge their secret identities to the government. Cap is initially assigned the task of enforcing the law, but after refusing to lead the hunt for unregistered heroes, SHIELD turns on him and tries to arrest him. In Cap's place, Iron Man takes charge and thus begins the clash between the two heroes in this story.

After a heart-breaking battle in *Civil War* #4 between Cap's anti-registration forces and Tony's pro-registration forces in which the hero Black Goliath is killed, Steve and Tony meet at the old Avengers mansion under a flag of truce to privately work things out one last time in *Iron Man / Captain America: Casualties of War*. During the conservation, the two men reminisce about previous conflicts between them, and as they do, the ideological differences between the two of them come out. Tony criticizes Steven for thinking that every superhero is like him: "You're the perfect man. You live by ideals and standards that are . . . impossible for anyone but you." He goes on to insinuate that Steve is out of touch with the real world: "You dig in your heels and fight even harder. Never mind whether you can win. Sometimes I think you'd rather go out in a blaze of glory than face reality."

For his part, Steve insists, "What's right is what's right. If you believe it, you stand up for it." While this stance may initially seem stubborn or naive, Steve reminds Tony how quickly 'reality' can change: "You don't know who could get elected, how public sentiment might change. I'm old enough to remember Japanese-Americans being put in camps because they were judged potential threats to national security." Not only that, but there are plenty of intelligent supervillains in the world who could hack whatever servers all of the superhero identities are stored in. Steve tells Tony that his problem is that "You've always thought you knew best by virtue of your genius" and that he uses that genius to manipulate others into the results that he thinks are best, like exploiting Spider-Man's need for a father-figure so that he would join the pro-registration forces. All that matters for Tony is the result.

Beginnings and Results

For Kierkegaard, a hero must rise above "the idea of the state or the idea of a society" (p. 62). Society and those who have security in this life want to judge great people and their decisions by the results, but heroes are concerned with how things begin. A hero risks being a scandal and an offense to the world and that means at times appealing to something higher than law, ethics, or reason. This is reflected in Captain America's response to Sharon Carter concerning the rule of law in *Civil War* when he tells her that the US "was founded on breaking the law. Because the law was wrong." (*Captain America*, Volume 5, #22).

Kierkegaard's go-to example for matters of faith is that of Abraham, who was told by God to sacrifice his only son Isaac; however, God spoke to Abraham right before he was about to kill Isaac and stopped him. God's command to kill Isaac and then spare him was in part a performative act to show that Abraham's God was different than other gods who would require child sacrifice, but does the result justify Abraham's initial act of obedience? Or was Abraham justified by appealing to something higher than reason, ethics, or society at the beginning without knowing how it would all end?

Steve's appeal to Tony is that the ends don't justify the means, but it is how one begins that matters. One cannot anticipate the result and the unexpected consequences of one's actions. In the case of the Civil War, Steve seems justified. A shape-shifting race of aliens called the Skrulls were able to infiltrate the superhero community and infect all of Tony's technology, effectively crippling the U.S. national security apparatus over which Stark Industries had a monopoly. Additionally, following the defeat of the Skrull queen by the villain Norman Osborn, a.k.a. the Green Goblin, Tony becomes a fugitive and is pursued by Osborn who wants to obtain the identities of all the registered heroes. Tony's genius didn't see any of that coming. But Steve knew that how you begin, you could say "in faith," is more important than any of the results that you might anticipate through reason alone. Society's fickle opinion and Tony's genius didn't ensure the best result, and led to something worse—*The Dark Reign* (or Norman Osborn).

A hero cannot determine the end, but they can believe and determine where they begin. It is the beginning, not the result that makes them a hero. Abraham began with faith and wrestled with all of "the distress, the anxiety, the paradox" that it involves (p. 65), and for Kierkegaard, this makes him greater than any hero. Faith is a passion, open to being misunderstood, but Iron Man's actions represent "an age that has crossed out passion in order to serve science" or a result reason can control (p. 7).

One Was Life, One Was Death

Jonathan Hickman's run on the Avengers was an ambitious project that started with "the great idea." That idea was the expansion of the Avengers roster to counter the ever-growing threats that the Avengers face. As Hickman narrates, this great idea "started with two men. One was life [Captain America]. And one was death [Iron Man]" (*Avengers*, Volume 5, #3). This was particularly true in light of how each man faced the looming threat of Hickman's run—multiversal incursions. For reasons revealed later in Hickman's run, the Marvel multiverse had begun to die as a result of the earths of different universes colliding with one another. If a universe's earth was destroyed, its entire universe died as well.

To face this threat, the Illuminati, a group of Marvel superhero leaders including Steve and Tony, gathered to discuss their options. Black Panther, having witnessed an incursion over his home country of Wakanda, had encountered a mysterious being named the Black Swan, who destroyed the other encroaching earth using an anti-matter bomb. Mr. Fantastic presents the Illuminati with the Black Swan's plans for the bomb, the implication being that it might present a worst-case scenario option, before Cap interrupts him: "Let me stop this conversation right here. We are going to handle this exactly like we normally would . . . Because that's what we do" (*New Avengers*, Volume 3, #2). As the Illuminati discuss the hard choices they have to make and talk about who among them might be willing to kill another world, Tony speaks up, "If this is the end of everything, then perhaps it's best for everything to remain on the table while we search for an answer." Tony's openness to such a deadly solution is met with horror by Steve, who replies, "Anthony, . . . what the hell is wrong with you?" Steve admonishes them all: "You just have to believe. Believe in the cause . . . believe in each other . . . this is all going to work out. I know it."

Steve is alone in his optimistic heroism. He is surrounded by men of learning like Tony Stark, Mr. Fantastic, and Doctor Strange and by shrewd kings like Black Bolt, Namor the Sub-Mariner, and Black Panther. But of Steve we can say, "That man was not a thinker. He did not feel any need to go beyond faith" (p. 9). Steve has "faith like a mustard seed" that can "move mountains" (p. 49). It is this faith that allows him to make inspirational speeches like this one:

> Doesn't matter what the press says. Doesn't matter what the politicians or the mobs say. Doesn't matter if the whole country decides that something wrong is something right. This nation was founded on one principle above all else: the requirement that we stand up for what we believe, no matter the odds or the consequences. When the mob and the press and the whole world tell you to move, your job is to plant yourself like a tree beside the river of truth, and tell the whole world—"No, you move." (*Amazing Spider-Man* vol. 1 #537)[1]

Shrewd people like Namor, Black Panther, and Black Bolt "always have great difficulty in making" this kind of "movement of faith" (32). Likewise, those who rely on human reason like Mr. Fantastic try to move beyond faith by human calculation.

Tony is a different than the other Illuminati. He still doesn't have faith, but he has resignation. He accepts the pain, loss, and the reality that, as the common refrain throughout Hickman's run reminded us: "Everything dies." In a final climactic battle in New York City during the final incursion as their world crashes around them and the inevitable doom of the multiverse becomes apparent, Steve confronts Tony with the ugly truth: "You knew it was a lie. You knew there was no stopping this" (*Avengers*, Volume 5, #44). As they continue fighting, Tony gets the upper hand and shoots a repulsor blast into Steve's face as they are both crushed by a falling helicarrier. As Hickman writes, "It started with two men. One was life . . . and one was death. And one . . . always wins. Everything dies."

---

[1] *I love him!* *(Get out of here, Deadpool! You have your own Popular Culture and Philosophy book!)* **To get this joke, read Deadpool and Philosophy.** *(Beat it!)*

Getting the World Back

But death is not the last word. Faith only becomes faith with the finality of death. Everything before that is probable or improbable. Shrewdness and calculation run into the wall of death, but faith believes for the impossible beyond death. As Kierkegaard writes, "Everyone became great in proportion to his *expectancy*. One became great by expecting the possible . . . but he who expected the impossible became the greatest of all" (p. 16). Kierkegaard is not referring to an afterlife and the belief in an immortal soul. Likewise, contrary to the accusation of Namor that Steve is only concerned about "the preservation of his soul at the expense of everything we hold dear" (*New Avengers*, Volume 3, #2), Steve's faith is "faith for this life" (p. 20).

Tony refused "to look impossibility in the eye" (p. 47). According to his human understanding, there was only so much he could do to save the world, but once his reason was spent, all that was left to do was give up as he and the rest of the Illuminati seemed to do after a tragic encounter with a team of superheroes (who looked suspiciously like the Justice League) whose world was destroyed by the Illuminati's anti-matter bomb (*New Avengers*, Volume 3, #23). That is not how Steve Rogers handles the impossible. Steve believes the world can be saved, even if only "by the absurd," by something beyond what reason can expect or calculate (p. 47). Steve, in the face of death, can last until the end, stare into impossible circumstances, and say, "No. YOU move." And indeed, Steve's faith is rewarded. Not only do the Illuminati's efforts prove to be fruitless (the death of the multiverse was inevitable), but the world and the multiverse is restored at the end of *Secret Wars*. Like Abraham with Isaac, Steve gets his world back. He didn't know how it might happen, but he believed there was another way regardless.

When Faith Benefits Reason

Kierkegaard writes, "Abraham had faith . . . he believed the preposterous" and became "a guiding star that saves the anguished" (pp. 20–21). Likewise, Captain America serves as a guiding star and exemplar in a way that Iron Man never can precisely because to Cap "there is always an alternative!" (*Captain America*, Volume 1, #268). And really, someone like

Tony has benefited numerous times from Cap's faith in the good of others. During the *Avengers Disassembled* story, Tony is manipulated by magic into acting drunk in his Iron Man armor while giving a speech to the UN General Assembly, and he threatens to kill the ambassador of Latveria, the country over which Dr. Doom rules. After a number of odd attacks on Avengers Mansion, Tony, Steve, Hawkeye, and Falcon are discussing the day's odd events when Giant Man storms in, yelling, "Tell them Tony! Tell them what you did!" (*Avengers*, Volume 1, #501). Tony explains that he thinks his behavior and the attacks on the Avengers are connected. After Giant Man tells Tony he doesn't believe him, Tony looks at the others and despondently asks, "Is that it? You all don't believe me." After an awkward pause, rendered beautifully by David Fitch and Brian Michael Bendis, it is Steve who speaks up and says, "I believe you."

In spite of all the evidence to the contrary, it is Steve's faith in the seemingly impossible and in his friends that allows him to overcome what seems "obvious" to human reason. It might seem like a shot in the dark, but sometimes trust can carry us further and help us find the truth better than reason's best calculations.

9
A Human Fighting the Gods

ROB LUZECKY AND CHARLENE ELSBY

He might be one of the physically weakest members of the Avengers, but Captain America doesn't leave being a hero up to the gods. Being a hero is something that is precisely human, and Captain America, as the exemplar of human perfection, is the greatest hero of the Avengers.

Our argument is that gods cannot be heroes, and the god-like members of the Avengers—Ironman, with a god's intelligence, Thor, with a god's strength, and the Hulk, with a god's rage—are not "heroes" like Captain America. He is a human hero, whose heroism is a result of an expression of his humanity. He always retains his humanity, even when this requires him to throw aside his shield. Captain America is heroic precisely because he is an example of what a human can do. Captain America is particularly heroic, in the sense that he rallies against gods in his constant redefinition of what a human can do.

Captain America Is the Best Human

When we, as humans, try to imagine an entity better than ourselves, we tend to start with a human as the basis. We think of a human, and then we think of all of the ways a human could be improved, and then we come up with an entity who's like us, but better. We eliminate the human flaws and then imagine something that isn't restricted by our particularly human limitations. We move slowly, we can't fly, and we suck at science. Most of us would never figure out that removing the pin at the bottom of a flagpole would allow us to get the flag at the top

(*Captain America: The First* Avenger). These minor failings are unremarkable in the normal course of the world.

Then horror descends upon the world. The horror is witnessed both on the terrible scale of the fire-bombing of cities and countries getting carved up by the treads of aggressor's tanks, and on the smaller but no less terrible scale measured by individuals' silent looking away as people of slightly different skin colors, who participate in a slightly different series of sacred practices, are first marginalized and then sent away to death camps. A town gets fired on by a tank. Cities get destroyed. The Tesseract gets taken by the Nazis (*Captain America: The First* Avenger).

Walls are built. Countries are turned into fortresses. The freedom to move between nations is diminished in the name of security. Those who have come into political power use their positions to demean those who oppose them. An angry man of limited intelligence has risen to power by guile and force. The madman in power rallies the worst of a nation to support him. Books are burned under the flags that symbolize all that is oppressive, racist, xenophobic, and horrible. Where once there was democracy, there is now fear. It is in this world that Hydra surveys the people it seeks to enslave. Now, when events have taken humanity to the precipice where the existential threat is real, being a five-foot-four, ninety-five pound kid with asthma and high blood pressure is not at all good enough. When the world grows dark, we seek heroes who are not beset by all the limitations that seem to define us as human beings fighting for existence. It is in times like these that the world needs Captain America.

A bunch of philosophers think that these circumstances of great turmoil have led to humanity's becoming aware of God. That is not to say that humanity created God. (That is outside the scope of this chapter.) But when humans try to *think* of what *a god might be*, they think of a creature that's like us, but without all of these pesky flaws. God has powers to act, like we do, but God's powers aren't limited, like ours are. God knows things, like we do, but isn't limited by our finite perspective, as we are. This process continues until we have a deity whose capacities are based, conceptually, on our own, but better. We like to imagine that God would not be a kid from Brooklyn whose parents died. We like to conceive of God as knowing how to defeat the enemies both foreign and abroad. The God that we like to believe in during the times when humanity is most under threat is a God who is greater than us in every sort of way.

But harkening toward this sort of God—while humanity falls to its knees in the moments of immanent catastrophe—is not the only way to save the day. Thor wasn't around in World War II. In addition to the utterly non-human gods that populate the Marvel Cinematic Universe, we can also recognize that there is Captain America, who is a completely different sort of entity than those who roam the streets and halls of Asgard. Unlike Thor and Loki, Captain America is a human being who has saved the day countless times before: seventy years ago he saved us on the Italian front (*Captain America: The First Avenger*); he gave the orders that stopped the alien invasion of the streets of Manhattan (*The Avengers*); a few years ago he came to the rescue in the rubble-strewn streets of Sokovia (*Avengers: Age of Ultron*); there was that time that he fought the mercenaries on the dimly-lit deck of a rusted-out freighter (*Captain America: The Winter Soldier*); most recently, he fought to protect a friend from the wrongful overreach of a government (*Captain America: Civil War*). Captain America saved us all these times specifically because he is a human. When Steve Rogers walked into Brooklyn Antiques, he was not turned into Captain America as a way of getting around the flaws of humanity. What Captain America is, is *more human*.

We all know that Dr. Erskine's super-soldier serum and the exposure to "vita-rays" just amplifies a person's nascent traits—just look at how the Red Skull turned out. Instead of conceiving of all of the bad parts of humanity and then eliminating them, the scientists responsible for Captain America conceived of all of the good parts of humanity and then amplified them. What Captain America is supposed to be is precisely *not* an entity better than humanity, but the best kind of human. His humanity is an essential part of how Captain America is a hero. He makes what seems impossible possible, and not for some abstract inhuman figure, but for humanity.

The Paradoxical Nature of Captain America

Albert Camus's existential definition of what it means to be human describes the nature of Captain America's existence. According to Camus and other existentialists, man exists in a paradoxical condition. The absurdity of the human condition is that it constantly strives for universality—a God-like status in some form or another. Meanwhile, we're stuck here in this world of particulars. It is always humanity's desire to strive for godliness, for perfection, and for freedom from the limitations of the material world. It is, however, an unattainable goal for someone in our condition—existing, as we do, as a subject within a world. To be in this state, in which we constantly strive towards something we're not, and inevitably fail in our attempts, is just what it is to be human. Captain America doesn't strive to be better than human; he strives to be the best human, and that means maintaining this paradoxical condition.

The danger in being self-aware, according to Camus, is that you're led towards nihilism. Being faced with the absurdity of your existence is like having the constant feeling that you're destined for something better that exists beyond the reach of humankind. We demand that the world make sense, and it fails to do so. We command it to follow the order of our rationality, and it defies us. In the face of constant defeat at the hands of the world itself, we're often smacked in the face with our own futility. But to accept the fact of that futility is to admit defeat. To fall prey to nihilism would be to give up one of the aspects of the human condition—what makes a human a human— which is specifically the fact that despite all evidence or action to the contrary, we *will* try to overcome ourselves. Steve Rogers knows that he can't join the army because of his health issues. Nevertheless, he tries. To accept that you'll fail and then to try anyway? That's what life is about. That is humanity's way. That is Captain America's way.

Camus uses the myth of Sisyphus to explain how it is that mankind can attain their fullest humanity. Sisyphus is the mythical figure who was punished by the gods, who determined that there would be no greater punishment than to engage in futile labor—to be forced to do something without purpose. Sisyphus, for Camus, embodies everything it is to be in humanity's present condition. Humanity has been abandoned by God, left to determine its own essence. Meanwhile, every attempt to universalize what it is to be human is negated. The analogy here is between Sisyphus's labor and human life in general. Once we recognize fully that there is no greater purpose to life, that humankind has no destiny except for what it makes for itself, then it seems that simply living is comparable to Sisyphus's labor. There's no point to it. There is nothing to be attained by doing it, and there is no way to do it correctly.

Not knowing what to do and not knowing how you're going to do it before you do it is precisely the situation that humans find themselves in when gods visit the Earth. A stranger walks menacingly into a room and rips out a scientist's eye (*The Avengers*). The crowd scatters in terror. Loki reveals his godly identity by presenting himself in all his Asgardian grandeur and demands that the crowd kneel. The god tells the cowering masses that there is nothing to fear and nothing to be ashamed of, because it has always been humanity's destiny to kneel to power. Loki wields his scepter and tells the terrified crowd that they need not concern themselves with the human (all too human) mad scramble for identity, through which we try to assert ourselves as beings who possess some sort of significance in the world. Some in the crowd look as if they disagree with this assessment of human potential, but Loki surrounds them. The message: humanity's fight for meaning was never really a fight, in the sense that it was just some sad illusion played out by a species that didn't know its place in the cosmic order. In but a few moments, with but the slightest of effort, Loki informs the crowd that that they (and all of humanity) are nothing but slaves.

All fall into place except for some old guy, who—after surviving the camps—is tired of being told what to do. Loki, as the embodiment of that which determines order, decides that this man must be killed. No one, not one in the crowd, knows how to save the old guy—or, indeed, if they should even *try* to save the old guy. They have just been told that it would be contrary to their very natures to perform any action that might be interpreted as anything but subservient. They have just seen the forces of legal authority stopped dead in its tracks. A god came to Earth and told us to give up. The trickster half-brother of Thor stands over the cowering masses, and tells us that our submission is good and fine, in the sense that it would alleviate ambiguities that define human life. Where once there were questions about what to do and how to do it, now there are only answers: grovel, and do so happily.

The godly authorities came to Earth and Captain America didn't like what they had to say. Long ago, back in the midst of the Second Great War, when he was just some kid from Brooklyn, Steve knew exactly what it was to exist in the paradoxical condition that Camus outlines. Back then, every authority that mattered told Steve that he was unfit to fight in the war. Even after Steve became Captain America, the government ordered him to be nothing more than a glorified performer. When Loki tells the crowd to kneel, and when the government tells Steve that he can't fight, both the government and Loki are enacting and enforcing limits on what humans can do. The positing of a limit by a government or a God is, in effect, the demand that humans surrender their ability to choose the course of their lives. When gods and governments speak up and tell us what to do, they're telling us to give up the paradoxical position where we don't know the answers to the questions that beset us at each moment of our lives.

This call to surrender in our paradoxical struggles is the call that a hero answers through resisting authority. In resisting authority, Captain America demonstrates what it is that makes a human a human. In resisting the gods and government, Captain America embodies the paradoxical nature of humanity. In a time when paradoxical entities find themselves under attack, it is precisely the entity who defiantly embodies the paradox who defines that what is human and most heroic.

Captain America Is Happy

In Camus's version of the story, Sisyphus is, in the end, happy. By fully accepting his paradoxical place in the universe, as he who engages in futile labor willingly and in good spirit, he comes to embody the full human potential. Other philosophers would choose to negate either one side or the other—the particularity of the human or its tendency toward the universal (the desire to become Godly). We can do so in all sorts of ways.

Friedrich Nietzsche, for instance, claims that the entirety of philosophy and religion since Socrates has attempted to deny the human (all too human) ability to overcome ourselves, which amounts to a denial of the existence of change in the world. Nietzsche claims, in *Twilight of the Idols*, that we must really hate the world and all that's in it, if we're to come up with other worlds and place them side by side with ours for comparison. But it seems that humanity is wont to do exactly that—we come up with other worlds, better worlds, without the flaws of this one, and then we declare some other world to be *the real one*, as opposed to this sensible but illusory world to which we are only temporarily bound. What this does, effectively, is eliminate one aspect of the human condition: the fact that it is a subject within a world. By declaring that this world is not real, we take refuge somewhere else, anywhere else, as long as it's where we are not.

According to Nietzsche, the people who make this conceptual move must really hate the world. One of the things which makes Captain America truly heroic is that he refuses to make this move. No matter how much the odds are stacked against him, no matter what the face of the enemy, no matter what the size of the army he is fighting, Captain America never gives into a hatred of anything, least of all humanity.

On the other hand, we might try to eliminate the universal aspect of humanity's existence. Having tried to get in touch with whatever it is that is universal within us and, finding nothing, we might resort to a nihilism that negates any further attempts. We become reductionists (we try to explain the incredible diversity of the world through reference to one thing, god, or cause), we explain away every sense of order and reason as merely illusory, and we try to take solace in the idea that, since it is evident that we can't be *good*, at least we can be *right*, even though what it means to be right is to accept the meaninglessness of existence. In *Captain America: The Winter Soldier*, we see examples of this sort of reductionism in the actions of Alexander Pierce. Having given up any notion of there being any possible order or good emerging from the chaos of human affairs, Pierce rigs three "helicarriers" (powered by new "repuslor" technology supplied by Stark Industries) to kill anyone who might come to challenge his view of what is right.

Such reasoning leads inevitably to the consideration of suicide, which is the guiding concern of Camus's essay (*The Myth of Sisyphus*). If there is no meaning to live, why live at all? Eventually, Camus decides against suicide, and he does so in such a way that leads these authors to conclude that Captain America is leading his life as a person should, if he is to accept his own absurdity and persist despite the odds. The battles Captain America fights are always against authorities that try to diminish the wonderful paradox of the human condition.

The forces against him in these battles are always great, and sometimes in the fight he loses a lot along the way. But every time, Captain America picks up his shield and uses it to strike a blow for the constantly fragile humanity of the "small guy" who became our greatest hero. Captain America's heroism teaches us that in the face of absurdity, we cannot find respite by eliminating either aspect of the human condition. Instead, we must persist, *especially* in the face of the immanent possibility of failure, in accepting the paradox of our lives.

10
Trust Systems or People?

DANIEL MALLOY

The core difference between Captain America and Iron Man is a philosophical one. Their main disagreement, and one that leads to the majority of their conflicts (including Marvel's *Civil War*) is about trust. Specifically, who and what is worthy of trust?

Cap trusts people. You kind of have to if you believe in things like freedom and democracy. He thinks that you make people better by treating them with respect—treat them like the people you think they can be, and they will become those people. He's done this over and over down the years, with some spectacular results. The number of former villains and borderline anti-heroes who've become pinnacles of the superhero community thanks to Cap is mind-boggling: Quicksilver, the Scarlet Witch, Hawkeye, the Black Widow, and most recently Deadpool. Cap can do that sort of thing because he trusts people.

Iron Man, on the other hand, trusts technology and systems rather than people. People, from Stark's perspective, are parts. The moving bits that make the machines work, or the unmoving bits that make machines necessary. That's not to say he doesn't care about them—he absolutely does. But he doesn't trust most of them. From Iron Man's perspective, people are machines that are likely to malfunction. So, there need to be redundant systems in place to keep them working properly, just as he needs his mechanical bits to prevent his body's natural processes from destroying him.

Both approaches can work, but only Cap's can preserve any semblance of freedom and individuality. Cap and Iron Man can both keep people safe and alive, but only Cap can explain why.

Iron Man's approach tends to focus so much on how to achieve the goal that it loses sight of why the goal is worth achieving in the first place.

Star-Spangled and Golden Avengers

Iron Man and Captain America both became heroes thanks to applied sciences, although it's significant that where Steve Rogers became Captain America due largely to the help of others, Tony Stark assumed the role of Iron Man primarily through his own genius. Tony is a self-made hero, while Steve is the result of a government program. Captain America began his career as a hero thanks to a team of people trying to make it happen, and then continued as a leader and partner through his World War II adventures. Iron Man, on the other hand, was a solo act until the fortuitous formation of the Avengers.

This distinction also carries over to their styles as heroes and leaders. Although Iron Man is an Avenger, he is still very much his own hero. Tony never quite buys into the team, in spite of leading it and funding it. When Iron Man leads the Avengers, the team isn't really a team: they're a group of individuals who happen to share a common objective. And that's the way Tony likes it; it's what he understands and is comfortable with.

Historically, the Avengers really only gelled as a team when Captain America joined. It wasn't that there was resistance to the team idea; it was just that the ostensible team leader, Iron Man, had no idea what a team really was. The self-made man could delegate, but that was about it. Cap, on the other hand, took the group in hand and forged them into a unit that was greater than its parts. The Star-Spangled Avenger understood not only that they had common goals and what abilities they each brought to the table: he understood how to combine them in ways that reinforced one another.

Put simply, the difference between these two leaders of the Avengers is that Iron Man trusts his fellow Avengers to do their jobs. Captain America simply trusts them. This may not seem like much, but it is, in fact, everything. The difference is that Iron Man treats them like employees. Cap treats them like people. Shellhead sees them as capable of choosing how they carry out the Avengers' common objectives. Glory Pants understands that his teammates have to have input on what those objectives are.

Cap's Kooky Quartet

Avengers #16 tells a remarkable story. It introduces the world to the radically new line-up of Marvel's premiere superteam. Following the departure of the team's founding line-up (Iron Man, Thor, Giant Man, Wasp, and the Hulk), Captain America was left to pick up the pieces and re-assemble the Avengers. The pieces he picked are what make this Avengers team so unusual. Being Captain America, he could have easily called on any number of superheroes—who wouldn't want to serve alongside the Sentinel of Liberty himself? But instead of looking for heroes with a proven track record, Cap recruited his "kooky quartet." This iteration of the Avengers was made up entirely of reforming supervillains, aside from Cap himself. Hawkeye was a failed would-be superhero turned criminal and Iron Man foe. The Scarlet Witch and Quicksilver were former members of the Brotherhood of Evil Mutants, and the offspring of that group's leader, the mutant terrorist Magneto.

From these less than obvious recruits, Captain America sought to forge his legacy as the sole leader of the Avengers. And they were hardly alone: over the years and under Captain America's leadership, the Avengers have continued to reach out to edges of the superhero community and into the ranks of their own foes for new recruits. When you look at the records of many members of Marvel's premiere superteam, it looks less like an elite fighting unit and more like a rehab program.

This is a risky recruiting strategy, and it doesn't always pay off. But it demonstrates that Cap doesn't just believe in second chances; he believes in people. The trust that Captain America puts in the people around him is emblematic of the kind of leader he is, and also it is part of what makes him a true hero. There are many facets of heroism: self-sacrifice, going beyond the call of duty, devotion to others, etc. But the one where Captain America excels above all is in his ability to inspire others. He can forge a legendary Avengers team out of a kooky quartet because he can get others to believe in him, in themselves, and in each other.

In a way, this is exemplified by Captain America's only real superpower: his ability to inspire. Cap is an exceptional athlete, a dangerous fighter, and an excellent tactician and strategist, but all of those abilities are simply at the high end of normal human range. He could win at the Olympics, but Quicksilver will always beat him in a foot race. He's a bright guy, but nowhere even close to Marvel's mega-minds, like Reed Richards, Hank Pym, or even, yes, Tony Stark. But what he does better than any of them—better than anyone, in fact—is get people to believe in themselves and each other. All because he trusts them.

The Old Man Trusts Him

There's a great moment in *The Uncanny Avengers* #1, when Cap hands Deadpool his Avengers ID card. Deadpool, the Merc with a Mouth, the man even death can't shut up for long, is momentarily rendered speechless. When he finally does speak—after Cap has left him—he doesn't crack a joke or talk about chimichangas or Bea Arthur. No. Instead, the motor-mouthed mercenary utters a simple, profound "Oh, crap." Deadpool, the unwanted and unwelcome interloper of the superhero community, has just gotten the ultimate validation. It's not the card, but the card is part of it. It's who gave him the card. It wouldn't have meant nearly as much coming from anyone else.

And, in fairness, almost no one else would have given Deadpool the card or made him an Avenger. It's one of the recurring conflicts in that Avengers team. The team's field leader, Rogue, doesn't trust Wade Wilson; but she trusts Cap. Spider-man even quits the team over Deadpool's presence. But others, even former enemies of Wade's, stay on. The reason is simple, and is nicely summed up by the Human Torch: "The old man trusts Deadpool. End of story."

Iron Man's Initiative

Compare the Star-Spangled Avenger's recruitment drives to those of the Golden Avenger. Iron Man has a history of suspicion not only of supervillains, but also of borderline heroes. When he needs them, it's not as teammates, but as employees. Hence when Tony Stark was named director of S.H.I.E.L.D. and began the 50-State Initiative, recruits were paid, and were aware, on some level, that failure could lead to exile to Prison 42 in the Negative Zone. Carrot, meet stick.

From a certain perspective, Iron Man's approach makes more sense. In order to get people to behave in certain ways, you offer incentives. You reward them for correct behavior, and you punish them for incorrect behavior. This is perfectly rational. More accurately, it is perfectly instrumentally rational.

That is the problem. People are like tools for Tony, means he uses to achieve his own ends. Now, he doesn't generally treat them in exceptionally cruel or immoral ways (most of the time), but he also doesn't generally treat people as though they were important in and of themselves. People follow Iron Man because he pays well; they follow Captain America because he believes in them.

Compare, for example, the way Iron Man's Initiative employs Deadpool to Cap's acceptance of him. When Wade decides to pick a side in the Civil War, he tries to join the Initiative (in a wrongheaded way, of course). He decides to bring in some heroes he believes are unregistered: the Great Lakes Avengers. The members of the GLA, as it turns out, are not only registered, they are the branch of the Initiative for their region. But Deadpool's skills get noticed, and he is recruited. A branch of the Initiative hires him, in his capacity as a merc, to go after his own best friend, Cable. While Iron Man may not have had anything to do with the decision, it's his style. Rather than trust Deadpool, he pays him. Rather than inspire him to be something better, he keeps him as a merc.

Demon in Cashmire

The source of Tony's problem is painted all over him: he's an engineer and a capitalist, both goal-driven professions. It may seem odd to think of being goal-driven as a bad thing, and often it is not. The problem is when achieving the goal becomes the total focus. When you worry exclusively about how to get something done, you tend to forget about what you're actually doing and why you're doing it. There are many ways to discuss this distinction: some call it the difference between strategic and communicative reason, others call it the difference between quantitative and qualitative thinking, and still others distinguish between instrumental reason and moral reason.

Philosophers Theodor Adorno and Max Horkheimer diagnosed the problems involved with this instrumental reason or means-end thinking just after World War II. In their classic *Dialectic of Enlightenment*, Adorno and Horkheimer argued that an exclusive focus on how to achieve our goals diminishes us in two ways, both of which we can see at work in Iron Man. First, in focusing on achieving a particular goal, we tend to lose sight of what we're doing in order to achieve it. Second, we tend to forget why the goal is important.

There are many instances of Iron Man not paying attention to what he's doing to achieve his goal. The borderline dictatorial powers he assumed during the *Civil War* is only one. A more interesting and clear-cut example is provided by the *Armor Wars* storyline. Tony discovers that some of his designs have been stolen and sold on the black market, and are now being used to enhance the technology of various Marvel villains. Angered, he devises a weapon of sorts that can deactivate any Starktech in the vicinity and then embarks on a crusade to reclaim all of his stolen technology. His target lock kicks in, and his adventures result in the death of Titanium Man and his own removal from the Avengers. He also put Captain America (or the Captain, as he was known at the time) in a coma. All because he lost sight of the possible consequences of how he was doing what he was doing.

On the other hand, Iron Man's actions during *Civil War* plainly show Tony forgetting why a particular goal is important. All of Tony's actions were supposedly directed to a single goal: keeping people safe. In order to do that, he assembled an army of super-powered people, heroes and villains alike, and declared war on the Sentinel of Liberty himself. The result was almost laughably predictable: massive destruction and death, Tony's humiliation, and the death of Steve Rogers. In order to keep people safe, Iron Man put everyone in a tremendous amount of danger.

Two Faces of Respect

Captain America and Iron Man trust different things. But their different styles can be traced a bit deeper than simply what they place their trust in. The reason Captain America trusts people while Iron Man trusts technology comes down to a question of respect. Both men respect the people they work with, but in different ways. To show this, first let's look at the connection between trust and respect.

All trust is based in respect. To the extent that the two can be separated, it's possible to respect someone or something without trusting them; for example, many members of the Marvel superhero community respect Namor the Sub-Mariner, but don't trust him. No one doubts his abilities or his honor. Namor will act according to his code, and pity anyone who doubts that within earshot. But Namor's code is his own and no one else's. Since others aren't entirely clear on what Namor's honor will lead him to do, they don't trust him. But the respect is always there.

The reason trust won't work without respect is because trust involves risk. Whenever we trust someone or something, we rely on them to act in particular ways without our input or control. Think, for example, of loaning someone money. Whenever a loan is offered, the loaner takes the risk that it will not be paid back. If the loaner trusts that the money will be returned, it is because they respect that the loanee is a person who keeps their promises. On the other hand, if the loaner does not expect the money to be returned, it's because they do not trust the loanee, and, in turn, do not respect the loanee as a person of their word.

But all respect is not the same, and different forms of respect give rise to different sorts of trust. Philosopher Stephen Darwall offers an influential distinction between recognition respect and appraisal respect. Recognition respect is the sort owed by equal, rational agents to one another. In recognizing another person as a person, I acknowledge that they are a free being, capable of making their own choices. Part of the respect I owe to them is an obligation not to unduly interfere with their ability to make their own decisions. Appraisal respect, on the other hand, is less abstract and more specific to the individuals we grant it to. Any rational, autonomous being deserves to be recognized as such. But we value different rational, autonomous beings differently based on the other qualities they have and the choices they make. For example, Steve Rogers made the choice to become Captain America. Recognition respect requires that we acknowledge that choice, refrain from interfering with it, and, since it is a good choice, support it. Appraisal respect, on the other hand, is the sort of respect we owe to Steve Rogers because he is Captain America

Cap's trust of people is based on recognition respect. This form of respect consists in acknowledging that human beings are rational and autonomous, and as such have the right to make their own choices. If we want someone to do something—to decide in a particular way—then recognition respect calls on us to provide them with relevant information and try to persuade them that this action is the right one. We can't, for example, threaten them or lie to them to get them to do what we want. We can attempt to persuade them or bargain with them, if we want to treat them with respect. That is how Cap leads the Avengers.

Shellhead, on the other hand, has appraisal respect. Appraisal respect is not grounded in rational autonomy, but in other qualities that distinguish one person from another. It might help to think of this as "respect-as." Tony respects Captain America, for example, but not as a person. He respects Captain America as a soldier, as a leader, and as a symbol. Stripped of those uses, Tony would have no respect for Steve Rogers.

Appraisal respect isn't always goal-oriented; that's just the most predominant sort in Iron Man's way of viewing the world. It's perfectly possible to have appraisal respect for someone or something one has no use for; as, for example, the respect that Tony has for Dr. Doom. They are bitter enemies, and Doom is a brutal dictator, but Tony would be the last person to question Doom's intellect or ingenuity, even though it causes him no end of grief. Tony respects Doom as an adversary and as an engineer and scientist, but not as a person. This is one thing—apart from high-tech battle armor—that Doom and Stark have in common. Doom has appraisal respect for some people (admittedly, not many). But, for example, he acknowledges that Dr. Strange's abilities in the mystic arts surpass his own.

The two kinds of respect lead to two kinds of trust. Cap trusts people to make their own decisions, good or bad. He will bargain, and persuade, and inspire, but he will also listen. He knows he may well be wrong, and others may well be right. Respect of this sort, recognition respect, goes both ways, as does the trust to which it gives rise. Iron Man trusts people to do their jobs—to display the sorts of qualities that he respects them for. And, he thinks, they should trust him based on his unique qualities. Since Tony Stark is undeniably one of the smartest people on Earth, his teammates and employees should trust him to make the best decisions in any given situation. Once he's made those decisions, they should be carried out—not debated or questioned.

Win by Dying

With their contrasting and conflicting styles, it's hardly surprising that Iron Man and Captain America wound up on opposite sides of the civil war. They don't see people the same way, and therefore didn't see the conflict in the same way. In the end, Iron Man lost. He lost because he trusted his tech more than his people or even himself.

Cap won because he trusted himself, his people, and, in the end, even Iron Man.

11
Fighting Ethical Relativism in *Tales of Suspense*

FERNANDO GABRIEL PAGNONI BERNS AND
EDUARDO VETERI

Moral values. Ethics. There are entire volumes written about these issues. Superheroes, as representatives of Goodness (that's right, with a capital G) are inextricably linked to moral values and ethics. When battling supervillains, rescuing cats stuck in trees, or in their personal civil lives, heroes are linked to morality and goodness. Not all heroes, however, understood "good action" the same way. Ask Punisher. He considers himself a good guy when he wipes the world of scum with bullets and fire.

Still, the clearest example about the ambiguity of "good action" is the relationship between Captain America and Iron Man, which is slightly tense even before the events of the best-selling *Civil War* arc. Both of them are good people and share preoccupations about the welfare of the citizens of America and the world. But while Iron Man answers directly to the predominant thinking of his era—he is, first and foremost, a capitalist fighting to make good actions *and* money—Captain America holds ahistorical moral values as his main belief.

Following Immanuel Kant (1724–1804), considered a central figure in modern philosophy, we maintain that the ahistoricity of Captain America makes him superior to his much-too-earthly frenemy Iron Man. *Tales of Suspense* (1959–1968), was an ongoing monthly comic-book edited by Marvel. This particular series had the advantage of putting together the adventures of Captain America and Iron Man for the very first time, since both superheroes shared each issue since #58.

A Little Tale about Two Superheroes and Their Philosophies

In *Tales of Suspense* #58 (October 1964), Tony Stark and Steve Rogers engage in a battle "to the bitter end" (as the colorful cover says). The villain known as the Chameleon deceives Tony Stark and leads him to a battle against Captain America. The latter does his best to calm down the situation ("Whatever is troubling you, let's talk!"), but the man in the golden armor is too thick-head to understand or listen ("There is nothing to talk about!").

At last, each superhero listens to the other, and they come to an agreement and defeat the Chameleon. Happy ending. In the last panel, Iron Man rationalizes the whole situation and comes to the conclusion that people should follow the advice of President Lyndon Johnson (he explicitly mentions his name) when he, the President, asks people to reason together. Probably, Stark is making reference to Johnson's politics of building a nation through agreement and concordance rather than with extremisms. To Johnson, the American president serving at the White House when the comic was published, all extreme views were equally bad, and only through meeting in the middle did the country have a future.

This little adventure points to Iron Man's philosophy: he is always a man of his time, whichever time it is. He is talking here about a *real* political point of view from a *real* president, rather than a fantastic president such as, say, Lex Luthor. LBJ will appear again. In *Tales of Suspense* #83, Iron Man engages in a battle against the Titanium Man, a giant enemy who puts the hero in serious trouble. The battle is televised and worried Americans pray for the safety of Iron Man and, by extension, the US as a whole. Among the citizens watching the battle, Lyndon Johnson himself is depicted in a panel. The president is depicted reaffirming his motto to another man (his secretary perhaps?): someday, all men will reason together rather than indulge themselves in violence. Up to that day, Americans are very lucky to have Iron Man on their side. As seen, the real president, real politics and the golden avenger seem to be in good relationships. Iron Man is depicted as channeling Johnson's ideals of politics and democracy.

Let's jump ahead many decades. In our globalized era, Stark is the person who would fully understand the implications of a world getting small. The need for state surveillance increases each passing day, as terrorism spreads like a disease all over the globe. In the arc *Civil War*, Stark agrees with the President's decision to enroll the superheroes into legit forces supervised by the government. Many refuse, fearing for their freedom and safety, but Iron Man insists: the world has changed and the time for outlaw vigilantes has come to an end. Again, Tony Stark embodies the thinking of his era, the philosophy of his time.

Decades had gone by from *Tales of Suspense* to the blockbuster *Civil War*. One thing remains, however: Iron Man adapts himself to each era, to its thinking on morals, economics, culture, and foreign relations. He is, truly, a man of his age. And this is one of his main advantages. He is adaptable; he understands how to swim within the changes of morals as the years goes by. And for all this, he is truly superior to other heroes, such as Captain America and his fossilized thinking. Right?

Nope.

Wrong.

Ideas, morals, and values are historical. In other words, they are inextricably related to the social and cultural contexts that produce them and thus, changeable through time. Understanding this fact is one of Stark's main advantages, but it is also his main problem. He is too attached to his time. As seen, he is only a little (golden) parrot to someone else's morals. He changes as the times changes. Captain America, by contrast (and probably because he is a man who was literally frozen in time), is a relic from the past. Good Cap holds high some ahistorical values, and thinks that there are such things as intrinsic human dignity and rights. There are things which come first, independent of who is occupying the main chair in the White House. There are things which exist independent of the prevalent social and cultural thinking of the era. Saving human lives and preventing suffering are his priorities.

In our current world's thinking, good and evil face the *philosophy of relativism* which turns them into "fragile preferences of a particular social group at certain place and time," according to Didier Pollefeyt in "The Morality of Auschwitz." Values such as good and evil are relative in the sense that they must be addressed in their proper context to be truly understood. What is evil for someone—a person, a nation—could be addressed as good for another. Good and evil are not, we know, essences *but social constructions*. Throughout history, people have decided, in agreement, what should be considered good and what bad.

Many times, however, the definitions were created to serve the needs of some hegemony. A little example: patriarchy allows men to do things which are considered bad if performed by women. Captain America, however, still believes in an ethical imperative that transcends history, society and culture. For him, human lives (that of friends, strangers or enemies) are the most important thing. Human life is sacred and must be preserved. For example, in *Tales of Suspense* #65, Steve Rogers almost blows his cover as a weak soldier (the worst within the platoon) when a case of sabotage ends with an airplane exploding in the sky. Mr. Maxon, president of Maxon Corporation and the man who actually paid for the new airplanes, worries for his reputation after witnessing his jet becoming a ball of fire. Rogers cannot hide his disgust and angrily makes his claim for the lost human lives, that of the pilots. As a consequence, Rogers wins suspension time: peeling potatoes at the kitchen for showing lack of respect. But that is Steve Rogers. He cannot simply pass the fact that human lives are lost, even if his objection somewhat cracks his cover as a spineless soldier.

Embracing a moral position is to take ethical values which cannot always be framed within relativism or subjectivity. Ethical values indeed exist outside human embodiment; they are an ethical imperative. As a man for the 1940s, Steve Rogers embraces with gusto this way of seeing ethics and values, as things that exist concretely, outside the temporal line and outside a given socio-cultural context.

This "relic" thinking proves Captain America as superior to Iron Man. Because he will be here for us, no matter what society could consider "good" at the time.

Billionaire Playboys Don't Read Kant

What is an ethical imperative, anyway? Why does Steve Rogers embrace it so passionately? Kant's "categorical imperative" is the way in which people determine what their duties are, what they should and should not do. It is categorical, because it applies (or should apply) to everyone, and it is an imperative, since it is a command. According to Kant, the categorical imperative is to act in such a way that you treat humanity always as an end and never simply as a means to achieve an end. Every person, by virtue of his or her humanity, has an inherent dignity which we have the obligation to respect. A hero must save any person, no matter who he or she is or what he or she has done.

According to Kant, the moral value of an action does not reside in the results of the action, but in the action itself. I do something because that action is good: the results do not matter. One way to test whether an action is truly good is to consider whether it could become "a universal law." This is Kant's test of *universalizability*.

Of course, Iron Man also helps people, *all* kind of people, without any payoff in mind more than being helpful. For example, Iron Man saves the life of Communist Black Widow in *Tales of Suspense* #53. Since she's a Communist and the decade is the 1960s, she is coded as "evil." Stark saves her anyway, mostly to demonstrate that Americans and capitalism are better. Iron Man understands goodness as linked to a particular thinking. He finds goodness in sitting together and using reason. Certainly, that is an idea filled with good intentions, but it answers to the political philosophy of the era.

Tales of Suspense #39 narrates the origin of Iron Man. Stark's inventions are weapons created to weight the balance in favor of America in the war against Communism. Iron Man's origin is framed by utilitarianism: win the war and take America to new heights. Turn the nation into a leader within the globe. And sell. And get richer. Further, his famous armor is built to escape from imprisonment in Vietnam, as a way to enhance the possibilities of his surviving. Lastly, his invention allows his heart to continue beating. In other words, his armor helps him save America but also, saves himself.

So, there are *many* reasons, *personal and political*, behind the origin of Iron Man. Even more, in *Tales of Suspense* #56, Tony Stark decides to abandon his life as superhero to live as a playboy, spending money, traveling through the world and romancing the most beautiful girls. In other words, Tony decides to follow the ideal of masculinity so heavily promoted by magazines such as the very successful *Playboy*. In *Tales of Suspense* #63, the men working in Stark's factories decide to begin a strike since a villain, the Phantom, is sabotaging the installations. Stark is worried: he understands his men, but he is concerned that the strike could economically ruin him.

Tales of Suspense #40 tells how Stark decides to change his first armor (colored gray) for a golden one. It answers to the fact that the previous one, according to a lady, is "terrifying," while a golden one would be more in concordance with the "modern times." Why gold is representative of "modern times" more than any other color is a mystery, but nonetheless, he agrees and changes his metallic clothes, again answering to what a particular era expects from him. He is gray (bad) no more but golden (good). And it is not coincidental that his foe in that particular issue is a Neanderthal monster, which refers to times of old, in heavy contrast with the modernity represented by Iron Man (and gold, of course).

In fact, Iron Man changing armors so they fit better the era becomes almost a recurrent joke within the series. He makes the prototype of his most famous armor (the golden and red one) in issue #48 of the series. A blurb screaming at readers the change of armor ("See the new Iron Man!") gets more space on the cover than the reference to Mister Doll, the main villain leading the adventure. Issue #54 has a cover which states: "Wait till you see Iron Man's new protective head mask! Ol' bullet-head seems to change his iron masks as often as a glamour girl changes her hair-do's . . . but this one is a doozy!" Basically, the cover says to us that Iron Man is an attention-seeker—, but even more important, that he is constantly changing his external aspect, refusing to get frozen in an era.

By contrast, good old Cap is a person literally frozen in time. Captain America's origin is also related to the supremacy of America in the world, as Steve Rogers was injected with a serum to make him a super-soldier strong enough to help the US win the war. There are, however, two slightly interesting bits to share: first, Rogers drinks the awful ambrosia that can kill him without any doubt. In issue #63, the doctors themselves state that the potion that could give Rogers super-strength can also kill him "in seconds," with poor Steve there, drinking and hearing all that cruel chat. Even so, Steve drinks the potion anyway; his life is just secondary if he can help people.

Second, there is a full temporal jump. Captain America's main mission was to fight German Nazis, but getting frozen in time, he awakes in his future, the 1960s. In this new temporal frame, his mission, his purpose, has changed. Following Kant, it can be said that the material aspect of human morality has changed: there are other values now, and Nazis are not anymore the enemy, but communists (previously, friends against the Nazis). Thus, there is a perceptible change of social values. However, the form of human morality remains: Captain America wants to prevent human suffering.

Kant mourns the fragility of innocence, the last stage of pure goodness. "Innocence is certainly desirable, only it does not last, and is easily led astray, for it contains no enduring principle. A man's desires keep on growing, and without realizing it he is out of his innocence" (*Lectures on Ethics*, p. 228). This is a topic framing the whole history of Steve Rogers. In *Tales of Suspense* #75, Rogers feels especially melancholic, lamenting that his time was really twenty years ago. He calls himself a "relic." As a man who has left part of his life behind, he will carry melancholia forever, achingly remembering those whom he has lost. Even so, he has no doubts in playing hero again, no matter which the year is. If people are suffering, he must come to their rescue.

Cocky Bucky

Captain America is a better hero than Iron Man because the former will be there for you no matter the circumstances, the socio-cultural context, or whether you are an enemy or a friend. Captain America holds high the value of human life. Human lives must be respected as the most sacred thing in the world, and that is not negotiable. In either time frame—1940s and 1960s—Steve Rogers protects life so fiercely that he risks his own.

In *Tales of Suspense* #61, Captain America travels to Vietnam to exchange his life for an American pilot who has been taken as prisoner. After a battle against Sumo, a villain who, of course, is well versed in sumo, Rogers rescues pilot Jim Baker. In the last, panel, Jim thanks Captain America for rescuing him. Cap's answer is very telling of his ethical point of view: seemingly, the engines of the airplane prevent Rogers from hearing what Jim is saying, a good way to politely reject any thanks.

Captain America does his thing (saving lives), expecting nothing in exchange, not even a simple thanks. In *Tales of Suspense* #68, an American general thanks Captain America for his services to the US. Captain America, of course, states that he is only doing his job. Next to him, however, his faithful sidekick Bucky thinks how good it feels to be the recipient of congratulations. Unlike Rogers, Bucky needs an end to act in a moral way. Kant calls this end "mediated," in other words, complying with the obligation because there is an interest—receiving congratulations, in this example. Through the mediated ethos, actions are morally neutral. Bucky does something good, but he is expecting a reward at the end. It is logical to expect a reward, but Bucky's moral is not at the same level that Captain America's total altruism.

But nothing screams "Kant's ethics" as boldly as *Tales of Suspense* #71. Captain America and his sidekick are battling Nazis (it is an adventure situated in the 1940s). Our heroes win, but the castle where the action takes place is falling apart because of a big explosion. While fleeing, Captain America insists on saving all the Nazis who he previously incarcerated within the castle. After freeing them, the Nazis only want to kill Captain America. Bucky, filled with anger, spits to Rogers that "these are the men you insist in saving," clearly chastising Captain America's decision (well, well, the little brat was not *that* sweet after all). For Bucky, the only lives worthy of being saved are those of non-Nazis while, for Rogers, every life is worthy.

In this sense, Bucky is closer to the philosophical thinking of Iron Man. Both men are essentially *good people*. Even so, Bucky does not believe in universal, ahistorical morals: the life of Nazis is not that important because Nazis are bad men. Further, both he and Iron Man are too eager to make good actions because of their ends: glory or keeping the factories running and the millions coming. Again, both men are good, doing their best to save people all around the world. But a person considered—because the social-political context—a bad guy, maybe, just maybe, neither Iron Man nor Bucky will try to save. This is a complex point, as Communists were coded as purely evil in previous decades. Now, Communism is accepted as an alternative ideology.

Captain America, on the other hand, will be there to save that person. He believes in the doctrine of objective moral value and the categorical imperative of doing good actions without any emotional or personal involvement guiding that action.

An early *Tales of Suspense* #81 finds Tony Stark considering revealing his true identity as Iron Man since "nobody is above the desires of his government," a situation that predates the *Civil War* arc by decades. Meanwhile, it is not that rare that Steve Rogers is the one who will stand against the American government if he believes it wrong. His code-name has the tag "America" but he fights for everyone, for every life. In issue #87, he calls this philosophy "his belief," and he is ready to die for it. And his philosophy is a gift for humankind: you know he will be there to save you, whoever you are—Communist, Nazi, or American—and wherever you are—in the 1940s, in the 1960s, or in the twenty-first century.

12
Champion of the People vs. Technology

CRAIG VAN PELT

IRON MAN: Change is in the wind, Cap.

CAPTAIN AMERICA: Change isn't always good Tony.

IRON MAN: Says the man who was frozen for seventy years.

CAPTAIN AMERICA: Technology has its place. But your dogmatic faith in technology troubles me.

IRON MAN: You put your faith in God, I put my faith in technology.

CAPTAIN AMERICA: That's the problem, Tony. Technology is created by man, and men are flawed, therefore technology will always be flawed.

IRON MAN: Some people say God was created by man, and men are flawed, therefore God will always be flawed.

CAPTAIN AMERICA: God created men. Tony, stay on topic. You want to protect people with robots.

IRON MAN: Yes.

CAPTAIN AMERICA: Robots designed by people . . .

IRON MAN: Designed by smart people. Like me.

CAPTAIN AMERICA: But there's a problem with human bias influencing how the robots are programmed and designed. Won't that human bias influence how the robots act and behave?

IRON MAN: Cap, you're totally overthinking this, which is impressive considering your brain was a ball of ice for seventy years. Whether you like it or not the Fourth Industrial Revolution is coming. You're about to become an antique in a brave new world.

In Marvel's *The Avengers*, the lifestyle of genius, billionaire, playboy, philanthropist Tony Stark provides a glimpse into the arrival of the Fourth Industrial Revolution. This rapidly emerging new age of computers and industry involves a cocktail of robotics, the Internet, artificial intelligence, nanotechnology, and other technologies. For example, Jarvis is Tony's personal artificial assistant that runs much of Tony's life and company; Tony Stark is seen at the end of Marvel's *Avengers: Age of Ultron* getting into a self-driving sports car; and parts of Tony's Hulkbuster suit fly autonomously to attach to Tony's Iron Man suit as he is flying through the air.

Jarvis, the self-driving car, and the parts of Tony's Hulkbuster suit all act independently of Tony. But they are acting based on programming written by human engineers. Humans are plagued with various flaws such as greed, anger, sadness, vengeance, racism, sexism, addiction, and other issues. These flaws may cause bias in how humans think about the world, and how they interact with other people. These flaws even cause problems in how humans design scientific research, create medicine, tell history, or even program artificial intelligence.

In other words, human bias may influence everything that humans attempt to create. This type of concern is a postmodernist argument. Postmodern philosophers aren't concerned that technology is evil, but that humans are flawed. Objective morals for robots, or artificial intelligence, are not possible because of human biases which may have crept into their design. Therefore, blindly putting trust in something created by humans is not a wise move.

Ultron, the *Terminator*, and even Dolores from *Westworld* are all fictional visions of the potential pitfalls of robots and artificial intelligence. Dolores is set on the quest designed by Dr. Ford, the Terminator is based on artificial intelligence that has gone rogue, and Ultron concludes that the only way to bring about world peace is to destroy all humans. They were all designed by humans, yet their moral objectivity is based on the positives (or negatives) of human engineering.

However, it's also possible for artificial intelligence, or robots, to perform perfectly without going rogue, and yet still be a threat to human existence because of the flawed designer. For example, think of Tony Stark. Despite Tony Stark's positives, he has some glaring character flaws. He doesn't play well with others because he is an anxiety-ridden narcissist, and often sought comfort for his pain with alcohol as well as entertaining a revolving door of women. While some people may feel comfortable with a billionaire-genius-philanthropist designing artificial intelligence, those same people may not feel comfortable with a genius-alcoholic-womanizer designing artificial intelligence.

While these concerns are common for fantastic science fiction, they are not the primary concerns getting attention around the world. The real threat to humanity, in the near future, may be the Fourth Industrial Revolution. Before robots destroy all life on the planet, they are more likely to bring major disruption to workers on every continent.

Basic Concerns about Technological Displacement

The Fourth Industrial Revolution will present more challenges to human existence than simply technology which may not be morally objective. In *Rise of the Robots,* Martin Ford discusses how the rise of artificial intelligence, and robots, may lead to widespread unemployment. This unemployment is due not just to job loss as technology replaces human workers, but also due to the sudden lack of new jobs for human workers. This may involve drones that deliver packages, drones that do farming, artificial intelligence that teaches classes online, robots that fill pharmaceutical orders instead of human pharmacists, artificial personal assistants similar to Jarvis, and a wide range of other applications for a blending and applicability of rapidly emerging technologies.

Furthermore, owners are interested in profit, so they seek technologies that can make their businesses, marketing, and communication both cheaper and more efficient. Many times a company's stock value goes up when it announces job cuts. This is because businesses are not in the business of job creation, but the business of profit creation. More than just profit, there is also the drive of capitalism. The drive to profit at increasingly more efficient rates will most likely guide many of the technological innovations as human workers are displaced by more efficient warehouses, delivery systems, billing systems, education systems, medical systems, tax accounting programs, robot chefs, and enhanced manufacturing capabilities.

Workers at all occupations whether they work in legal, education, customer service, cooking, medical, agricultural workers, and other professions once thought to be human laborer safety nets may be vulnerable to technological innovation that rapidly displaces workers. Autonomous cars may only be the tip of the iceberg to usher in the Fourth Industrial Revolution.

CAPTAIN AMERICA: You think the rise of technology is a good thing. But you have no plan for how to employ people who will lose their jobs.

IRON MAN: People can repair robots and drones.

CAPTAIN AMERICA: Until robots can repair robots and drones. Where are people at in this fantastic future of yours?

IRON MAN: Why am I debating science with a man who doesn't understand science? Artificial intelligence can already beat humans at chess. Artificial intelligence can beat humans at poker. The future is already here. Get with the program.

CAPTAIN AMERICA: Tony, I don't need to understand science. I understand humans. Humans are flawed, and their flaws will infect the designs of the robots.

IRON MAN: Cap-

CAPTAIN AMERICA: Ultron.

Iron Man thinks for a moment.

IRON MAN: Touché. But Steve, open your eyes. You are the result of a science experiment that generated the absolute best in human physical capabilities. You are pound for pound the best there was, but even on your best day you can't compete with a machine. Twenty-four hours a day, seven days a week, a machine is going to work longer and harder than you. Even if the machine takes off some hours for maintenance, you can't win.

CAPTAIN AMERICA: It's not just about the work. It's about the profit margins. The advances in technology are going to generate fewer jobs, and higher profits. It's capitalism on steroids.

IRON MAN: You're criticizing capitalism?

CAPTAIN AMERICA: It's not the best invention mankind has ever created. Tony, you of all people know the dangers of capitalism.

IRON MAN: You know Steve . . . you are Captain AMERICA. You are America's champion. How can you protect America but not like capitalism? Because capitalism and America go together like steak and potatoes; like the Beatles and the sixties; like Han Solo and the Millennium Falcon.

CAPTAIN AMERICA: Well—

IRON MAN: Steve, are you saying that capitalism is bad? Because if you're against capitalism, that's practically un-American. Are you a Marxist?

CAPTAIN AMERICA: Tony, I'm a champion of the people. I don't care if people are capitalists or Marxists. If people are being bullied . . . if they need my help . . . I'll be there.

IRON MAN: Some people might say America is a bully. What do you say to that, Oh Champion of the People?

CAPTAIN AMERICA: I am Captain America. I believe that all men and all women are equal, that they have the right to freedom and liberty. And it doesn't matter if those people are in the United States, Mexico, China, or any other country. I fight for all people. I know . . . that the United States was invented by people. Capitalism was invented by people. Even the United States dollar was invented by people. None of those inventions have been great for all Americans, let alone the rest of the world. And those human inventions, which have been vigorously modified over time, are still flawed. With that as a clear indisputable fact, there is no way that a human-created robot, or a human-created computer program, can be designed without flaws. You put a flawed machine to operate within a flawed economic system . . . and lots of people are going to suffer. That, Tony, is the bottom line.

Basic Income in the Face of an Economic Crisis

There are proponents of an idea called basic income, a.k.a. universal basic income. This idea posits that all people, regardless of income level or employment status, should receive a check from the government. Basic income proponents approach the problem of human access to necessary resources required for living, such as food and shelter, not as a resource problem but as a money problem.

Capitalism may accelerate profits in the Fourth Industrial Revolution, while leaving poor people vulnerable because of even fewer income opportunities in the job market. Through poverty, money creates an invisible barrier, a social rift, that prevents people from accessing available life-saving resources. Basic income may be a way to counteract this social rift.

The basic income check may be enough to cover basic costs such as food, shelter, and medical expenses. For the richer citizens, whatever taxes they pay would be more than the basic income check they receive. For poorer people, they may still get a check even when unemployed. Basic income is one potential answer to the problem of technological displacement during the Fourth Industrial Revolution.

Critics of basic income wonder if it will increase dependence on state welfare systems, whereas not having basic income may encourage more innovation, entrepreneurship, and self-reliance. Critics also wonder if people might become lazy. If the state is going to provide enough money to survive, many people may not be motivated to work even if they are physically and mentally capable of working. Making basic income work in a free market could be a big challenge when labor, as well as commodities, are sold on markets where the monetary price rises and falls based on supply and demand.

Would basic income be feasible in a free market? Whether basic income is possible or not, through technological displacement, the problem posed by the Fourth Industrial Revolution is that an even larger segment of society which wants to work may not be able to work. People are separated from basic life-saving necessities by money. When money is the key instrument used to grant people access to food, shelter, and healthcare . . . something will need to change if jobs disappear.

IRON MAN: You fight for the little guy. You are a champion of the people. I get it. You don't like bullies.

CAPTAIN AMERICA: That's right.

IRON MAN: What about the poor people working horrible jobs. They lose fingers in machinery, develop arthritis working terrible repetitive jobs, they get cancer inhaling dangerous fumes. Medical costs will go down as people stop working. You want people to keep working these dangerous jobs?

CAPTAIN AMERICA: I said the system was flawed.

IRON MAN: You want evil capitalists to profit off the broken backs of poor people?

CAPTAIN AMERICA: Of course not.

IRON MAN: I believe the Fourth Industrial Revolution is going to protect people, and you say it's going to hurt people. But our current system hurts people, and you have no answer to make the current system better. My answer is technology.

CAPTAIN AMERICA: The current system is designed by people. It's flawed. People get hurt. Any technology that emerges during the Fourth Industrial Revolution is going to be flawed because it was designed by people.

IRON MAN: So anything created by humans is flawed?

CAPTAIN AMERICA: Humans are not perfect.

IRON MAN: Okay, smart guy. What's your answer? You don't have one. The Fourth Industrial Revolution is coming whether you like it or not. But on your best day you can't compete with a machine. There are people who spend their entire lives working in coal mines, or fields, or factories . . . and then they die from cancer. Or they suffer a debilitating injury, and then they're replaced by another poor person who works that kind of job. Their lives are less fulfilling. But you want to keep going down this same road of dangerous jobs for poor people. Captain, I am the real champion of the people, because I don't think people should be in those jobs.

CAPTAIN AMERICA: Tony, I don't think people should be in those jobs either. And I think machines replacing people in those jobs is probably a good thing.

IRON MAN: Then what's your problem?

CAPTAIN AMERICA: My problem is people like you . . . who so blindly believe in technology, and its ability to fix problems, that you ignore all the problems technology creates.

IRON MAN: I believe in science. As science learns, it refines itself, and it gets better over time. It's just like wine.

CAPTAIN AMERICA: You believe in science, and technology, and that somehow science and technology will some day in the future be able to solve all of life's problems . . . even if it can't solve those problems today. Even when technology can't solve the problems it creates today, you have a blind faith that it will somehow fix those problems in the future. But Tony, a lot of people can't wait for the future. You don't have a plan for all the jobs that are going to be lost. You seem to believe that life acts on some linear progression, that when one job closes another job opens. But that's not how life works. In life, Tony, when one job closes . . . people scramble to find a new job. They migrate to new states or new countries, desperate to find work because they need money. Thousands of people die each year migrating to find new jobs. You have no answer for the job loss Tony. You're so focused on trying to perfect technology to prevent another Ultron that you can't see how technology impacts people on a basic everyday level. And that's why you and I are different Tony . . . because I grew up a poor kid in Brooklyn.

IRON MAN: Oh, and I was born with a silver spoon in my mouth?

CAPTAIN AMERICA: Well . . . you were definitely born with a silver spoon stuck somewhere.

In Captain America versus Iron Man, it is Captain America who clearly emerges as a champion of the people. Captain America's concerns about the Fourth Industrial Revolution are not based on naive fears, but instead grounded in the bleak reality of human economic history. The idea that a multi-billionaire can truly understand the everyday challenges of working people, and then create answers that will benefit the poor and middle-classes, is something that Captain America questioned about Iron Man's faith in technological advancement. Captain America, who at times may appear a Luddite, presents a dystopic vision of the economic impacts the Fourth Industrial Revolution can bring.

13
Iron Man Was Paradoxically Wrong!

MAXWELL HENDERSON

Sure, Iron Man's pretty cool. He's dated supermodels. He built his first suit of armor to save himself from a complex medical condition—oh yeah, while simultaneously using it to break out of captivity from a bunch of bad guys. Hell, he *proposed* to his girlfriend by getting an entire Russian town to spell out his proposal! He—

> **CBR:** [*ahem*] That *wasn't* actually Iron Man.
>
> **MAXWELL HENDERSON:** . . . uh . . . who said that? Hello?
>
> **CBR:** I mean, sure it was *technically* Iron Man. But come on! This is the Iron Man vs. Captain America and Philosophy. Surely you're thinking about the Iron Man of Earth-616, in which there was the iconic Marvel Civil War. You know, the main Marvel Universe!
>
> However, you're referring to the Iron Man from Earth-1610, commonly called the "Ultimates" universe, who proposed to Black Widow.
>
> **MH:** Okay. Who are you? Now.
>
> **CBR:** Well . . . I should introduce myself. I'm the Comic Book Reader, or CBR for short. If there's a comic out there—you name it, I've read it! From *Maus* to *Ultimate Spider-Man*, *What If?* to *Invincible Iron Man*, I've read them all! Heck, some of them I read a couple times. In fact, you might call reading comics my real superpower!
>
> **MH:** So . . . okay that's great . . . but wait, how are you *here* though? This isn't a comic, it's a book . . . and geez, you're *inside* the book! How does that even happen??

CBR: Ah, so that I can explain . . . turns out that my superhero power of reading comic books all day and all night had a bit of a . . . drawback? You might say? Basically, I didn't really know it, but it turned out that I pushed my power a bit too far. One night, on a real marathon comic reading session, I accidentally got pulled *into* the very comic I was reading!—

MH: [*sigh*]—say no more, I get it, I get it. Okay, Mr. CBR, so why are you here? Are you particularly interested in philosophy?

CBR: Not exactly . . . look, not to be "that guy," but not every superhero movie has been amazing, and I assume the same holds true for chapters in a book about superheroes. And do you know the main thing that *makes* them letdowns? It's when they blatantly disregard the majestic comic book lure that the very movie (or chapter) is based on! I just am here to make sure you stay on track and . . . correct.

MH: You're my . . . fact checker?

CBR: . . . correct.

MH: [*Sigh*] Look that's totally fine. In fact, that's great. I'd rather have someone making sure that I'm giving the *other* readers nothing but the finest information about Captain America and Iron Man.

CBR: 👍

MH: Why . . . what are you even doing?

CBR: What? I like emojis. Just because it's a book doesn't mean I can't use emojis.

MH: But you can't even . . . never mind! Getting back to my original point . . . Look, all I was trying to say is that Tony Stark, or as he is better known, Iron Man, is an incredibly smart, sophisticated, and innovative character. If there is ever a seemingly hopeless situation, Iron Man defines himself as a superhero by consistently finding an option no one would have thought about—or might have even known existed!

But I think that Iron Man has still made his share of mistakes over the years. And of those biggest mistakes? He almost broke apart the Marvel Universe through the Super Hero—

CBR: Superhuman Registration Act, SRA. Or SHRA if you spell it out a bit—

MH: —yes, thank you, almost broke the Marvel Universe because of the SRA.

CBR: Well, duh. Passing the registration act pitted hero against hero, friend against friend! . . . Although, it was pretty dope to see them whaling on each other. Oh man, and the part with Punisher?? Man, he was so cool in that series. Remember how he saved Spider-Man in the sewer from Jester and Jack O'Lantern??? And the Jester got surprised because first the bullet went right through Jack O' Lantern's head and—

MH: Anyway—

CBR: —I mean, who knew pumpkins had *so many brains* in his head, you know? 💣 🎃

MH: ANYWAY—

CBR:

```
    _ / _                      _ / _
   / ~ , ~ \        —>        / X , X \
   \  \_/  /                  \  XX  /
```

MH: . . . Are you using ascii art now?

CBR: ;—)

MH: [*Sigh*] Anyway—what if I told you that the biggest issue with the SRA wasn't that it would pit hero against hero, ultimately culminating in Iron Man and Captain America fighting to (practically) the death? What if I told you the real big deal was that the SRA almost broke the Marvel Universe through **paradox**?

CBR: Huh?

Illogical Iron Man?

MH: That's right—introducing the registration act into the Marvel Universe is where it all went haywire. By forcing superheroes into revealing their secret identities and registering with the government—that ultimately led to a condition for many superheroes that was akin to a paradox discovered long ago by the philosopher and great logician—Bertrand Russell.

CBR: Bertrand Russell . . . why does that name seem so familiar? I feel like I've seen him in something before . . . (—_—) ˃̫

MH: Well, I know you're an avid comic book fan, so that wouldn't surprise me—there was an excellent comic called *Logicomix* about Bertrand Russell's life!

CBR: Ah! Well, maybe you know a bit about comics after all! Hm, thinking back to that comic, I *do* remember something about a paradox. But I don't really remember exactly what it was? I think I remember getting a bit frustrated with it.

MH: Ah, don't worry about it—it's a pretty tricky paradox! Heck, if it was easy, mathematicians and philosophers would have discovered it a long, long time before Russell did!

Basically, Russell was a philosopher—but his first and most notable claim to fame came in the field of logic!

CBR: Logic, huh? Most of the time I hear anyone describe themselves as logical, that seems like it's pretty much code for "No, you *can't* steal any of my french fries!"

MH: I . . . can't speak to that exactly? When we speak about logic in a formal manner, we really mean that we are talking about a way of reasoning or thinking that has to obey a pretty strict set of rules—it's like math! We both know that Tony Stark uses logic all the time—he's one of the most brilliant men on the planet, a scientist and engineer extraordinaire. And Tony isn't just logical in this thinking about scientific matters—he also tends to rely on logic for how he considers all kinds of day—to—day problems, like ethics.

Did Tony have to use logic to construct his many suits and weapons? Of course, but that was logic in a strictly mathematical sense. But we also saw him use logic in the Marvel Civil War when confronted by a mother spitting on him outside a church funeral. I don't have to tell you (obviously, you've read the Civil War who knows how many times), but that mother was spitting on Iron Man because in some sense, he represented all super heroes—and a super hero had killed her son, along with hundreds of other innocent civilians in an accidental massacre.

Now, while Tony's response was no doubt influenced by the passion of this grieving mother, his true response was to open his eyes to the facts of the situation: superheroes running free were an extreme danger to society, and logically speaking, Tony could not abide that fact. If we thought about a civilian who had the power to pose an extreme threat to society, that civilian would have to get a license or permit for whatever tool or weapon they were operating that would pose such a threat. So, if a normal citizen had to have a license or permit—if they had to 'register' themselves so to speak—to wield such power, why should superheroes be any different?

CBR: Hm, . . . I suppose that makes sense, from a logical perspective. If we let superheroes obey different rules than normal people, it seems like we would have an inconsistency.

MH: Yes! That's exactly the point—

CBR: CONTRADICTIONS!!! THE MOST VILE OF OFFENSES AGAINST THE COMIC BOOK GODS!!!!

MH: —uh—

CBR: Don't act like you don't get where I'm coming from!!! That's the SECOND most annoying things about a bad comic book adaptation—when it's inconsistent! Sure, Okay—I buy the fact that Superman can go faster than a speeding bullet, fly into a sun and somehow just get *stronger*, or get hit with a nuke and suffer no real damage. But if all of a sudden Superman died because he came down with a bad case of the sniffles? Inconsistencies like that are where I call bulls—

MH: ANYWAY—you are absolutely in good company in that regard. Being logical isn't so much about the premises—the beginning ideas—it's more about staying consistent once you accept certain things as true.

Back in Bertrand Russell's day, logic (as it is today, anyway) wasn't really a thing yet! Logic really emerged out of the intersection of philosophy and math—no one wanted to make philosophical arguments that were inconsistent! And at the heart of logic is exposing bad arguments—especially those with contradictions like you just mentioned.

CBR: Oh, sure, you don't need to be a logician to understand a contradiction. You can't have something being a thing and *not* a thing at the same time. If I am reading comic books about Captain America, I can't also NOT be reading comic books about Cap at the same time.

MH: Precisely—anything with a contradiction in it seems like it must be false. But . . . let me ask you this—what if I told you that you really *were* both reading and not reading a comic book about Captain America right now?

CBR: I'd say you broke my 🧠 hat does that even mean? I just said, you can't be reading and not reading at the same time—how does that even make sense?

MH: Well Comic Book Reader, you basically described the literal definition of a paradox.

CBR: Huh?

MH: A paradox is really a statement that you just said—it isn't as simple as being true or false. A real paradox is . . . kind of outside true and falseness! It's something that you can't even say that it is true or false.

CBR: Hmmm . . . that's interesting. Wait, so this gets back to Russell's paradox then, right?

MH: Absolutely. Russell found a huge paradox that seemingly upset the entire world at his time. I think, given your massive interest in comics, that the easiest way to explain this paradox is through a super—example.

CBR:

MH: [_shudders_]

Everyday I'm Russelling

MH: So . . . Russell's paradox revolved around a big idea concerning math and logic in his day—and this idea was about _sets_. Sets were basically a collection of things: items, ideas, you name it!

CBR: Okay . . .

MH: —so as an example! We could have a set which contained the names of all of Iron Man's suits of armor.

CBR: Oh! That's so easy!! Stealth armor, space armor, Hulkbuster—

MH: —right so you don't have to actually _name_ them, I'm just saying, that's an example of a set.

CBR: Right, right, right.

MH: —but one thing to notice in our previous example: that set doesn't contain itself.

CBR: Come again?

MH: If we named the set of all the names of Iron Man's armors "Iron Man Armors," then "Iron Man Armors" would not be part of "Iron Man Armors."

CBR: ☐ ⌇ ☐

MH: Okay . . . maybe that was too crazy an example. How about this: obviously, you have been using the alphabet a lot now. Let's pretend "The alphabet" is the name of a set. That set ("The alphabet") contains all twenty-six letters of the English language.

CBR: Okay . . . so obviously, that set would only be twenty-six "things" long—

MH: —right—

CBR: So "The alphabet" set would not contain "The alphabet" inside itself!

MH: Exactly! And there are tons and tons of sets like that—sets that don't contain themselves. Let's call all those sets type A.

CBR: It seems like all sets are type A then; what kind of set could possibly contain itself?

MH: Good question . . . what happens if we had a set called 'adslfjadf' which contained the *names* of all sets?

CBR: . . . hm, well since 'adslfjadf' is also a set, and since 'adslfjadf' contains the names of all sets, then 'adslfjadf' must be in . . . itself! Does . . . how . . . how does that even work??

MH: It's not as crazy as it sounds! It really just means that the set should have itself *in* itself—we aren't breaking any rules with that! It's like Superman flying faster than the speed of light. Does that make sense? Well, no, not according to the laws of physics. But is that consistent with Superman's powers? Sure! So, the idea of sets containing themselves might be a bit odd, but it fits within the system we have for sets.

CBR: Okay, I can buy that. So where's the paradox here then?

MH: Well, it comes when we ask a very specific question. Remember how we have A sets—those are sets which don't contain themselves? Well, we also have 'adslfjadf' sets—let's call them B sets—those are sets that DO contain themselves.

What happens if we have a set C: which is a set of all the A sets?

CBR: Psh, what's the problem there?

MH: Think about it.

CBR: [*sigh*] okkkkkay.

WE NOW PAUSE FOR THIS BRIEF INTERMISSION

°°◻️∅,,,∅◻️°°`°°◻️∅,,∅◻️°°◻️∅,,,∅◻️°°`°°◻️°°◻️∅,,,∅◻️°°`°°◻️∅,,∅◻️°°◻️

Okay, Done?? . . . You didn't try to actually figure this out, did you? Haha, with your puny brain??

WE NOW RETURN TO OUR CURRENT THINGAMAGIG

CBR: . . . I . . . I see it now.

MH: Go on.

CBR: If set C is the list of all A sets, it is really the list of all the sets that don't contain themselves. That means that C, at the beginning would not be part of its own set.

MH: Now you're getting it.

CBR: . . . but . . . if C does *not* contain itself—that means it is a type A set—because type A sets don't contain themselves! But that means that if set C is a type A set, since set C is the list of all type A sets, it should be in its own set! Which means it no longer is a type A set—

MH: Keep going—

CBR: —which means that if set C no longer is a type A set, that means that set C no longer contains itself, which means that it belongs in set C again . . . and . . . ahh!!! I FEEL THE PARADOX!!! I FEEL IT IN MY VERY COMIC BOOK PAGE BONES!!!

MH: There's the rub. Russell's paradox was all about exposing a fundamental problem with math, logic, and philosophy that the system itself couldn't quite explain.

And in a big way, that is my biggest issue with Iron Man in the Civil War. He invites paradoxes into the Marvel Universe that seem frighteningly similar to the paradox uncovered by Russell. Not exactly the same—but similar.

CBR: (⌐■_■) lay it on me.

Where It All Went Right Then Wrong Then Right Then Wrong Then . . .

MH: In my mind, the very idea of a superhero is to protect the lives and security of the people around you—*especially* the people who are closest to you. Superheroes will go to extraordinary length to do the right thing, to protect the weak, and even sacrifice themselves to save someone else. So in a way, the SRA makes total sense—again, like a driver's license, people that have the power of driving a car should have to be registered to wield that power.

But there is a huge difference between a just—turned—16—and—way—to—excited—to—drive—teen and Spider-Man getting a license: no one is out there trying to *hurt* the teenager getting their license. And certainly, no one is trying to hurt the teenager's *family* for getting a license! But that's simply not true for heroes like Spider-Man and Daredevil.

Captain America understands the hearts and plights of the more underground heroes, who have worked their entire lives to keep their identities a secret. Only though this secret can they protect their loved ones while helping the public at large. But Iron Man's support of the SRA forces these heroes into an awkward position. Iron Man claims that the superheroes registering their identities with the government will provide some kind of accountability—some sort of oversight for the heroes that would end up saving lives. And this argument makes sense—but for the superheroes themselves, it also seems like they get stuck in a very sticky spot.

CBR: (°ロ°)!!!

MH: Giving up their identities to the government seems to be the "right" thing to do, protecting citizens. However, by giving up their identities, they are invariably increasing the risk to their family and loved ones, who would be obvious targets by the bad dudes. And thus, superheroes in these conditions wind up in a no—win situation: a paradox of what they should do.

If the superhero elects to give up their identity, they put their families in danger. Superheroes by definition have to protect citizens, especially their families. So, that means that the superhero can't reveal their identity. But, not revealing their identity means (according to Iron Man) that more citizens will be in danger. So, the superhero has to give up their identity—

CBR: —I'll stop you there—that *is* interesting. I can see the analogy to Russell's paradox; it's like trying to decide what kind of set C is. If it's A, then it's B—but if it's B, then it's A!

MH: Smiley face.

CBR: . . . did you just *say* 'smiley face'?

MH: I . . . I was trying to be cool like you—

CBR: Dude, you can't be me, okay?

MH: [*sigh*]

CBR: Also, wait—I feel like something is a bit off here. Wasn't Russell's paradox really arising out of a problem with logic itself? It doesn't seem to me that the same exact thing is happening here.

MH: That's a great point—however, as it happens, that is *exactly* what is happening here . . . in a way. Russell's paradox was truly a paradox, because using the rules of the very system (in this case, of logic), it exposed a question that really couldn't be answered. Not just right or wrong—but just couldn't be answered, according to the rules of the system.

I think that's very similar to what happens with the Civil War in comics. Comics *aren't* bound by the same rules of math, and obviously don't rely too heavily on hard science—

CBR:—you're telling me people CAN'T randomly fly through the air on a whim, or get hulk powers from a nuclear blast??

MH: — BUT I *do* think the underlying system governing comics is: the nature of the Superhero. Superhero comics are okay with breaking laws of biology, chemistry, physics—but the one thing a superhero comic should *not* do is allow for something to happen which directly violates the law of the Superhero. This is why, placed in seemingly impossible situation *physically*, heroes like Captain America and Iron Man almost *reject* the physical to obey the much stronger law—the law of the superhero. Somehow, against all odds, the superhero will always figure out a way to never give up their superhero-ness while at the same time, saving the day.

But the Civil War forced our beloved superheroes to paradoxically look in the mirror and try to answer a question that superheroes cannot answer: "What happens when you have to hurt someone innocent, someone you want to protect?" Obviously, there are pragmatic answers to this: try to pick the option that hurts fewest people, try to do the thing that will work best . . . but these are pragmatic solutions that we'd use in the *real* world! In the superhero world, these questions ultimately have no good answer! A true superhero would sooner break the laws of physics then knowingly choose a path that hurts someone.

CBR: . . . wow. For all the comic books I've ever read, I've never quite thought of it like that.

MH: Well, this is exactly why we need more philosophy comic books out there.

CBR: Ha . . . well, I'll admit it ¯_(ツ)_/¯ I was expecting to come here to be correcting you, making sure you weren't allowing any more filth into the comic book world. But not only did you impress me, you actually taught me a thing or two! I gotta hand it to you, next time I pop back inside the *Civil War* comics, I'll be shaking my head a bit more at Iron Man's decisions.

MH: That sounds great—and it has been great to make your acquaintance, CBR! Can you tell me where you are off to next?

CBR: Well, I've got a lot to think about, and I feel like I need to relax a bit. I was thinking about heading back to one of my favorite comics.

MH: Oh that sounds fun. . . . Any particular reason?

CBR: Remember when I said I could . . . *feel* things in the stories—

MH: GOODBYE

CBR: (☞ﬁ∀°)☞ (((

14
The Gods of Marvel

GERALD BROWNING

For decades, Marvel Comics has been known for telling epic-style tales that entertain millions of men, women, and children around the globe. Their larger than life characters could not be contained on the page. So, for nearly twenty years, the Marvel Cinematic universe releases have dominated the summer blockbusters on our silver screen. Characters like Spiderman, The Avengers, X-Men, and Deadpool (to mention only a few) have ruled ticket sales because of their larger-than-life stories, amazing special effects, and—most importantly—ability to stimulate our imaginations.

However, these stories are nothing new. These wonderful characters, while new to our younger generation, and the fodder of nostalgia to those of us who grew up (years ago) with these characters, have actually been around for thousands of years.

Characters very much like Captain America and Iron Man have been performing awesome feats long before our great grandparents and even *their* great grandparents. Today, we call these characters "superheroes." In ancient Greece and Rome, they called them "gods." In ancient Greece, Captain America was a demi-god called Heracles and Iron Man was a god called Hephaestus.

Mythology and Marvel

Marvel Comics has used directly mythological heroes and villains in their comic books for decades. The most obvious example is Thor, the Norse god of thunder, as well as characters in

Thor's adventures such as Loki, Odin, and other Norse gods and goddesses. But ancient Greek characters such as Heracles have also become important characters in the Marvel Comics universe.

Mythology and comic books have a strong relationship. It is all too common for religious and mythological heroes and heroines to appear on the pages of graphic novels—Marvel in particular. Many of the tales of the gods, goddesses, demigods, and the like have been depicted in ancient drawings, paintings, and sculptures. It is also quite interesting to see how the mythology has influenced and inspired some of the Marvel's greatest heroes and characters. Tales such as the *Iliad*, the *Aeneid*, and the *Epic of Gilgamesh* have enthralled children and grownups for many centuries.

Forging the Myth

The story of Tony Stark (aka Iron Man) has been told on the page and on the screen. Technology genius and philanthropist Tony Stark, captured by terrorists and wounded by a grenade, forges a mini-reactor to save his life and fashion a suit of armor to escape his captors. Tony Stark has proven himself to be a very smart, crafty, inventive, and cunning superhero. The more that we learn about Tony Stark (and his alter ego Iron Man), the more parallels we can draw between Iron Man and the ancient Greek god Hephaestus.

Hephaestus, the god of blacksmiths, metals, craftsmen, and artisans was well known for his abilities to create and build, especially weapons for the gods. The symbols of this crafty god were known to be an anvil and hammer. Much like Hephaestus, Stark used the hammer and the anvil to create his iron armor. Much like the Greek god, the iron hero is known for creating weapons like no other.

Another trait that both god and hero possess is their ability to overcome their physical limitations. Hephaestus has been named "the lame one" due to a deformity in his foot. Some suggested that it was Zeus that hurled him from Mount Olympus, which caused his deformity. Whereas, some believe it was Hera that maimed him. Whoever caused the deformity, it was Hera who ejected Hephaestus from Mount Olympus because of his deformity.

In both the popular movie *Iron Man* (2008) and the graphic novel series, billionaire Tony Stark was captured by terrorists and wounded in an attack. Shrapnel from a booby trap (or terrorist assault, if you're watching the movie) left metal in his chest. In order to stop the shrapnel from entering his heart, Stark, managed to fashion a high tech magnet to keep the shrapnel at bay. This is the prototype for the arc reactor that is constantly imbedded in his chest.

During the scene where Stark builds the reactor, he is inside of a cave and we see him building the arc reactor and the Iron Man armor. Stark is surrounded by darkness, open flames, and steel. This is the birthplace of Iron Man. From then on, he uses his technology to keep him alive as well as create weapons to fight evil. This very scene is very reminiscent of images of Hephaestus working in his forge. Favoring volcanoes and volcanic islands, Hephaestus works in darkness, using his anvil, hammer, and open flames, to manufacture his formidable weapons and tools.

Both Hephaestus and Iron Man use their intelligence as a way to make a name for themselves. Both men are known for their crafty nature. Being a thinking man's hero, Stark is just as known for his intelligence and ability to create, as he is known for his glamorous alter ego. Hephaestus produces weapons so powerful that even the gods themselves fear what the god of smiths can create.

Stark as Iron Man is known for his diverse kinds of armors. His armors (created to aid him on various missions) have been modified on multiple occasions. Each one possesses an upgrade that turns each suit into a more powerful weapon. Much like Hephaestus, Stark created armored suits that might threaten even the gods themselves. For example, Stark's "Thorbuster" armor (which first appeared in *Iron Man*, Volume 3, issue #64) was created just in case Thor went rogue and had to be put down. The armor was powered by an Asgardian crystal. Ultimately, Thor was able to destroy this armor.

The god Hephaestus has a direct connection to robots. In Homer's epic *Iliad*, the god of smiths shaped conscious humanoid beings out of gold and bronze. In order to help him with the design and blacksmithing, he fashioned thinking women out of metal. Hephaestus also created a metal guard for King Minos of Crete. So Tony Stark isn't the only one who has been known to create metallic heroes.

Demigods and Super Soldiers

Not quite a god, but not quite a human, some super-powered beings have to walk the boundary between being the "average Joe" and something more than a mere mortal. Two characters who have experienced difficulty walking this line are Greek mythology's Heracles, the son of Zeus, and Steve Rogers, better known as Captain America. Heracles was known to both the Romans and Marvel as "Hercules."

Heracles was down to earth enough for people to relate to him. He had a lot of the same struggles that ws humans had. He constantly rebelled against his family. His father's wife, Hera, continually made obstacles for him to overcome due to the fact that she was jealous that her husband Zeus had sired the demigod by having an affair with a human. Heracles was a man of utmost bravery who performed tasks that tested his strength and courage.

Just like the mighty Heracles, Captain America is a man who is more than just a "mere mortal" yet he isn't as "god-like" as characters such as Galactus, the Silver Surfer, Apocalypse, or Thanos. "Cap" is a hero who is grounded in the reality of the world around him. Millions of readers are fascinated as a "kid from Brooklyn" from a different era attempts to stay rooted to the land around him, yet is a symbol of freedom and justice and uses his might to fight enemies, domestic, foreign, and otherworldly.

We see some conspicuous differences between Rogers and Heracles. Rogers was born a weak and frail person. It took the US military's science division to create a "Super Soldier" serum that the patriotic Rogers took in order to become the mighty Captain America. Heracles, on the other hand, was born with his superhuman abilities since he was the son of the most powerful of the gods. Yet, when we delve into these two characters and the times in which their popularity was at its zenith, we can see that both characters, and their origins, were shaped to cater to the demands of the populace.

As for Heracles, he was Greek demigod during a time where people admired the heroics of Achilles, Ulysses, and the like. Heracles was a character who was larger than life yet retained his humanity and human attributes. The character was still relatable, yet possessed powers that were equal or superior to those of the strongest human beings. The mythology of the times spurred the imaginations of the young with amazing stories, taught lessons, and explained even the mundane occurrences such as why the seasons change, why the sun sets and rises, and how our lives are predestined to occur as they will. All of this created a world where there was magic in the little things in life.

Captain America likewise appealed to an audience of his time. Captain America was created in 1941. His character was revived in the 1950s during the height of the atomic horror movie. Science and science fiction were becoming more popular. Atomic horror films, science fiction, and fantasy were beginning to capture the imaginations of young and old in the United States. The notion of Captain America appeals to the wonders of science and the patriotism of a nation that was struggling through World War II.

Captain America: The Winter Soldier (2014) really dramatizes the disconnect that Rogers has with the America that he has been thrust into. The Marvel cinematic universe has told the story of Captain America in a way that really exposes this disconnect. *Captain America: The First Avenger* (2011) was set during the World War II conflict. This period piece shows Rogers in his element. He grows into the hero that America needs at the time, to defeat the evil Nazis. *Captain America: The Winter Soldier* and *The Avengers* (2012) display Rogers as a man out of time.

Due to his deliberately out-dated language (Joss Whedon is well known for us snappy and intelligent use of dialogue) we are constantly reminded that even though Cap is out of his comfort zone, he is still the personification of a "hero." No matter the era he is in, the concept of what it means to be a hero is the same. Captain America and Heracles are well known for being brave adventurers who exhibited heroism and kindness for their fellow man. In a remarkable parallel, Captain America has battled Thanos and Heracles fought Thanatos, meaning that both men have struggled against the personification of Death.

Both Heracles and Captain America use their brute strength and also employ iconic weapons that are primitive in nature. Heracles is known for wearing a lion's skin and wielding a club. Both are symbols of his masculinity and aggressive nature. Captain America, however, also has an iconic weapon that is quite primitive. Steve Rogers wields the iconic shield made of Vibranium. The weapon, made of the Wakandan metal, is impervious to most known metals (second only to Adamantium). Both the club and the shield are weapons used by ancient tribes. In many depictions of Heracles, we see him wielding his club. And now it's virtually impossible to think of the Captain America uniform without the powerful shield.

Brains vs. Brawn

What makes a good story? What does it take to have a great tale that adults and children alike can gravitate towards? It would appear that the ingredients for a good story are the same now as they were thousands of years ago. In fact, some of the same stories have been told over and again for generations.

We have two types of heroes which span generations. The first type of hero is one who uses on technology and craftsmanship as his weapons. This particular hero relies on his sharpened mind in the way a warrior relies on his sharpened blade. Sometimes this hero uses his mind to take the place of a weakened body.

The other type of hero is one who relies on his strength and bravery to see him through battle after battle. These heroes are the ones who thrive on the battlefield. These are heroes who are the first one into a skirmish and the last one to leave the field of combat. At times, they can be gentle, but only at the appropriate time. These heroes have symbols of their brute strength, but their body is their main weapon.

The differences between these heroes was never more evident than in the movie *Captain America: Civil War* (2016). In this film, the rift between the Avengers widens and the main schism is between Captain America and Iron Man. The bond between these two superheroes breaks when we see that their ways of problem solving start to drive a wedge between them. Iron Man sees the super-powered beings as a potential threat (in much the same way as he created a "Thorbuster" in the comic book). He believes that there should be a registration for new heroes who are coming out of the woodwork, thanks to the "Incident" that occurs in *The Avengers* (2012).

Rogers does not agree and sees this registration in much the same way as the time when Hitler (and Hydra) registered the

Jewish people. Stark sees the logic of registering super-powered beings and Rogers looks into his heart to know what is right and wrong. His moral compass does not veer. It is this very difference between these two heroes that divides them.

The Good Soul

Both Iron Man and Captain America embody characters and stories that arose long before their time. Both are iconic superheroes who have inspired the imaginations of millions across the world. If we look at both of these characters for the heroes that they are, both Heracles and Captain America embody the adventurer and personality traits that make a hero heroic.

With Hephaestus and his modern counterpart, Iron Man, we notice that these characters have the potential of being heroes and achieve heroics, we see that Iron Man is a scientist and has the ulterior motive of satisfying a curiosity. This is not to say that Iron Man isn't a hero nor capable of achieving great heroics, but Rogers has a more of a "purity" about his agenda that we cannot question.

Both men are brilliant minds. Stark has a genius intellect which allows him to fashion weapons to save mankind. Rogers is a brilliant tactician who has a mind for war and strategy. Much like Heracles, Rogers has an idealist point of view, whereas Stark has a more realist point of view. If we look at the "registry" plotline that we see in Civil War, it is plain to see the dividing line between these two "titans" (no pun intended). Both men fought for their principles and did what they did in order to save lives.

Like his ancient Greek counterpart, Tony Stark's most powerful weapon is his mind. With a genius intellect, he is able to create weapons and suits to combat evil. Stark's greatest weakness seems to be his ego. It appears that the very thing that makes him such a brilliant superhero is the weakness that he harbors, which is the perfect ingredient for a tragic hero.

Steve Rogers's greatest strengths are his brilliant strategic thinking and his physical prowess (both of which, arguably were enhanced by the scientific project that gave him his extraordinary abilities). The super soldier has such an indomitable spirit and a passion for helping others, which was a personality trait that he fostered since he was young (which was probably what drove him to participate in the super solider project to begin with). Both heroes have used their particular traits to push through the darkest of points in their lives.

Who's the better hero? In the comparison between these two heroes, we can find many similarities, but also major differences. In order to be a true hero, you need to be selfless. "Selfless" is not in Tony Stark's personality. His ego wins out in many of the verbal sparring matches that he has been in.

Steve Rogers can be selfless in the true sense of the word. He has a good soul and is very focused on saving as many people as he can. Ultimately, when we strips these characters of their power, all that's left is the personality. In which case, from this writer's experience, the winner of this round has to be Captain America.

15
Iron Kant or Captain Kant?

NATHAN BOSMA AND ADAM BARKMAN

Captain America and Iron Man you already know: both are superheroes and Avengers, who fight the good fight against the baddies. Immanuel Kant you may not know, but he was an eighteenth-century German philosopher who argued that rightness and wrongness are objective and absolute.

The view that ethics is objective and absolute contrasts with the competing view that ethics is a matter of evaluating the consequences of each action. So Kant claimed that some actions are just right or wrong, regardless of any good or harmful consequences that may happen to follow from them. Murder, for example, is objectively wrong, regardless of the possibility that some murders may have more good than bad consequences. This view, that ethics is objective and not dependent on looking at consequences, is called *deontology*.

The original Avengers' Charter states that the Avengers—including Cap and Iron Man—"dedicate themselves to the establishment, growth, and preservation of peace, liberty, equality, and justice under law" (*Avengers Annual #1*). This charter seems to agree with Kant's deontological view of ethics. But does this mean that all the Avengers—Cap and Iron Man specifically—would agree on what is or is not a duty and the particular application of moral principles?

Nope. In both the comics and the cinematic universe, the two superheroes come up against each other when the government tries to interfere with their actions. In the Civil War comic series, the US government calls for the Superhuman Registration Act (hereon referred to as the SRA), requiring superheroes to reveal their identities and act under standards imposed by them. In the Marvel Cinematic Universe movie *Captain America: Civil War*, the United Nations calls for the Avengers to submit themselves to the Sokovia Accords, placing the power of the Avengers under a UN board that will control their actions and powers, and the registering of all people who either have superpowers or are considered "of interest."

In both the comics and movie, Iron Man sides with the various government registration acts, and Captain America fights against them for the freedom of superheroes. On Kantian absolute ethics, this means that only one of them can be right. Who—if any—is right?

Universal Reach (But Not of the Thanos Sort)

Kant believed in a moral law that we all have a duty to obey, and insisted that by philosophical reasoning we can determine the proper action in any circumstance. He called this law the "Categorical Imperative," and formulated it in many ways. However, for the sake of simplicity, look at the first, and by far the most famous, version—stated in his *Groundwork for the Metaphysics of Morals* (1785): "Act only according to that maxim whereby you can, at the same time, will that it should become a universal law."

While this at first seems somewhat Thanos-like (universal domination is a favorite of his!), the idea behind it is pretty clear. What Kant calls a "maxim" is the principle that motivates you to do something. When he speaks of "willing to be a universal law," he means you should only do something if you were willing that everyone always be recommended to do it.

Kant also devised a three-step test to find out whether your action would be in line with your moral duty. The first step is to find your maxim: for example, if Pepper Potts wants to lie to Tony Stark, her boss, about her hours, she has the maxim, "It is okay to lie." The second step is to generalize that principle, making it a universal law: "It is okay for everyone to lie." The final step is to ask yourself two questions: Could you act on that maxim in a universe where it is a maxim that everyone follows? So, this argument appeals to the question people often ask about matters of ethics: What if everyone did that?

The answer to the first question is no: If everyone knew everyone else was lying to each other, there would be no point in your lying because whomever you're lying to knows you're lying! The answer to the second question is probably also no, as most rational people don't want to live in an entirely deceitful universe. Kant says we must be able to rationally answer both questions with a "Yes" if it is moral for us to act upon the maxim.

Kant was also a champion of acting out of motivation to be ethical, stating in *Groundwork of the Metaphysics of Morals*, "An action from duty has its moral worth not in the purpose to be attained by it, but in the maxim in accordance with which it is decided upon." While at first this quote seems too complicated for all but Reed Richards, the concept is simple: Unless your action is done purely out of the will to follow your moral duty, you are not acting morally.

Let's explain this by continuing with the lying example: Pepper wants to lie to Tony, but she knows that if she is caught lying, she will probably be fired. Too scared to risk it, she tells the truth. While she might be doing the right thing, it is without moral value, because she did not act out of duty to the moral law. Kant believed that these ideas were the backbone for the universal moral law of rational beings. With this in mind, we can go forward and check which of our fearless Avengers are in the right!

Iron Man: The Guardians Need to Be Guarded

Let's start with Iron Man. In the comic book series, after a confrontation between superhumans causes the death of hundreds of people, including dozens of children, the US government asks superhumans to register their true identities and accept government regulation and monitoring, all of which Iron Man accepts. With the Sokovia Accords, he is approached by the government following a series of destructive events, such as the destruction of Sokovia in *Avengers: Age of Ultron* and Lagos in *Captain America: Civil War*.

He's also asked to hand over control of the Avengers to the United Nations to supervise their actions in order to balance the protection of the Earth *by* the Avengers with the protection of the citizens of Earth *from* the Avengers. Again, Iron Man agrees to do so, and signs the accords. How is he justifying this? Let's examine his arguments to see if we can discover his maxim for acting.

In the Cinematic Universe, Iron Man is extremely moved upon hearing the story of a young man who spends his summer in Sokovia building sustainable housing who is killed by the actions of the Avengers while they were trying to stop Ultron from destroying the Earth. He says, "We need to be put in check, and whatever form that takes I'm game. If we can't accept limitations we're boundary-less, we're no better than the bad guys" (*Captain America: Civil War*). He believes that while the Avengers are doing good things, they're doing them in the wrong way, and with deadly consequences. Innocent lives are lost on his watch—deaths that could have been prevented had there been better regulation of their actions.

In the comics, Iron Man is initially against the SRA when it's first considered, and even hires someone to attack him following a speech on it in order to prove that superhumans needed to be free to act quickly in order to protect the nation. However, following the explosion in Stamford (causing the death of many, including children), the public lashes out against superhumans and the government quickly imposes the SRA (*Civil War #1–2*). Iron Man accepts this, his main argument being that the superhumans cannot self-regulate themselves without collateral damage; he also argues it would be impossible to resist this and it would be forced upon them if they didn't sign on.

Let's do a Kantian breakdown to find out if he is acting according to the moral law. There are multiple maxims we could use in this situation. We could make the maxim "I should protect the people of Earth," as he seems to be moved by the fact that innocents are dying on his watch. However, this will probably be problematic, after all, he was protecting the people of Earth when he was asked to submit his powers.

This may be an emotional factor for him; however, it is not the reason he decides to go along. If this were his true maxim, he would have sought regulation before it was asked of him. In both cases, he backs up his arguments to sign the regulation with that it is impossible to avoid the government enforcing it upon them. A more accurate maxim would be "I should obey the government." This seems like a strong maxim, so let's test it.

He has two choices: obey the government or disobey the government. Generalizing "I should obey the government" leads to "Everyone should obey the government." For many, this might seem perfectly fine, so let's test the other choice, namely, "I should not obey the government" or, generalized, "Nobody should obey the government." This *is* problematic. In a world where nobody obeyed the government, there would be no way to have any political structure, and there would be no government for people to disobey! This, therefore, fails. Iron Man seems to be making the right choice by siding with the government.

However, it should be noted that he says that this is unavoidable—not exactly a moral reason. In the MCU, he says "If we don't do this now, it's gonna be done to us in the future" to justify signing the accords against Cap's arguments of surrendering their power (*Captain America: Civil War*). After being kidnapped and seeing innocent people killed by his own weaponry, he shuts down the weapons program of Stark Industries, saying, "I had my eyes opened. I came to realize that I have more to offer this world than just making things to blow up" (*Iron Man*).

In *Iron Man 2*, he downright refuses to have James Rhodes take the suit to the military, getting into a drunken fight (which he loses), and seeming to believe that he is the only means necessary to protect humanity, saying things like, "I am your nuclear deterrent" and "I have successfully privatized world peace" (*Iron Man 2*). By *Iron Man 3*, however, he allows Rhodes to act as "The Iron Patriot," using the technology for military purposes, and when *Civil War* comes around, he surrenders his power to government control.

Since Iron Man's move toward registration and government conformity is gradual, it's not easy to see his motivations, but if it is simply that it is inevitable, then that would negate his moral reason for wanting to obey the government. But let's give him the benefit of the doubt; let's allow that he really believes that everyone should obey the government simply because it is the right thing to do.

Captain America: The Guardians Don't Need to Be Guarded

Let's now turn to Captain America. Things certainly seem quite bleak for him right now. Iron Man's maxim of "I should obey the government" makes it seem obvious that Captain America disobeying the government is morally wrong, and that if Cap refuses to sign off on the accords he is a criminal-vigilante.

However, all is not lost for Cap. What he needs is to come up with another maxim to justify his actions, though, one so powerful that it could be a seventh Infinity Gem. A good first step for him to do is to break Iron Man's maxim. Captain America fought personally in World War II, so let's use an example from then.

During and after the war, Cap criticized the government bombing of Hiroshima and Nagasaki (*Captain America Volume 2 #7*), but if the government had come to Cap and asked him to fly the jet that dropped the Fat Man bomb on Nagasaki, he would had to if he were to act under Iron Man's maxim. However, there would be a conflict of interest: in acting under Iron Man's maxim, he would have been the cause of death of hundreds of thousands of innocent civilians: this would have been murder. So, let's test it: Cap's "I should murder" becomes "It is okay for everyone to murder," which is plainly absurd. Cap would definitely not enjoy living in this world (although Punisher might), and, in this case, it becomes clear that Cap would be right to disobey the government's order to murder. So, he needs a new maxim. We will look at his origin story to fight out what this might be.

When Steve Rogers first tried to fight against Axis forces in the Second World War, he was not physically fit to do so. However, he did so because he knew that it was the right thing to do. He knew that the atrocities committed by the Nazis were some of the most horribly wrong things in all of the Nine Realms! In the Cinematic Universe, America is at war, and in the comics, they are not. In both universes, however, he knows he should join the war.

He is not drafted, and is in fact rejected when he tries to enlist, due to his physical health (*Captain America Volume 1 #109, Captain America: The First Avenger*). Despite this, his bravery and virtue lead him to be offered a chance to participate in a performance-enhancing experiment to become a super-soldier, which he accepts despite a high risk of death. He takes on the name of "Captain America," to serve as a symbol for exactly what he wants to fight for: freedom and justice. Therefore, his maxim becomes "I wish to fight for freedom and justice." Universalized, this becomes "Everyone should fight for freedom and justice." Because he is not forcibly enrolled into the army, we know that his central maxim is *not* "I should obey the government."

In fact, in the Cinematic Universe, his first actual mission is going against the orders of the government to rescue captured soldiers. Ultimately, it is this that earns him the respect of his officers and allows him to become a frontline soldier to fight HYDRA. Clearly, he is acting on the maxim of fighting for freedom and justice, not the maxim to obey the government. This is not to say, however, that Cap is a vigilante: he submits readily to his superior officers as a soldier. So why does he disobey the government in the original case, and criticize the atomic bombings of Japan?

The answer is in his maxim of fighting for freedom and justice, but especially justice. Captain America's maxim for obeying the government is not "Always obey the government," but "Always obey a *just* government" or "Always obey a government that asks you not to, among things, kill innocent non-combatants." Anyway, let's test this. If we go with "Always obey a just government,' then this becomes "Everyone should obey a just government." This, again, seems fine and this allows Cap to have two linking maxims: when he is obeying a just government, he's fighting for justice; when the government is not being just, he does not need to obey them, and fights for justice himself.

When his superior officers tell him they will not try to save possibly captured soldiers, or the government wishes to blow up entire cities of civilians, they are not being just. When the government does not act to save the soldiers, they have the maxim, "I should not save captured soldiers," which becomes "Nobody should save captured soldiers." This is not necessarily a contradiction, because in a world where no captured soldiers were saved, there would be no expectation of the government to save them. However, it is almost certainly not a world rational people would want to live in. When it comes to the atomic bomb, however, we have already determined that the killing of innocent civilians is wrong. It follows, then, that the govern-

ment is acting unjustly. Therefore, Cap can disobey them without going against his maxim of obeying a just government, and
still follow his maxim of fighting for justice.

So, despite being so frozen that Iceman himself would have
been impressed, and not waking up for seventy years, Captain
America still maintains these maxims. In the Cinematic
Universe, at the funeral of his former love Peggy Carter, Captain
America is presented with a speech that causes him to realize
these maxims when confronted with the Sokovia Accords. He
hears these words: "No one wanted to see a woman succeed at
either; and she said compromise where you can. But where you
can't, don't. Even if everyone is telling you that something wrong
is something right" (*Captain America: Civil War*). Cap realizes
that just because the United Nations and over hundred countries are behind the Sokovia Accords, it does not make them
right. Morality is not something that comes through a mass vote;
it is something that comes through careful reasoning and doing
the ethically correct thing based upon such reasoning.

When Cap is approached by the government and asked to
sign on to either the Sokovia Accords or the SRA, he needs to
ask himself whether or not he should side with the government.
In the case of the SRA, he is asked if it is just for the American
government to simply force all of the super-powered individuals
to give up their identities. They have the maxim "It is okay to
force people to give away their identities," which becomes
"Everyone should force people to give away their identities."

As well as his statement about choosing to do only what can
become a universal law for everyone to do, Kant also gave
another way to explain his Categorical Imperative:

Act in such a way that you treat humanity, whether in your own person or in the person of any other, never merely as a means to an end,
but always at the same times as an end. (*Groundwork for the
Metaphysics of Morals*)

Kant is saying that it's wrong to use some person (including
yourself) purely as means to accomplish some purpose you
have, without respecting that person, as an end in themselves,
independently of that purpose.

If the American government asks all super-powered individuals to give up their identities, this doesn't treat people as ends

in themselves and doesn't give people the dignity owed them by the government, and so Cap can disobey the government with a clear conscience. In the case of the Sokovia Accords, the UN has the maxim "It is okay to force Captain to fight for my specific agenda," which becomes "All superheroes should fight for the UN's agenda." But this becomes a dangerous build-up of power, and what happens when the government, and not one's conscience, starts telling us who the bad guys are?

When the government demands the Sokovia Accords, they are asking for the Avengers to become merely a means to defend the world, and nothing else: the government has no respect for them as people with potential desire to disagree and act otherwise. The same applies to the SRA: the government does not see the people behind the mask, only their superpowers. Once again, Cap can see that the government is acting unjustly under a test of both formulations of the Categorical Imperative, and can disobey the government in clear conscience to defend justice and freedom.

Captain Kant

So how does this fight end? Captain America is justified in his actions to not sign on to the various types of government restriction. While at first it may seem that Iron Man may have been making the right choice in creating a maxim "I should obey the government," this maxim falls apart under a more rigorous examination.

When the government acts justly, it seems right to obey it. But what would he do if Doctor Doom were to take over the government and ask him to use his powers to kill innocent people? Surely he would want to say no: but he would be going against his maxim, and thus no longer be acting in accordance with his duty. And so this shows an important weakness in Iron Man's maxim. In addition, we aren't totally convinced that Iron Man himself knows what his real reason is for signing on to the SRA or the Sokovia Accords: is it for a high ethical reason or some sort of non-moral impulse? In the end we side with Captain America, who tells Iron Man:

> If we sign this we surrender our right to choose. What if this panel sends us somewhere we don't think we should go. What if there's

somewhere we need to go and they don't let us? We may not be perfect, but the safest hands are still our own. (*Captain America: Civil War*).

After a close examination of both of our heroes' ethical maxims and duties using Kant's Categorical Imperative, Captain America beats Iron Man in this civil war of deontological ethics!

III

It's a Tie
(Lets Go Again!)

16
Would You Buy a Used Car from This Avenger?

ARON ERICSON

The question "Would you buy a used car from this man?" is a classic litmus test for trustworthiness. So let's ask that question in relation to our marvelous heroes, Tony Stark a.k.a. Iron Man, and Steve Rogers a.k.a. Captain America.

Would I buy a used car from Tony? If I could afford it, absolutely! The man's got really nice cars. If I was unsure about the shape the car was in, which is of course the worry when buying a used car, I'd only have to appeal to the mechanic in him and trust that his compulsive side would not let any problem go unfixed.

Steve is another story. We remember the crappy Volkswagen Beetle that he, Falcon, and the Winter Soldier take for a road trip in *Captain America: Civil War* (2016), and it does not put us in a buying mood. That car was chosen, admittedly, for the purpose of keeping a low profile while on the run from the authorities, but maybe used cars just isn't Cap's *métier*. For better or worse, however, questions of trust extend beyond used cars.

Trust is as necessary as it is fragile. In your everyday life, you need to trust that the food you eat has not been poisoned, that the building you're in is well-constructed and will not collapse, that the book you read does not contain a code that triggers a mind-control put in your mind by HYDRA scientists to turn you into an involuntary killing machine, and so on. At the same time, deep and meaningful trust takes a long time to build up and it can be quickly destroyed.

Stark Trusts Me About as Far as He Can Throw Me

Carolyn McLeod lays out these three criteria that most philosophers agree are required for trust.:

1. **vulnerability to others (risking betrayal)**

2. **thinking well of others (optimism about their intentions)**

3. **optimism about the competence of others (that they can do what I trust them to do).**

Tony Stark seems to have trouble with all three. Beginning at the end of the list and working our way up, we know that Tony is a smart man, and he's usually correct in thinking that he's way ahead of others when it comes to figuring out the solution to a problem. He also has more enemies than most, so maybe pessimism about the intentions of others is not an ill-advised go-to attitude.

Still, for all his faults, Tony doesn't strike us as being jealous (with the exception perhaps of Steve having a better relation to Tony's father, Howard Stark), and when he sees greatness in someone else, which doesn't happen all that often, he is quick to celebrate and endorse it. So does Tony really have such a hard time trusting? Black Widow quips, in *The Avengers* (2012), that Stark trusts her about as far as he can throw her, but thinking about it, at least when suited up he can throw someone pretty damn far. But, I want to insist, Tony has trust issues. He's not incapable of trust, but he has a hard time with it. And his major problem has to do with accepting vulnerability.

Tony's not big on asking for help. In *Iron Man 2* (2010) he's dying but doesn't tell anyone. Rhodey sees that everything is not as it should and tells Tony that there's no need for him to go through it alone. Tony doesn't take the extended hand: "You've gotta trust me. Contrary to popular belief, I know exactly what I'm doing." Really, Tony seems to have no idea what he's doing, and Rhodey shouldn't trust him. But Tony cutting himself off is also understandable.

Rhodey says Tony doesn't have to do "the whole lone-gunslinger act," but he can't help him with the palladium poisoning and maybe sentiment is not something Tony wants at that moment. Trust must be freely given and cannot be forced or coerced. This means, with regards to the criterion of vulnerability, that the one who trusts must freely accept this risk. None of us are all-powerful, so we are dependent on others, more so than we usually acknowledge. That we are vulnerable is an inescapable fact about human existence, but for there to be trust one must accept this vulnerability and be optimistic that others will help us in our precarious situation. Trust always involves a decision like that. You can believe someone to be both willing and able to carry out a task you want done, but still withhold trust. Maybe they annoy or bore you, and you don't wish to tie your life to theirs, with the vulnerability this entails, by entering into a trust relation.

Trust connects us, but Tony wants to remain at a distance from others. However this distance-keeping is not altogether strategic on his part. Poor Tony is just not very good with people! Even with Pepper, whom he loves and trusts deeply, he has a tendency to talk too much, make one too many jokes, and ruin an intimate moment.

Tony is a genius when it comes to science, but trust doesn't have a calculable logic. It calls for a different kind of approach. Philosopher Adriaan Theodoor Peperzak says that the verb to trust belongs alongside verbs like to greet or to address as "kinds of turning toward someone or something, without objectifying the intended reality." This is contrasted with verbs like to study, to manipulate, and to determine, all signifying objectifying activities. Scientific activity, and philosophy for the most part, deals in the latter. So does Tony.

When Tony joins a discussion, he doesn't really enter into any true dialogue. Rather, he does the talking and the others should listen and trust him. He seeks to control, or objectify, his surroundings. Call this the objective approach. The approach needed for trust, on the other hand, we can call interactive. Dialogue, a free exchange of views, is perhaps the clearest example of this approach, where what I say affects what you say, and vice versa.

In trust too, our lives become bound up with one another. I entrust you with some part or aspect of my life, I come to depend on you for the success of one of my projects. Our respective lives come to overlap in some areas. Likewise, at least if the trustee is aware of having been entrusted with something she cannot avoid reacting to it, positively or negatively, accepting or refusing the trust. Trust requires freedom on the side of the trustee as well; it can always be refused, and also, the trustee can just pretend to accept the task—hence the vulnerability to betrayal for the trustor.

The objective approach is important for deciding when to place trust in whom—for example, we may be prepared to entrust the Hulk with the task of smashing, because after careful study we have found good reason to think that he is indeed both willing and able to do so—but no amount of objective data can make the decision for us, it is something we must do ourselves. This decision, the very act of entrusting, requires the interactive approach.

Can we say that the difference between the objective and the interactive approach is also, to a large extent, the difference between Tony Stark and Steve Rogers? I think we can. When they evaluate the situation they're in, Steve gets his information from his interactions with people while Tony is a guy who likes to take a step back and do the math. This means that Tony will have trouble with the relinquishment of control necessary for trust. This is not meant as a criticism, or rather, to the extent that it is, it is one directed to many in addition to Tony.

It's not a bad bet that many people drawn to a book of philosophy will tend toward the objective approach, that they (we) like to take a step back and contemplate things. This, I dearly hope, is not a bad thing, but, Tony and we alike should keep in mind the limitations of this approach and humbly accept our limitations and dependences.

In Heroes We Trust

The movie in the series that most clearly has trust as its theme is *Captain America: The Winter Soldier* (2014). It even finds its way into the tagline used in the promotional material: "In heroes we trust." Captain America—whom we've gotten to know as the epitome of earnestness and always willing to believe the best in people—here finds himself bang in the middle of a conspiracy thriller where nothing and no one is as they first seem.

From *The Avengers* we have the metaphor of superheroes as soldiers. (Writer-director Joss Whedon explained that the reasoning behind this, from his point of view as a storyteller, was that the only way he could possibly fit so many heroes into the same story was to use the structure of a war movie.) We see this most clearly with Black Widow. As Hawkeye points out to her when she sets out to join the battle, this is new for her; she's a spy, not a soldier. But signing up to be an Avenger is signing up to be a soldier.

This opposition between soldiers and spies is continued in *Winter Soldier*, now as an opposition between trust and distrust, with Cap contrasted against Widow—back to her spying ways—and Nick Fury ("the spy," as Tony called him in *Avengers*). Of course, there can be trust between spies—Widow and Fury is ample evidence of this—but the fact remains that they lie for a living. For a soldier like Cap, trust is essential, and he tells Fury this: "Soldiers trust each other. That's what makes it an army and not a bunch of guys running around shooting guns." "Last time I trusted someone, I lost an eye," Fury replies.

We know that Steve is the guy who can be entrusted with superpowers precisely because he doesn't want to be *super*—he doesn't seek to be better than others. It's an idea reminiscent of the one Plato (427–347 B.C.E.) had, that political power should only be given to those who do not want it, because they are the ones who won't abuse it. (That a philosopher like Plato *just happened* to think that philosophers were the ones who fit that bill puts a bit of a kink in his nobility armor.)

In contrast to Cap, for Fury, keeping the world safe means being one step ahead of everyone else, to be in control. Trust isn't too high on his list of priorities. He tells Steve a story about his grandfather (is it a true story? With Fury who knows?) working in a nice neighborhood and walking home at night with a bag of tips he'd gotten at his job as an elevator operator. He would greet people, and was greeted in return. "Time went on, the neighborhood got rougher. He'd say, 'Hi.' They'd say, 'Keep on stepping.'" Rougher times in a neighborhood means rougher times for trust, and Fury, Sr. started packing a loaded gun in his lunch box. Fury concludes, "Yeah, Granddad loved people. But he didn't trust them very much."

A rough world calls not for trust but for big guns, and S.H.I.E.L.D. has built themselves the biggest. Captain Trust is not pleased: "Holding a gun to everyone on Earth and calling it protection. This isn't freedom. This is fear." For Fury, an attitude of distrust amounts to taking the world as it is, not as we'd like it to be. Is the optimism required for trust a naïve, rose-tinted way of looking at the world? It can be. To trust blindly, without reason, is irresponsible and dangerous. Trust, as we've said, always involves risk, and the difficulty lies in placing it correctly, to strike the right balance and find a middle ground between gullibility and paranoia. Taking unnecessary risks becomes quite uncharming quite fast.

We must use caution when we decide in whom or what we place trust. We try to determine if the trustee is trustworthy. Still, there is no way to make ourselves impervious to betrayal. Even Fury, a guy who doesn't place his trust willy-nilly, is fooled, by his mentor Pierce; as Fury says, "This man declined the Nobel Peace Prize. He said peace wasn't an achievement, it was a responsibility. See, it's stuff like this that gives me trust issues." This man, who seemed to almost out-noble Cap, turns out to be a HYDRA heavyweight, leading a takeover of SHIELD from within. This reminds us that there are no one hundred percent sure-fire guarantees that someone is in fact trustworthy. And if there were any such guarantee, then it wouldn't be trust.

If this lack of guarantees strikes you as unbearably frustrating, then HYDRA might be the organization for you! Founded on the belief that humanity could not be trusted with its own freedom, HYDRA seeks to eliminate the annoying uncertainty that freedom carries with it. The SHIELD weapons arsenal will grant them absolute control, where obedience can be ensured by threat, coercion, and failing that, murder. Such control would, it is true, ensure stability and order in ways impossible in the fragile nature of relations of trust. Cap's words, rallying the resistance, "The price of freedom is high, it always has been, and it's a price I am willing to pay," can be heard in two ways. The intended meaning is that to fight for freedom may very well cost you your life. The other meaning would be that the price of allowing humanity their freedom is to wave goodbye to certainty and to risk betrayal.

Pierce, in a last-ditch effort to win over Fury to HYDRA's side, appeals to Fury's fondness for order: "It's the next step, Nick. If you have the courage to take it." Taking a page out of Cap's book, Fury replies, "No. I have the courage not to." Freedom is worth the risk, and relations of trust are preferable to relations of control.

It's Not You I Don't Trust

There is some debate among philosophers thinking about trust when it comes to the importance of knowing someone's motivations. My own view is that questions of motivation really only become essential when we turn to the question of self-trust. An inkling about another's motivation can be useful when assessing if they will be willing to do the thing I'm considering entrusting them with, but really I don't need to know *why* they are willing, only that they are.

Self-trust differs from trust in others in its scope. Trust in others is necessarily partial. As Peperzak explains, it is impossible to entrust another with your life in its entirety since the act of entrusting would still remain your own. That can't be handed over, and, again, if your possibility to give your trust is taken from you, then the relationship would not be one of trust. Loki's mind-controlled recruits in *Avengers* do not really trust him. Questions of self-trust can also be partial like this, where the relevant questions are if you are willing and able to carry out a task. But we also find a different sort of questioning here, of the "Who the hell am I?"-variety, where we become unsure of ourselves in a way more intimate and all-encompassing than in trust-relations to others.

"It's not you I don't trust," Banner tells Black Widow at the beginning of *Avengers: Age of Ultron* (2015), introducing issues of self-trust as a theme of the movie. What is it about ourselves we have problem trusting? Let's see what the film has to say.

"Language!" Cap protests after Iron Man swears. Embarrassed, Cap adds, "I *know*. It just slipped out . . ." Sometimes things just slip out, and reveal things about us that we don't wish to acknowledge. Sometimes we react unpredictably and not very rationally. When Tony is caught with his fingers in the Ultron jar, his reaction is a nervous giggle. Cap's moralism about swearing is of the harmless variety. At most, it is a little humiliating for him. More harmfully, Banner's hulking out when angry is the extreme here. And anger is definitely an instance where the part of oneself that one try to keep suppressed rises to the surface.

When things slip out, my own self is revealed to me (and others, who perhaps often see this self more clearly than I do) in ways that often surprise me and I try to disavow. Selfhood is revealed to have a double structure, where I can be mistaken about myself. I am myself, but I do not possess myself. As Peperzak puts it, "The self in me is not sovereign because it is driven by a desire that I can neither choose or abolish. Without having chosen it, I am this desire: obsessed by a drive or pathos that cannot stop my reaching out to an unknown but fulfilling mode of being myself perfectly alive" (Peperzak, *Trust*, p. 78).

This desire, drive, or pathos, is who I am, but I am not its master. We don't choose to come into being, but find ourselves in a world that is not of our making, that is resistant to our plans. We found ourselves already driven and we find out about ourselves as we go along. The desire that I am is different from the multiplicity of desires that I have. The latter kind—for some shawarma, say—can be fulfilled easily enough, but soon the satisfaction dissipates. The former is the desire that guides all the particular desires. It is my deepest motivation, and it is perhaps unfulfillable. If we are, to a sufficient extent, fine with the particular desires that we are aware of having, then we trust ourselves. For most of us, however, there are at least some impulses that we'd rather do without. If these unwanted impulses become to frequent and demanding, then self-trust becomes hard to maintain, and the harder you try to silence the unwanted desire, the louder it gets.

The desire will not be abolished, but it can be refined. You can find an outlet through which the desire can come to fruition in useful ways. This is what in psychoanalytic theory is known as sublimation. Again, the Hulk provides the clearest example. Banner does what he can to keep "the other guy" down ("You really have got a lid on it, haven't you? What's your secret? Mellow jazz, bongo drums, huge bag of weed?" as Tony asks in *Avengers*). The danger with such repression is that the worst part of us will suddenly erupt—it just slips out—usually at the precise moment it does the most damage. Sublimation, on the other hand, would be to transform that potentially destructive passion into something worthwhile—say art, philosophy, or avenging.

It's the difference between the destructive Hulk and the avenging Hulk. If we can accept the worst in us, it will help us uncover the best in us. Banner doesn't get to a position of trusting himself without help. Tony is his unlikely spirit guide ("You're tip-toeing, big man. You need to strut."). It is very true that what makes it possible for us to trust ourselves is often the encouragement and trust of others (this is the role of the therapist in psychoanalysis), just as degradation and distrust from others often makes us doubt ourselves.

Tony Does Not Have Syphilis, But

In *Age of Ultron*, the dreams Scarlet Witch induces in them show the Avengers that they are not who they thought they were, and thus make them less certain in their self-trust. She doesn't change our heroes but instead reveals a truth about them that they have hidden from themselves. "I wasn't tricked, I was shown," as Tony says. We have heard that the effect of the Mind Stone in Loki's scepter, from which Scarlet Witch's powers originate, is "more than knowledge, it's truth" (Selvig in *Avengers*).

For those of us fascinated with psychoanalysis it's tempting to rip that statement out of its context and think about it in the way Jacques Lacan uses that distinction. The way Lacan uses the terms, truth is something unpredictable and surprising that unsettles the self-certainty of knowledge. The dreams in *Age of Ultron* work precisely in this way.

Tony has come a long way from the carefree playboy he was when we first met him. Back then, an irritated Rhodey described Tony as "constitutionally incapable of being responsible." In *Age of Ultron* his being is instead constituted by an overwhelming, hyperbolic, sense of responsibility. His dream shows him his Avengers comrades all dead, Cap's dying words to Tony being, "You could have saved us. Why didn't you do more?" To coin Loki's phrase from *Avengers*, Tony is burdened with glorious purpose. Also like Loki, he is damaged enough to think that he can and should be the one to fix the world.

Tony chooses Fury as his confessor: "I'm the man who killed the Avengers. I saw them all dead, Nick. I felt it. The whole world, too. Because of me. I wasn't ready. I didn't do all I could." Tony is driven by a sense of responsibility for the entire world, and the Avengers in particular, and it is tearing him apart. Fury tries to calm him down: "You've come up with some pretty impressive inventions, Tony. War isn't one of them." This is true of course, and if it was a trial then Tony would go free, but ethical responsibility is different from legal culpability. The ethical responsibility he feels is infinite. Is this the purest altruism or the height of narcissism? I don't know whom we'd trust to judge.

On the list of eccentric geniuses, Tony is joined by a number of characters from the history of philosophy. High on that list is Friedrich Nietzsche (1844–1900). "For I am strong enough to cleave the history of mankind in two," Nietzsche writes in a letter to Strindberg in December 1888. In the same letter, he notes that he's just finished writing his autobiography *Ecce Homo*, where the four chapters have the titles "Why I Am So Wise," "Why I Am So Clever," "Why I Write Such Great Books," and "Why I Am a Destiny."

The title *Ecce Homo*—Pilate's words to the crowd when presenting them with the scourged Jesus—is ironic coming from the dude who famously pronounced that God is dead, but the logic of cleaving the history of mankind in two very much brings the thought of a Messiah to mind. One month later, Nietzsche's personal history would be cleaved in two as he suffered a mental collapse, caused by tertiary syphilis, never to regain his sanity. One effect of syphilis is megalomania, and it is tempting to understand some of the wilder pronouncements in Nietzsche's late work as symptomatic of his illness.

Tony, as far as we know, doesn't have syphilis (with all the blood-testing in *Iron Man 2*, I'm sure he ran an STD panel at some point), but sometimes one has to wonder if our Iron Man has lost his mind. We could imagine that Tony's autobiography—*A Cheap Trick and a Cheesy One-Liner* is a title considered for it in *Iron Man 3* (2013)—would have chapter titles rivaling Nietzsche's in the hubris department. Like Nietzsche, Tony has a desire, and believes he has the strength, to cleave history in two. It is something we see already in the opening of the first *Iron Man* movie (2008) in the sales pitch for his new missile: "I prefer the weapon you only have to fire once. That's how Dad did it. That's how America does it." The same ambition, on an even larger scale, is found in *Age of Ultron*, where Ultron is first envisioned as the security system that will ensure world peace and render the Avengers obsolete, as Tony's responsibility would be fulfilled. He keeps dreaming of a miraculous invention that will put an end to all problems.

Ultron doesn't turn out as planned, of course, and emerges instead as a murderous robot threatening to bring about the extinction of humanity. This doesn't weaken Tony's resolve, however, but only strengthens it. With an addict's logic, he looks at the devastation caused by what he's done, only to go right back to do it again, this time wanting to put his computer system Jarvis into the android body that Ultron has built for himself. "I'm in a loop!" says a despairing Banner when his science brother asks him for his trust and help. "This is exactly where it all went wrong!" The pep talk Tony comes up with shouldn't exactly calm Banner's worries: "We're mad scientists. We're monsters, buddy. We've gotta own it. Make a stand." It's interesting to note that this pep talk mirrors the one he gave to Banner in *Avengers*: accept your inner monster and it might just save the day. It's not pretty, but it's all we've got.

The way Banner in the first movie could choose to bring the Hulk out, Tony in the second chooses to bring forth what is the greatest threat but also their best hope. (In both films this trust is rewarded.) In a register that at least aims for reassurance, Tony promises Banner, "It's not a loop. It's the end of the line." Again, Tony dreams of an end, a radical break in history. And say what you will about Tony, but you've got to hand it to him, he actually succeeds in creating his Messiah! Out of his monstrous, mad science emerges Vision. Vision isn't Jesus, of course, but the film is not overly subtle in its use of Biblical imagery here, most explicitly perhaps when Vision introduces himself as simply "I am" ("I'm not Ultron. I am not Jarvis. I am . . . I am."), echoing Jesus's self-description in John 8:58, in turn echoing God's words to Moses in Exodus 3:14.

Vision is also a special case when it comes to the question of trust. I've been banging on about how there are no guarantees when it comes to trust. The newborn Vision, *as he is telling the Avengers that there may be no way for him to make them trust him*, lifts Thor's hammer and hands it to him, thus guaranteeing his status as (trust)worthy. Let's call this instance of a guarantee in the realm of trust the exception that proves the rule.

I Don't Want to Stop

Having created a Messiah, is Tony satisfied? At the end of *Age of Ultron* he has decided it's time for him to tap out, that his days of avenging have come to an end. Moving on to the next chapter of the saga, *Captain America: Civil War*, we see that this retirement was short-lived. He's found that he's not, and perhaps never will be, ready to leave the hero lifestyle behind, and this has led to a break-up between him and Pepper. This forces him to do some soul-searching about his motivations: "A few years ago, I almost lost her, so I trashed all my suits. Then we had to mop up HYDRA. And then, Ultron—my fault. And then, and then, and then . . . I never stopped. Because the truth is I don't wanna stop." He doesn't want to stop. This realization makes him question what his mission is, and if he has been self-deceived in the past.

Cap learned a similar lesson about himself in *Age of Ultron*. Does Cap want peace? He would say yes, but does he deep down harbor darker desires? Ultron sees darkness in him ("God's righteous man. Pretending you could live without a war. I can't physically throw up in my mouth, but . . ."), and the dream put in his mind by Scarlet Witch confronts him with the same troubling message. In it, he's at a ball celebrating the war's end. He is reunited with his love Peggy who tells him, "The war is over, Steve. We can go home. Imagine it." Trying to imagine it, Cap sees nothing. There is no life for him without war. The man of the people can imagine no ordinary life for himself.

A scene with Tony and Cap chopping wood at Hawkeye's farm is especially interesting here. Trust is what keeps the team together ("A team that trusts is a team that triumphs," as a character in TV's *Marvel's Agents of SHIELD* likes to say) and Scarlet Witch was able to tear them apart "like cotton-candy" (did I mention that trust is fragile?). Tony notes that Steve doesn't seem overly perturbed by what his dream showed him (we don't know if Steve has told the others about what he saw, it seems like he has not). For Tony, Cap's stalwartness is cause for suspicion ("I don't trust a guy without a dark side."). No one can be that perfect, and if he is, then that would in itself be suspicious.

Steve scolds Tony's recklessness in carrying out experiments that would affect the team. Tony (not yet uncertain about the purity of his motivations and still intent on cleaving history) bites back, and unwittingly hits directly on what is Cap's dark side: the research was meant to not only affect the team but to *end* it: "Isn't that the mission? Isn't that the 'Why We Fight'? So we can end the fight. So we get to go home!" Having been confronted with the challenge to his self-image, this must hit Steve where he lives. His reply to Tony—that every time someone tries to win a war before it starts innocent people will die—is not dishonest, but Steve must wonder if his motives are in fact not as noble as he would like. By the end of *Ultron*, Cap leaves it to the results to decide if he's trustworthy ("Ultron thinks we're monsters. This isn't just about beating him. It's about whether he's right."), and, pleased enough with the Avengers' victory, he finds a sort of peace in the acknowledgment that he'll never be at peace, a home in the inability to ever find a home.

Back to *Civil War*, where Tony and Cap clash over the Sokovia Accords, a piece of legislation that would place the Avengers under the rule of the UN. Tony is for it, Steve against. This marks a clear shift in attitudes from when we first met them. Tony, in the first *Iron Man*, is determined to keep the invention of the Iron Man suit secret, as he doesn't trust the people around him: "I don't want this winding up in the wrong hands. Maybe in mine, it can actually do some good." By the second movie, the technology is no longer a secret, but he's still unwilling to share it with the government. When we get to *Civil War*, with his newfound self-distrust and presented with the collateral damage of his ass-kicking, he no longer thinks his own hands safe enough.

Cap has gradually outgrown his role as the order-taking company man. Fresh from finding out that SHIELD was in fact a mask for HYDRA, he's not thrilled about the idea of handing over the reins to any large organization, even the UN: "We may not be perfect, but the safest hands are still our own." For Cap, the ones best qualified to understand and assess the successes and failures of the Avengers are the Avengers themselves. It is not that he refuses accountability, but his point is that there is no independent standard against which to judge. There isn't really anything to which one could compare the Avengers, and in the absence of that, Cap reasons, judgment is best left to themselves, the ones who best know the challenges they face. He sees signing the Accords as an out-sourcing of responsibility, a shifting of blame.

Tony's point is that they've tried doing it Cap's way, and it lead to unacceptable losses of civilian lives. To go on trusting that M.O. is not a valid option: "We need to be put in check! Whatever form that takes, I'm game." That Tony wouldn't go along with literally any form of oversight is a given, but the statement reveals how Tony and Steve are talking about slightly different things. Cap has considered the alternatives and thinks that their own hands are still the safest. Tony doesn't really have an alternative thought out, he's just convinced that their own hands are not safe enough.

The real blow to their relationship, however, comes when it is revealed that Cap's best friend since childhood, "Bucky" Barnes a.k.a the Winter Soldier, during his stint as a brainwashed assassin for HYDRA, killed Tony's parents, and furthermore, *Cap knew this but didn't tell Tony.* Tony, rightly, takes this as a betrayal of his trust. Blows are traded, sparks fly, hearts break. When we leave our heroes they are far apart, but Tony receives a letter from Steve, an olive branch expressing regret that things turned out the way they did, and hope for the future. Steve gets to the theme of trust: "My faith's in people, I guess. Individuals. And I'm happy to say that, for the most part, they haven't let me down. Which is why I can't let them down either."

Steve believes in people, that a small number of individuals can come together and form non-hierarchical relations based on trust, and achieve something extraordinary. That the fact of his trust being rewarded leads him to want to be trustworthy himself is not a necessary logical inference, but in practice it often seems to work this way. At the same time, this is a hell of a thing to write to the friend you just betrayed. But Cap is quick to admit guilt: "I know I hurt you, Tony. I guess I thought by not telling you about your parents I was sparing you but I can see now that I was really sparing myself. And I'm sorry." Given how pissy Cap was about Fury's compartmentalization of information in *Winter Soldier* and Tony's secrecy in *Age of Ultron*, this should be quite the revelation for him.

Trust sometimes breaks down. If Tony and Cap are to win theirs back, there would need to be forgiveness. Forgiveness requires its own analysis, but we can briefly note some similarities between forgiveness and trust. We speak about "earning trust" and "earning forgiveness," and have a fairly good idea about what is meant by such statements, but in neither case can there be a list of actions that if I do them, then you are forced to trust or forgive me. When it comes to trust, and forgiveness, a decision is required (in contrast, no decision on our part can change that two and two equals four).

So when it comes to trust, I have the power to decide, but slightly paradoxically, when I decide to give my trust to someone I accept a certain amount of powerlessness, in surrendering control and risk betrayal. By the end of *Civil War*, Tony seems to be on his way to forgive Cap, and while that doesn't guarantee that he will also trust him again, it at least allows for the possibility.

In heroes we trust, and, like heroes, sometimes trust goes awry and away. Sometimes, pretty extremely far. But, like heroes, it'll come back. Because we'll need it to.[1]

---

[1] I would like to thank Staffan Ericson, Hanna Kinnunen, Ylva Nordström, Lotta Rönn, and Björn Waller for their comments, all trustworthy.

17

Please Hold for a Call from God

CHRISTOPHER KETCHAM

Saint Thomas Aquinas looked up from his cloud. The white rotary dial phone was ringing. God.

God had not yet gone digital, didn't trust it. Didn't sound right. In fact, even the phone was something new, which Aquinas was just getting used to. He knew this would be long distance because God was hundreds of light years away, observing the Frethmuspus-9 and the Click-bop-tick-tick-whatap-whatap troubles. Each side was threatening to hurl supernovae at the other. Abraham, Mary, and six of the apostolic saints had been dispatched to the negotiations as off-the-shoulder advisors.

Aquinas picked up the receiver. He said, "Hello, Aquinas here."

"Thomas, God. Listen, this shitstorm isn't easing up any and the damn apostles are totally ineffective. Are you ready for this? Your buddy Abraham is off somewhere on another toot. All the time and effort I spent on his rehab just got flushed down the toilet. But we've got other troubles not far from where you are down on Earth. That yellow bustard of an American president is stirring things up. He's making a mess out of things with all the walls he wants to build and tariffs he wants to impose.

Thomas, you saw how stupid walls in Europe were against the sappers and the guns that came after. And this was after the Chinese spent trillions and snuffed out the lives of whole generations building that damn interminable wall over there. I thought they had learned a wall-building lesson. Shit, no.

And tariffs. Until recently I was certain that the economists had drummed it out of people's heads . . . You tell me . . . how stupid were the damned allies after World War One to load up reparations on Germany?! Only made that bastard spawn of Satan—Hitler—a hit in Germany. Tariffs are punitive economic bullshit, Thomas—look what happened to the world with the Nazis. Believe you me, I hear about it every day from the Hasidim. They post me endless messages on their wall. My fault, my fault. But I vowed then and I vow now I will never let that happen again, so help me . . . Christ—That is, Christ and I want you to see if you can sort things out down there. Specifically, I want you to use your logical process, you know the one you use in the *Summa* . . . ah . . . *Summa*—"

"—*Summa Theologica?*" asked Aquinas.

"Yeah, that. Speaking of interminable . . . Anyway, we want you to look into those two mutants, that Captain America jerkoff and the block of iron, what's his name?"

"Iron Man?" asked Aquinas.

"Yeah, both of them. Find out who would be better . . . What I mean is that we've got two scenarios. First, that the yellow bustard just turns everything to shit and there's a huge worldwide depression. Second, that things get so bad that we come to the brink of another world war again. You heard about that hermit in North Korea shooting missiles left and right. Someday he's going to hit something other than a breaching whale. So, find out which one of those superhero freaks would be best to stop them starting a war and which would be best lifting them out of a friggin economic meltdown. Just when we got a world that seems to be starting to work together, we are right back with threats of war and the possibility for another depression that will send millions to the proverbial bread lines. Pisses me off, Thomas. I don't have time for this nonsense. Damn it, I've got entities threatening to throw suns at each other, here. I can't afford another escalation down there on Earth. You know how it is: first nukes, then suns. So, get back to me, say in a week or so, on what you have found . . . Hey, what are Peter, Paul, and Mary doing down there?" The phone clicked off to dial tone.

Aquinas thought to himself that this certainly was a different type of calling than that which turned him towards the priesthood. However, this was the same deity to whom he had pledged his existence nearly an earthly millennium ago, so he was bound to serve. Just how, he wasn't quite sure. So, he took up his pen and a fresh sheet of paper to begin the process that had been so successful for him in life and now in his five thousand six hundredth point of inquiry for his *Summa Theologica*. At the top he wrote, "New Point of Inquiry to Address an Old Topic."

Whether Comic Book Heroes Should Be Let Loose Upon the World

His original points of inquiry while he was alive were all about Christian theology and issues closely associated with theology, such as "just war." After his death, sainthood, and direct appointment by God as the Dominican Order Ambassador, Aquinas had been asked to consider other points of inquiry. The point of inquiry, "Whether emerging civilizations should have polytheism for a period of time" proved vexing because Aquinas's whole life had been oriented towards monotheism and against paganism. However, the one point of inquiry, number 5,073, that was coming back to haunt him was, "Whether comic book superheroes should be let loose in the world."

Aquinas constructed a series of strong objections and counterarguments both ways, but ultimately answered against the idea. He felt he had logically proved that supernatural creatures like Captain America and Iron Man, if loosed upon the world, would conflict with the image of an all-powerful God. God did not dismiss his objections, counterarguments, and answer entirely, but decided that he could persuade superheroes to do his bidding.

Secretly, though, Aquinas knew he was right—especially after Deadpool's rampages. However, now he had to somehow deconstruct his original proof of point of inquiry 5,073, and come up with new points of inquiry and arguments for the two queries that God wanted him to undertake, now that superheroes were running amok in the world.

Aquinas spent time composing, editing, and deciding upon his point of inquiry, given the premise that the only choices he had for "whom" in this exploration were Captain America and Iron Man. He also had to assume that both were existents in the world, which they, of course, are.

He wrote, *"Whether a superhero must use his/her powers to resolve an economic crisis"* and was satisfied with his work.

Now he began to work on his objections, counterarguments, and answers.

THOMAS AQUINAS'S OBJECTION 1: What do superheroes know of economics? They are blunt instruments tasked with flushing out and dispatching evil actors in the world.

THOMAS AQUINAS SAYS ON THE CONTRARY: In the present analysis we have Iron Man, who underneath all that metal is Tony Stark, a billionaire. If anyone should understand economics, it must be a billionaire.

THOMAS AQUINAS'S OBJECTION 2: While billionaires may understand specific aspects of economics associated with their own businesses and investments, unless they are trained in international macroeconomics, would they not become a blunt instrument where nuance is required? However brilliant he is, Tony Stark is an engineer by training and has inherited his wealth.

THOMAS AQUINAS'S OBJECTION 3: Both superheroes are superb representatives of the capitalist ideal, but their long-running battle against Communism is not the issue facing the world today. The dismantling of the global economy in favor of protectionism and tariffs are sowing the seeds for the next global super-recession.

THOMAS AQUINAS SAYS, ON THE CONTRARY: The Captain America suit and persona have been donned by a number of individuals, good and bad. These include Steve Rogers and his sidekick Bucky (James Buchanan Barnes) and even the villain Acrobat. While Steve Rogers' serum made him the superhuman that he is, it is not brawn that is needed, but strength of character and intellect. Which Steve assuredly does possess, but he is not an economist. If we don't need a good physical fighter, a respected economist surely could be persuaded to don the suit. Look at how many physicists agreed to leave to parts unknown to build the bomb in World War II. Intelligent people know when they are needed.

THOMAS AQUINAS'S OBJECTION 4: Captain America is too connected with the image of protectionism and rabid patriotism. He punched Hitler in the nose, remember. Viewed as a protectionist, he may play well in Turkey, Venezuela, and the Philippines, but what about the rest of the world?

I, THOMAS AQUINAS, ANSWER THAT: Iron Man and Captain America present images, respectively, of the billionaire and the "ugly American."

Therefore, both present themselves to the world in the guise of the person who will likely be one of the causes of the super-recession. While both Iron Man and Captain America are strong, courageous, and highly intelligent creatures, they both bring symbolic difficulties regarding who could be a person who could lead the world out of its economic malaise. Captain America has transformed himself from Hitler scourge to capitalist ideologue. He has been reported dead and then returned. So, too, has Iron Man. Iron Man lately has shown he is a human, with foibles and imperfections just like everyone else. God frowns upon Tony Stark's alleged use of intoxicants while in the guise of Iron Man, which is a huge negative. While many will sympathize with Tony Stark and his human frailties, and he does have an enormous stake in the world economy as a member of the billionaire clan—self-dealing will seem like a conflict of interest and could undermine his efforts in this cause.

On the other hand, because Captain America has been a Lazarus many times before, he could return from the dead again. His words, his beneficence as having, like Lazarus, been returned from the dead after a Christian miracle will overcome the negative symbolism and assure him both the respect and admiration of Christians around the world. Those of different faiths will respect his beatitude even if they do not accept his return from the grave. However, we must provide this beatific Captain America with a Nobel Laureate economist as a sidekick who can guide his actions to restore the economies of the world. He wrote in bold and underlined his answer.

Captain America must use his powers to help with an economic crisis.

Aquinas was pleased with his work, and began the search for economists who would work with Steve Rogers.

Treatise on Theological Virtues, Question 40, On War

With the next point of inquiry, Aquinas struggled. For guidance, he returned to his earthly work in the *Summa Theological* under the heading, *Of War*. Here he had worked through four points of inquiry: "Whether some kind of war is lawful," "Whether it is lawful for clerics to fight," "Whether it is lawful for belligerents to lay ambushes," and "Whether it is lawful to fight on holy days." He knew that Captain America had helped the American effort in World War II, and nobody in that war took Sunday off. Aquinas had no idea just how or between whom the next world war would come. However, there were significant complications if a world war would break out in the early decades of the twenty-first century. First there was the bomb, and likely both (or more!) sides would have them. Second, even with the isolationist policies that many countries were espousing, the global supply matrix was so complex that even a minor disruption would cause considerable economic angst, if not downright collapse, almost everywhere. The carnage to persons, property, and the environment would be considerable even if the conflict were limited to conventional arms. It would be the first shooting war where space would become involved, and that was getting awfully close to heaven. Could Iron Man intercept and render a North Korean missile harmless? He wasn't so sure. Would Captain America equivocate on who is right and wrong and hesitate too long? Aquinas cringed at the thought. Terrorists and religious extremists would lay ambush. Certain clerics would fight in the war as they had been doing in the conflicts that had arisen beginning in the latter decades of the twentieth century.

In his first point of inquiry whether war can be just, Aquinas listed three requirements: it must have been ordered by a sovereign, there must be a just cause, and the belligerents must have a rightful intention towards the good or to avoid evil. Aquinas was certain there would be sovereigns, even democratically elected ones, to declare war. Everyone would declare their causes just and their missions towards the greater good or against evil, likely calling the opposition dotards, rocket men, religious extremists, terrorists, or despot lunatics. The clarion cries would drown out all opposition and quickly escalate the tensions. Perhaps neither Captain America nor Iron Man would be needed if that happened. This surely would help Aquinas get out of a jam of recommending the wrong superhero for God. He could shelve that decision until a real conflict came to a head.

Aquinas, in his lifetime, addressed the question about clerics fighting with the admonition that they should lend spiritual help to their flock, but not actually engage in the fighting. That surely would be ignored by some clerics. At least there were no cleric superheroes! He had it on good authority (the comics) that neither Iron Man nor Captain America had any leanings towards the priesthood. Ghastly thought. He erased those notes. Can't give God any ideas on that subject, he said to himself.

This exercise was not helping at all. Much of what he had written about war simply put the two superheroes on basically the same level. He needed to find tangible differences to make a good case for God. He looked at ambushes next.

Much as he disliked the issue of ambushes because they are deceptions and deception quite often involve a lie told . . . ambushes and deceptions had become a fact of existence on the battlefield and in political discourse. Both Captain America and Iron Man could suddenly appear and take down their enemies. Deception is honorable when superheroes face a formidable foe who has used deception to get the world into trouble in the first place. Deception was becoming a real problem in the twenty-first century and not just on the battlefield. The idea that there could be 'alternative facts' without any evidence attached, that even intelligent people accepted as truths, completely vexed Aquinas. Surely, the comics were just as complicit in this 'alternative facts' conspiracy as all the others. How often did Iron Man and Captain America go missing and be presumed dead, only to surface later? The writers had a field day selling scads of issues when they published these salacious stories. All the while, they knew that they were just selling 'alternative facts,' which they would revise in the future with more 'alternative facts.' Nauseating, Aquinas thought to himself, but in a channel not accessible by God. God loved the comics. Most of them, anyway. Deadpool reminded him of his battles with Satan. God became quite grumpy when the movie was made. However, he made sure Deadpool would not get a best actor Oscar nod. But 'alternative facts,' however aggravating, were not Aquinas's mission. He now knew he was stuck.

Aquinas understood that his mission was to determine who would be the heroic actor to diffuse tensions of the world on the brink of war. Both Captain America and Iron Man had called themselves or had been called into service many times since their creation to undermine the sworn and presumed enemies of the United States. Aquinas was flummoxed; he had not found any good reason to choose one over the other. Both Captain America and Iron Man were loyal subjects of what most certainly would be one of the major combatants. The United States was not likely to be all that 'clean' from stirring up the belligerency. So, he composed what he thought would be a provocative point of inquiry: *"Whether a loyal subject can choose the good over the sovereign during war."* Finally, Aquinas smiled. He kissed the cross that hung from his neck and began to write with renewed vigor, betraying only a smidgen of saintly emotion.

What pleased Aquinas was that he saw that he was moving towards the most important aspect of the matter. This returned God's focus back to the earliest times and the Book of Genesis, where God ordered Abraham to sacrifice his son Isaac. Abraham was about to carry out the act when God intervened. You see, God was adamant that He be obeyed, no matter what. Adam and Eve discovered the price for disobedience: they got thrown out of Eden. This point of inquiry would likely cause God to pause, and this is just what Aquinas wanted to happen. So, he began his analysis.

THOMAS AQUINAS'S OBJECTION 1: Military leaders in the United States report to the civilian authority and cannot countermand that authority or go out on their own. The question is whether Captain America is a member of the military, now or ever. His powers come from an experimental serum he received from the government in World War II. They called him a super soldier, but he served out of uniform. He did serve his country then and after, but in what capacity? Was he a spy? We conclude that he is an independent operator with loyalties to the United States and not to any particular administration or leader. That he assists the military does not necessarily mean he is a member of the military.

THOMAS AQUINAS SAYS, ON THE CONTRARY: Iron Man served world-wide efforts against communism. He did this for the cause of advancing American business and its technical expertise. He continues to advocate American capabilities and ingenuity even today. Therefore, his agenda is more aligned with the military-industrial complex than it is with political ideology. More recently, he has served his industrial brethren by fighting terrorism. He is not averse to going after hackers, pirates, copyright infringers and others. However, his agenda is slanted towards other industrialist billionaires like himself. If the war-like actions of an administration should cause the stock markets to soar, he will have mixed feelings. Even though he will profit from belligerency, if the actions against other countries are ill-conceived or simply wrong, what will Iron Man do? Industrialists have always profited from war. Iron Man is no exception—his firms make weapons. He is a government contractor and would lose contracts during a tiff with any administration.

THOMAS AQUINAS'S OBJECTION 2: In my treatise on just war, I affirmed that it is the sovereign's prerogative to initiate and wage war, not the civilian. I repeat my objection here. "First, the authority of the sovereign by whose command the war is to be waged. For it is not the business of a private individual to declare war, because he can seek for redress of his rights from the tribunal of his superior. Moreover, it is not the business of a private individual to summon together the people, which has to be done in wartime" (*Summa Theologica*, p. 3074).

THOMAS AQUINAS SAYS, ON THE CONTRARY: This point of inquiry as stated does not say that the superhero initiates the war, but, rather, countermands the sovereign who is waging (presumably) an unjust war. I quote Augustine here: "A just war is wont to be described as one that avenges wrongs, when a nation or state has to be punished, for refusing to make amends for the wrongs inflicted by its subjects, or to restore what it has seized unjustly" (*Summa Theologica*, p. 3075). Therefore, if the war is not just, what rights do civilians have to withdraw from such a war or countermand their sovereign, even if it will be called mutiny or unpatriotic or worse? The question does not advocate regicide, assassination, removal from office or governmental change, just an effort by the superhero to end or prevent an unjust war.

I, THOMAS AQUINAS, ANSWER THAT: Once the sovereign has initiated war, at least in the US, with the approval from Congress whether in a police action or in an actual state of war, the sovereign is given the authority to continue that war until its conclusion or until Congress itself shall undertake to withdraw the sovereign's authority to wage war.

However, superheroes are a unique bunch. They not only have superior physical capabilities, but both Captain America and Iron Man have outsized intelligence. Regardless, both were and still are human. Therefore, they have human flaws. They are not God. To ask a superhero—any superhero—to second guess the actions of a government with checks and balances like the US is to suggest that this form of government has been proven to be inadequate.

However, if God were to command a superhero to second guess the government or go even further—what are the implications? Jesus declared that peace and love were the antidote to the Roman occupation and suppression of the Jews in Jerusalem. He railed against the moneylenders who had infected his father's house with avarice and greed. He was just a lowly citizen . . . but we all know that he was the son of God. Jesus was a superhero of sorts with divine powers not wrought by serum or other human-created elixir, but from God, his father.

On the other hand, God has not declared kinship to either Captain America or Iron Man. If he should, we would expect recriminations not unlike that which Jesus experienced. Rather than declare kinship, God wants to know how to forestall war in a world where war has become increasingly deadly, not only for its people but for the planet, itself. If humans wrought most of the superheroes, then the question is for what purpose? Certainly, there are evil superheroes, but God chose to focus on two who have been servants of the good for their entire existence as superheroes. I am not one to second guess or even challenge God's insight or purposes. However, both Iron Man and Captain America in the role of superhero leader, usurping the duly-elected leadership and congress of the country they serve, represent a clear and present danger to its constitution and the republic it founded.

The choices we have for such a difficult task include a war hero and a billionaire arms dealer. General MacArthur quoted a line from a song in his farewell speech to a joint-meeting of Congress, "Old soldiers never die, they just fade away." He had just been fired by President Truman for disrespecting the presidency. Said Truman later, "I fired him because he wouldn't respect the authority of the President...I didn't fire him because he was a dumb son of a bitch, although he was." The Second World War is now but a distant memory to most. Resurrecting Captain America the war hero likely will not sit well with those who did not experience what FDR said about fearing fear itself and the horrors of that global conflict. He doesn't have the patriotic punch he once had. He might suffer the same ignominious fate as MacArthur and be banned or tweeted out of service to the people . . . "@Yourefired."

The world has become the province of billionaires. They control the economies, spend untold millions to influence elections and support candidates of their choosing. What rights do they have over ordinary citizens to do this? These rights have been legislated and court-tested to give those with money the power to choose who leads and who does not. What we have with Iron Man is the gravitas he has simply by being a member of the billionaire's club. The rights affirmed to him in that capacity make him above the ordinary citizen. In addition, he has accumulated a measure of goodwill and trust by becoming a recognized superhero, and one who sides with the interests of democracy, industrialization, and a family of billionaires.

As a billionaire industrialist, he has become sovereign-like and, as such, has the authority to rally other billionaires to just causes, like the ending of an unjust war. Aquinas paused, then wrote in bold and underlined the sentence:

Therefore, we can only conclude that the billionaire superhero Iron Man should be tasked with choosing the good over the sovereign where necessary in any war.

This was the only option, the clear path, the path he would send God down so that God would realize that there is no other option but Iron Man when it comes to ending a war. Yet Aquinas had this nagging doubt . . .

He continued his thoughts on billionaires, not in the context of economics, but power. If other billionaires rally against a rogue billionaire sovereign, it shows the world that the billionaire clan sees right over might. This will ultimately give them even more power . . . I trust in my belief that God will duly consider this consequence. Rather than hope, Aquinas wrote down on his paper that one of the issues that God would have to deal with is that the billionaires would see an opening to power and would take it. They would ride the coattails (figuratively, of course) of Iron Man to take even more of the pie away from others. When God needed money, he just told Judas to mint more silver coins for heavenly needs, but he refused to create new wealth on Earth. "That's humanity's job," he said, when Aquinas and other saints would beg for just a few more alms for the poor. Then there is the other matter, that other superheroes will want to get involved in the war as a way of increasing their own visibility, power, and, of course, wealth.

God will also have to decide whether he wants the other Avengers, perhaps including Captain America, in this endeavor. Certainly, a half dozen or more superheroes present a force multiplier, but they are a complex bunch with different personalities. What this effort requires is a true leader who has the respect of a broader cross-section of his peers. Even though the only choice for Aquinas was Iron Man, he worried about that outsized ego. Perhaps the Avengers would be able to steer Iron Man in the right direction

Aquinas put down his pen. His hand shook. He looked down at the world of blue water, white clouds, and continents of green and sand and Beijing smog. He had watched for a long time the decline in reverence for God, for something more powerful than themselves: a power for good to assuage evil. He caught the whiff of Satan and a chuckle from hell. The smell of brimstone had always haunted him—"There but for the grace of God go I." He knew he couldn't keep this thinking or his recommendation from Satan. There were no secrets in heaven; that was for hell. God knew Satan's secrets. Aquinas did not. Aquinas worried that Satan had understood the reasoning he had used to choose Iron Man. Satan was adept at controverting such things. Whether Satan could tempt Iron Man into doing something that both God and Aquinas would regret, he did not know. This worry suddenly began to weigh heavily upon Aquinas's soul.

He got down on his knees to pray. Tears came to his eyes. This being so close to God was not what he had expected. He thought that the cloud would be a place of peace, reverence, and elegiac wonder. Instead, it was the proverbial cloud that software vendors were selling. He was nothing more than a productivity assist to the Almighty. "Oh," he cried out, "oh!"

Please Hold for God

Aquinas published his two points of inquiry and their analyses. He regained his composure with the thought that God knows what God is doing. However, God was spread quite thin these days. He hoped that he, Thomas Aquinas, had provided good service to the Lord with his work. He waited and prayed.

The white rotary dial phone rang again, exactly one week after it had the first time. Aquinas picked up the receiver and said, Hello.

"Thomas, God again. Can you hear me? There's a lot of static on this end."

Aquinas: "I can year you."

"Good. Hey, the damned wormhole is down again. It just barely transmits this call. I don't know which of you cretins convinced me to contract the lowest bidder, but bloody hell, this is the third time in a thousand years. I still kick myself that I put a speed limit on light. It would have been much simpler than this buggy hole in space thing to just blow through the universe like a screaming banshee. Anyway, things are pretty well resolved here, no help from your brothers the apostles. It would have gone on for millennia and fucked up two whole galaxies if I hadn't stepped in."

"Wonderful news," said Aquinas.

"Wasn't the way I wanted to do it. Had to give them the old Godfather 'offer they couldn't refuse.' Well, they both chose existence over extinction. I hate to go there because then we get the whole 'vengeance God' thing, and that's just a pain in my ass. So, what do you have for me, Thomas, on the thing with the two mutants down there on Earth?"

"Well, . . ." said Aquinas.

18
Red vs. Blue or Both Simply Leviathan Green?

NICOL SMITH

What happens when blue leather/spandex and a red snap-on codpiece smack into each other? Well . . . apart from a weird, slapping sound—WARRE!

Yes, I wrote "war" in ye olde English because two of the Marvel's most popular frienemies have a story as old as time. It's a tale of friendship, betrayal, drama, intrigue, civil war . . . and a giant being killed by the clone of a Norse lightning god. Like I say, old as time.

The two individuals in question are obviously Captain America and Iron Man. Two guys who are friends as well as heroes and should therefore not be leading two armies in a war against each other, right?!? Well, dear reader, we're talking about two characters who both have domineering personalities and a very determined view of how the world should be and what a superhero should be. It was only a question of *when* their epic struggle for the control of superherohood would get started.

Tin Men, Captains and Tyrannical Kings

For the most part, they're like night and day, like fire and water. Captain America, Steve Rogers, is the pinnacle of human perfection and super-humanly athleticism, whilst being a hand-to-hand combatant and tactician of note. On the other hand, Tony "Iron Man" Stark is the good-looking billionaire playboy who is highly intelligent and technologically creative enough, making up for his lack of natural athleticism through mechanical augmentation.

Yet there's one major thing they do have in common—apart from both being human and having boy bits: their egos. Both want to lead and both always seem to think they know what's best. What happens when two potentially destructive forces like water and fire meet head-on? Steam. Steam has a tendency to scald or burn, just like a lot of characters got burned during the conflict of the Marvel *Civil War*. Now it might seem that I am being a bit harsh on Cap and Shell-head but their actions leading up to and during the civil war seem very similar to that of a *Leviathan*.

"*Leviathan*? You mean that goofy little Hydra-wannabe secret society from the Secret Wars Saga?" Nope. Neither am I referring to the huge sea monster that is being kept in check by another comic book publisher's version of the Submariner. *Leviathan* is actually the name of a book written by philosopher Thomas Hobbes (1588–1679) back in 1651 when the world was still in low-res black and white and dial-up internet a mythical dream. His book focused on the creation of civil society and how it should be ruled by one supreme ruler or sovereign.

The supreme sovereign/king/ruler/main poohbah, has absolute say in the state, from what is to be taught at educational institutions and which public opinions should be allowed expression, to how religious institutions should conduct their business. He (Sorry, ladies, this harks from the time when you were considered to be merely irrational peddlers of the flesh that led rational men astray) also makes the laws and enforces them with the threat of punishment to those who would dare be stupid enough to break these laws. The sovereign does not necessarily have to be a nice guy (chances are that he would not have been with that much power); he simply has to ensure that everything runs the way he feels it should and that order is maintained. So why would anyone in their right mind want to subject themselves to a ruler that would most likely be oppressive?

Hobbes decided that the easiest way to explain why there should be one supreme ruler is to start by describing a hypothetical situation so bad that we would do anything (like submit to a sovereign) instead of having to live in such a situation. This hypothetical situation he called the "state of nature"; it was supposedly a "time men live without a common power to keep them all in awe, they are in that condition which is called war; and such a war, as is of every man, against every man." The state of nature was a war-like situation in which mankind existed without any form of government or organized rule. It was supposedly very violent and Hobbes described the life of man under the state of nature as "solitary, poor, nasty, brutish, and short." (p. 84).

All of this unpleasantness happened because there was no big official body to tell us to stop killing and stealing from each other. Hobbes further said that all this stealing and killing happens because people are all selfish and born equal. Everyone is born free and has the rights to ownership and to punish those who wrong them. It doesn't take much imagination to see how this could quickly get out of hand. If you were to steal my goat and I am either in a bad mood or just vindictive, I could deem it reasonable punishment to kill you and your whole family. This, in turn, could spark a quest for vengeance from kin who survived my attack or happened to be away learning some mystical fighting art. Then there would be more violence. All of this happens because there is no one in charge to say, "Enough is enough!" and judge how wrongdoers should be dealt with. Think of this like a playground without any competent adult supervision, or like most parliaments around the world.

Your Signature Here . . .

Now how does this relate to Iron Man and Captain America? Well, this is exactly the kind of situation in which the heroes and villains of the Marvel universe find themselves prior to the civil war breaking out: there is no overseeing body to hold heroes accountable for their actions. Sure, the police hunt most of them at least one time during their caped careers but mostly the heroes are left to their own devices—whether tight spandex suits that shoot sticky white stuff or assault rifles—and they are never really called to task for damage inflicted to property or unintended harm that may have been caused when they clash with villains or other heroes (usually while under some form of mind-control).

So when Speedball and the New Warriors' surprise attack on Nitro in Stamford gets close to 700 people killed, this is the tipping point which forces the citizens of the USA to say that enough is enough and call for the regulation of superheroes in the form of the Superhuman Registration Act. In the *Captain America: Civil War* movie, it is after a successful mission in Lagos, Nigeria, has been sullied by the many innocents who died because of Scarlet Witch's miscalculation. This is after the Avengers save/wreck New York and kill a bunch of people by creating Ultron, who attempts to drop the city of Sokovia out of the sky.

In both the movie and comics, the superheroes and supervillains are expected to consent to an agreement that binds them to certain regulations. In exchange for their consent, they would be signing a contract that allows them to carry on brooding on top of gothic buildings as employees of a governing body. Those who do not want to comply are hunted down as outlaws who face imprisonment.

This bill to regulate the heroes and villains is very similar to what Hobbes would've described as the way out of the state of nature. For Hobbes, people would've found it more feasible safety-wise to band together and form a social contract which would allow them to move from the violent war-like state of nature. This social contract basically means that the people involved will give up certain rights (such as inflicting punishment on those they feel have crossed them) and agree to live together under the law of one supreme ruler. This supreme ruler not only makes all the laws but maintains them through the threat of punishment if these laws are not obeyed. Hobbes thought that this would be a natural step, as it made more sense to live together more peacefully—though constrained—than to carry on living in a state of war.

So where did this comic version of the social contract leave the Marvel superheroes? Not with a lot of options, I'm afraid. It becomes a Red vs Blue situation and everyone has to choose sides. They have to. Even if the heroes were to choose against registration and remain fugitives, would it not be safer to remain a fugitive with a whole bunch of other super-powered fugitives?

Those few who are brave enough not to, like the X-Men and Dr. Strange, are clearly treated with disappointment or merely shunned like Marvel's madman superhero Moon-Knight. And let's be honest: what are you to do as a superhero in a situation like this? Two of the biggest heroes have drawn a line in the sand, and if you are enough of a heavy hitter, both of them are going to try and recruit you. And how can you honestly say No to Captain America or Iron Man? They are legends and core members of the Avengers, which is the most elite superhero group in the Marvel universe. Even Spider-Man had to wait and jump through seemingly countless loops before he was accepted to join them. Spider-Man! And here one or both of these legends are now asking you to join him. How can you say No to one of these legends and his particular cause?

By joining team Iron Man, you're clearly signing a social contract in the form of, well, . . . uh, a legal contract. Signing up for Cap's team is more of an unofficial social contract, but you still have to follow his rules and plans. Those who work with or for Iron Man have to do the same. Tony's camp rules: be a good government employee and chase down those who will not join and put them into prison. Cap's rules: join the Resistance and be unofficially disorganized but don't kill (like the Punisher did when he joined team Blue).

You're starting to see where this is going, right? When the guy in blue who likes to play with a glorified Frisbee and a certain red Tin Man unifies the heroes who are in a philosophical state of nature into two organized groups, they both take it upon themselves to provide guidance and leadership. It's not so much a case of the two of them being voted into power by the members of their respective groups as both of them basically saying, "Look, this is how I'm going to do things and you are either with me or against me." This is pretty much the stance that Hobbes's Leviathan takes when it comes to ruling a state.

A Stark Resemblance

So let's look at how Iron Man is similar to Hobbes's legendary supreme ruler. Let's start with his membership of the Marvel universe's *Illuminati*. Yup, you read correctly: there's a select group consisting of Marvel's most influential and brightest who form a secret society to make serious decisions, such as what to do with the Hulk and the constant threat that he keeps on posing. They end up deciding to shoot him up into space (which might not have been the best idea, as he eventually comes back and whoops all of their butts during the World War Hulk saga). Naturally, Tony Stark is part of this cloak-and-dagger-type megalomaniacfest along with Mr. Fantastic, Black Bolt, Namor, Black Panther, Doctor Strange, and Professor X.

It's also during one of these meetings that Tony first brings up the idea of the Superhuman Registration Act. This causes a huge rift within the group and it is disbanded. Iron Man, however, never gives up on this idea, and once The New Warriors play a role in the accidental death of all those Stamford innocents, it is all Tony needs to go ahead and push for the bill to be passed. With the backing of Mr. Fantastic and size-obsessed Hank Pym as well as Spider-Man (who would later change his mind), the bill is passed and all superheroes are expected to make their secret identities known and basically become super-powered employees of the US government.

Iron Man uses his wealth and influence to become the figurehead of this movement and helps with the funding and development of more effective weapons for capturing resisting superheroes and villains and also the building of a maximum prison in the Negative Zone.

Like a sovereign ruler who maintains order through punishment, Iron Man enforces his will—or, rather, his vision—for what would be best for the super-humans of the United States. There is no democratic vote, only incarceration for those who dare defy his view of the future. Sure, an argument could probably be made that the government is technically in charge of the super-human registration act, but realistically the US government is merely a means to Tony's ends and his vision of the regulation of every super-powered being. He does, after all, manipulate scary crazy Norman Osborne (Green Goblin) with nanotechnology to attack an Atlantean ambassador in order to solidify the public opinion for the need of a super-powered army, should the Atlanteans choose to go to war.

I could've very easily written this from the perspective of how Machiavellian Stark is. But to be fair to Iron Man, he genuinely believes that this Registration Act will be the best thing for the greater good, and the consequences of the conflict with Cap's team weighs heavy on him. After the death of Black Goliath at the hands of a clone cyborg Thor that he helped to create, Iron Man is nearly driven to alcoholism again. That being said, Iron Man is still not willing to back down. Like a true Leviathan, he continues his onslaught on Captain America's rebel forces. Now, if we're honest, no one is ever really surprised by this kind of behavior from Iron Man, as he has always been known for his egoistic stubbornness and willingness to fight for what he wants.

Liberty, Justice, and the Leviathan Way

But what about Cap? Captain America is supposed to be the antithesis of Iron Man in the civil war. When he learns about the Superhuman Registration Act, he not only outright refuses to register and hunt down those would also not register, but takes it upon himself to start a guerrilla war against Tony and those who join him. He takes up this cause as a protector of personal freedom and privacy, but in the end, he's really no different than Iron Man. As Marvel's resident moon-obsessed madman vigilante, Moon Knight, put it to Cap when he initially came around recruiting:

> You're right. It's a mess out there. People fighting. Dying. People being murdered while you and Stark and your pals play capture the ####ing flag. You self-righteous son of a bitch. Coming in here. Acting like this is anything but your regularly scheduled grudge match to work out your differences. All of you trying to prove who has the biggest super power. And for what? For a law? Man, a person who cares if there is or isn't a law telling them that it's okay to put on a mask and fight, they should be doing something else. Anyone who has a choice, doesn't belong in the first place. Why don't you and Stark just get a room. And leave the rest of us out of it.

Moon Knight pretty much tears Cap a new one with this scalding remark that cuts straight to the bone on the matter of Cap's ego being just as out of control as Iron Man's. And how does Captain America respond? With a "Yeah, I never really wanted you anyway because you are crazy." Someone being crazy does not mean that they are wrong.

Moon Knight is spot-on about Cap when it comes to the civil war. It is a clash of egos taking place and it is quite surprising to see Cap outright ignore an idea that is aimed at doing something for the greater good. He, instead, flatly rejects it and goes to war for what he perceives to be the greater good: that the superheroes need to retain their secret identities (wayyy too late for some) and that they be allowed to continue operating above the law, as this will prevent the heroes and villains possibly being utilised as an army for US global domination.

His beliefs will not allow him to even consider that the registration act might have some merit to it. Just like Iron Man, he opts for an all-or-nothing "My way or the highway" approach and ironically does not realise that this attitude is the catalyst for the civil war which he warned Maria Hill of SHIELD about. He lobbies just as hard as Iron Man to get some heavy-hitters onto *his* team. Not "Team Superhero Liberty," Team Cap. Team Blue. And they are fighting Team Iron Man, which is red.

When Leviathans Collide

Captain America's fight against his friend and former ally is a fight that he would label as a fight against tyranny and he most likely would've had no qualms about labeling Iron Man as sovereign of a Leviathan. The irony is that is he is just as much of an absolute ruler himself.

What neither Cap nor Iron Man seem to have taken into account is that their actions during the civil war are comparable to that of some would-be tyrants they stopped together— Thanos, Kang, Apocalypse; or any of the other would-be conquerors the Avengers have charged into battle against. All of these villains have had subjugation in mind and would not have hesitated to instil brutal, tyrannical rule over those they conquered. Similarly, the egoistic feud between these two heroes leads to the subjugation of all the superheroes and villains to their ideals. This subjugation, in turn, leads to a war, and war is exactly what the state of nature is, according to Hobbes. This new state of nature, in turn, leads to the need for an absolute sovereign. So where does this leave us—apart from confused? I guess one of these two Leviathans ultimately has to win in order to resolve this the new war-like state of nature. In the end, one does: Iron Man was victorious and ended up having his Registration Act enforced.

Tony's side of the issue may not necessarily have been a bad idea, as it does seem to be a bit more organized and co-ordinated than having a bunch of people who can manipulate matter or destroy buildings with a single punch fight it out amongst themselves as they see fit. As such, freedom for the heroes and villains is, indeed, a state of nature similar to that

Hobbes described. This is, however, not the point. Neither is Captain America's fight for the protection of civil liberty and the prevention of the heroes and villains being militarized by the US government. The point is about how these two icons of the Marvel universe have simply hi-jacked the role of leader and taken it upon themselves to decide the fate of the rest of the heroes and villains that are merely being dragged along for the ride. They are two Leviathans fighting for dominance and damn the rest—especially all the innocent civilians that they are both supposedly trying to protect.

19
The Superhero Challenge to State Sovereignty

Jeffrey A. Ewing

Central to the traditional definition of the modern state is its territorial "sovereignty," its existence as the supreme authority within a territory. This authority is often backed by having a relative monopoly of the means of violence within that same territory—you cannot be a sovereign state unless no competing powers overawe your coercive capacities.

Simultaneously, issues of sovereignty permeate the recent superhero blockbuster *Captain America: Civil War*, where the superhero community of the Marvel Cinematic Universe (such as Iron Man and Captain America) are divided and fight over the Sokovia Accords. The purpose of the Sokovia Accords is to establish a UN panel to oversee and control the Avengers, pulling them into the international framework of nation-state control and giving the UN some authority over an independent team of individuals with nearly unchallengeable powers.

The *Avengers* are indeed a challenge to state sovereignty— what state can truly challenge the Hulk or Thor? How can US weapons easily counter Iron Man armor? What are the implications of superpowers for contemporary state sovereignty?

This Doesn't Have to End in a Fight

In *Captain America: Civil War*, the Marvel Cinematic Universe finds the superhero community torn apart. One year after the events of *Avengers: Age of Ultron*, the Avengers are pursuing Brock Rumlow, attempting to keep him from stealing a biological weapon in Lagos. In an act of desperate defiance, Rumlow detonates and Wanda Maximoff (Scarlet Witch) throws the explosion into the sky, damaging a nearby building. In a resulting meeting with the Avengers, Thaddeus Ross (US Secretary of State) informs the Avengers that the United Nations is working to pass the Sokovia Accords, whose purpose is to fold the Avengers into the UN, imposing a panel to oversee and control the team.

The argument for these Accords is that the unchecked power of the Avengers has, in the UN's judgment, endangered the world (citing such matters as Lagos and the creation of Ultron), and international oversight is a necessity:

> THADDEUS ROSS: Huh. Five years ago, I had a heart attack. I dropped right in the middle of my backswing. Turned out it was the best round of my life because after thirteen hours of surgery and a triple bypass, I have found something forty years in the army had never taught me... perspective. The world owes the Avengers an unpayable debt. You have fought for us, protected us, risked your lives. But while a great many people see you as heroes, there are some who would prefer the word "vigilantes".
>
> NATASHA ROMANOFF: And what word would you use, Mr. Secretary?
>
> THADDEUS ROSS: How about "dangerous"? What would you call a group of US-based, enhanced individuals who routinely ignore sovereign borders and inflict their will wherever they choose and who, frankly, seem unconcerned with what they leave behind? New York, Washington DC, Sokovia, Lagos . . .
>
> STEVE ROGERS: Okay. That's enough.
>
> THADDEUS ROSS: In the past four years, you've operated with unlimited power and no supervision. That's an arrangement the governments of the world can no longer tolerate. But I think we have a solution. The Sokovia Accords. Approved by 117 countries. It states that the Avengers shall no longer be a private organization. Instead, they'll operate under the supervision of a United Nations Panel, only when and if that Panel deems it necessary.

These accords divide the Avengers—Tony Stark supports them, partially from guilt in his role in the creation of Ultron, while Steve Rogers rejects them. The stakes are raised when a bomb explodes in the Vienna conference where the Accords were supposed to be ratified, killing King T'Chaka of Wakanda.

Evidence suggests Bucky Barnes (the Winter Soldier and Steve Rogers's longtime friend) planted the bomb, further dividing the superhero community as the manhunt commences for Barnes while Rogers works to get the true story.

While the divisions in the superhero community form the centerpiece of the action in *Civil War*, the Sokovia Accords are at the center of its philosophical heart. Their stated purpose is clearly in response to the power that the Avengers team wields (alongside other superpowered individuals or groups). In open recognition that the world has often benefited from their work, global governments nonetheless have decided that their power is a danger to the world if unchecked given their lack of supervision and training. Classifying power rankings is central to the Accords once adopted, as evidenced in the *Agents of SHIELD* episode "Emancipation," as the events of *Captain America: Civil War* force the registry of Inhumans.

> LINCOLN CAMPBELL: How does this registration thing work? You put us on a list then what?
>
> GLENN TALBOT: Well, we collect fingerprints, DNA samples. We run a power analysis to categorize your threat level which is also used to determine health risks.

Concern over power is an argument that Tony Stark finds persuasive in *Captain America: Civil War*:

> TONY STARK: There's no decision-making process here. We need to be put in check! And whatever form that takes, I'm game. If we can't accept limitations, we're boundaryless, we're no better than the bad guys.

Simultaneously, the philosophical essence of the Accords is not merely the danger of the Avengers. The existence of superheroes as unchecked powers challenges the sovereignty that is essential to modern states—and the challenges superheroes pose to this order is the ultimate philosophical issue underlying the Sokovia Accords that divide the superhero community.

Preventing the War of All Against All

Central to the definition and practice of modern states is the concept of *sovereignty*, meaning its supreme authority within a territory. *Sovereignty* was first formally integrated into the European state system in the 1648 Peace of Westphalia. Here, states were legally recognized as the sole form of constitutional authority in Europe within their respective territories (versus imposing claims by the Holy Roman Empire or other states).

This did not end wars and other challenges between states, nor did it simplify the complexities of sovereignty with regard to issues such as globalization or rights in an international framework, but it did establish the important notion that a core component of an established state was its exclusive claim to govern within its recognized borders. A key part of that territorial governance was a state's relative monopoly over the use of force within these borders—no competing state or power exists with the state's territory to challenge its claims to rule. As a core element of the state system, numerous political theorists have analyzed aspects of sovereignty to gain a clearer picture of its traits, operations, and limitations.

The first European philosopher to extensively theorize sovereignty was the French philosopher Jean Bodin (1530–1596). Writing *The Six Books of the Republic* (1576) in the height of a French civil war between Calvinist Huguenots and the Catholic monarchy, Bodin was deeply concerned with political order and the need to have political unity of the kind which could (in his analysis) only be guaranteed under the guidance of a supreme territorial political authority. Bodin extended the concept of sovereignty so far as to define it as "absolute and perpetual power vested in a commonwealth," not subject to *any* competing claims to authority, control, or law within its territory.

The English philosopher Thomas Hobbes (1588–1679) similarly wrote during a time of civil war and responded with a passionate defense of absolute state sovereignty. In Hobbes's account, political authority within a political community inheres in the populace, but they must alienate their individual sovereignties to a central political authority, the Leviathan, to protect the community and the individuals within it from the dangers of interpersonal chaos and violence. Hobbes writes that "during the time men live without a common power to keep them all in awe, they are in that condition which is called war, and such a war as is of every man against every man"— unchecked political chaos demands an absolute sovereign with a monopoly over coercive force within a territory.

While these early philosophers writing under conditions of civil war argued for the centralization and control of coercion for the common good (echoing the arguments of Tony Stark acting in the context of a 'civil war' within the superhero community of the Marvel Cinematic Universe), the controversial notion of the 'sovereign' (or now, the 'state') as supreme uncheckable authority is often subject to severe critique in subsequent critical thought. Nonetheless, a state's monopolization of the means of violence within its territory is widely recognized as a central element of state sovereignty, necessary for its claim to statehood. As the critical theorist Jurgen Habermas identifies:

> The *state* on the modern conception is a legally defined term that refers, at the level of substance, to a state power that possesses both internal and external sovereignty—at the spatial level, to a clearly delimited terrain, the state territory, and at the social level, to the totality of members, the body of citizens or the people. . . . the territorial state, with its monopoly on the legitimate use of violence and its differentiated administrative apparatus financed by taxation, was better able to cope with the functional imperatives of social, cultural, and, above all, economic modernization than older political formations.

In short, modern states definitionally require the sovereign centralization of control over the legitimate use of violence (among other features), and the totality of these features grant advantages to states over other historical forms of political organization. The absence of monopolized control over such legitimate use of violence is a strong challenge to state sovereignty, both in political theory and in terms of the legal framework that governs states and their interrelations in the wider system of states. It is this notion that creates the perceived need for the Sokovia Accords in *Captain America: Civil War*: their power is a power that needs to surrender to the control of the United Nations, to be folded in as a weapon of the international state system rather than as a challenge to the power of states in which the Avengers operate.

Ignoring Sovereign Borders

The explicit justification for the Sokovia Accords, to reiterate, is formed around recognition of the power of the Avengers, and the dangerous implications of that power. Thaddeus Ross explicitly makes this clear in his rationale over the Accords, that they don't stem from a belief that the Avengers are necessarily harmful; they stem from concerns over their unchecked power. Ross acknowledges that the Avengers "have fought for us, protected us, risked their lives," often serving the common good, yet he refers to the Avengers as "dangerous":

> What would you call a group of US-based, enhanced individuals who routinely ignore sovereign borders and inflict their will wherever they choose and who, frankly, seem unconcerned with what they leave behind?

Secretary Ross acknowledges both the good done by the Avengers in the world, and the harm that they've occasionally left behind, but while potential harmfulness raises the stakes for the issue, many of the arguments for the Sokovia Accords straightforwardly suggest the largest issue provoking their adoption is the challenge to state sovereignty that an unchecked Avengers may have.

The Avengers violate the principles of state territorial sovereignty in nearly every way imaginable. First, while they are physically based in the US, they routinely operate within the territorial borders of other states the world over, without formal consultation of those governments. While they are not formally agents of the US government or citizens, they have entrenched histories with the US government (such as Stark's history of weapon sales, Steve Rogers's long history with the US military and literal superhero identity as Captain America, or James Rhodes's career as War Machine while serving as liaison between Stark Industries and the US military). Their disdain for non-US borders, though understandable (why hinge saving the world on the results of other states' bureaucratic hierarchies?), is simultaneously worrisome for the international community. On that level, folding the Avengers into the political representative body of the community of nations, the United Nations, makes sense.

At the same time, while the Avengers have saved the Earth from multiple apocalypses, local territorial states are held responsible for the aftermath—cleaning the streets, rebuilding buildings and infrastructure, comforting the populace, and restoring order. Surely the damage is not the fault of the Avengers—it isn't as if they sent a horde of extraterrestrial invaders (blame Loki) or made a world-ending insane robot like Ultron (. . . okay, maybe that one's on Stark—perhaps Ross's points aren't all that bad). Regardless, the damage occasioned by other parties, which they defeated, and the damage wrought is generally the fault of the aggressors. Still, with states facing massive damage from city-spanning battles, it makes sense again that the international community would want some accountability, at the very least to have a point of appeal for help in the aftermath.

Finally, and perhaps most importantly, beyond the violation of territorial borders or the practical messes left behind the existence of superheroes challenges a central definitional element of state sovereignty—its relative territorial monopoly over the use of coercive force. Even street-level antiheroes like Punisher challenge state sovereignty in their refusal to leave investigating crime and inflicting punishment to state authorities. Beyond this, how can states be said to have meaningful territorial control over violence against the impossibly mighty, like the Hulk? Or against a literal god like Thor? Or the reality-warping powers of Doctor Strange or the Scarlet Witch? The very reason why superpowered threats like Loki or Ultron require superpowered opposition like the Avengers is exactly the reason why the Avengers violate sovereignty—in the absence of vastly amplified coercive force (such as superior technology, mystical arts, or similarly powered yet state-subordinate heroes) states are easily overpowered by the most powerful of heroes. If they have to contend with heroes that cannot be effectively countered, state sovereignty is rendered effectively meaningless.

The fact that the MCU *civil war* erupts as heroes that support the Sokovia Accords are enlisted to take down those who aren't proves this exact point, where the currently most powerful state (the United States) cannot effectively challenge the might of these heroes without enlisting *other members* of their own team. Here lies the challenge that inspired the Sokovia Accords—the existence of superheroes deeply challenges the monopoly of violence that state sovereignty requires, as enacted in the international state system or theorized by thinkers like Bodin or Hobbes or Habermas.

In short, in order to be sovereign in a territory a state needs to face no significant challenge to its coercive monopoly. Thus, if heroes exist which states could not check, *that state would not have sovereignty* and would maintain the illusion of sovereignty at the whim of said superpowered beings. Imagine for a moment that Doctor Strange, the Hulk, Thor, Scarlet Witch, and Vision decide to conquer the Earth with their vast combined powers. Unless other superpowered beings, powerful technology, or other powerful defenses come to the Earth's rescue, who could stand against them? Recall for a moment a conversation between Nick Fury and the Avengers in *The Avengers* (2012):

> BRUCE BANNER: I'd like to know why SHIELD is using the Tesseract to build weapons of mass destruction.
>
> NICK FURY: Because of him! [*points at Thor*]
>
> THOR: Me?
>
> NICK FURY: Last year, Earth had a visit from another planet that had a grudge match that leveled a small town. We learned that only are we not alone, but we are hopelessly, hilariously outgunned.
>
> THOR: My people want nothing but peace with your planet!
>
> NICK FURY: But you're not the only ones out there, are you? And you're not the only threat. The world is filling up with people that can't be matched, that can't be controlled!

States recognize that in the face of superpowered entities, superior technology, alien forces, and mystical threats, their claim to sovereignty is effectively nonexistent. They cannot match their coercive potential, and thus they cannot control them. In this regard, the biggest conceptual weakness in the Accords is that their enforcement still requires other *compliant* heroes, as by definition the system of nation states may not be able to enforce them otherwise. And what alternative do they have—*kill* the hero community, and have no real challenge to villainous entities and organizations? To be blunt, the existence of the super-powered community renders *state sovereignty* effectively meaningless, and these superpowered entities are closer than states are to attaining the characteristic sovereignty that political theorists have attributed to states.

Disclosing Shocking and Fantastic Abilities

To reiterate, the central conflict in *Captain America: Civil War* stems from the challenge superpowers pose for state sovereignty (for example in their disregard for state borders and the lack of consultation with state personnel). Most important, though, is the challenge superpowered individuals pose to the monopolization of violence that is necessary to state sovereignty as we know it. The existence of teams and individuals with features such as godlike might (such as Thor, Ms. Marvel, the Hulk), control over weather or the elements (Storm, Iceman), cutting-edge or unique technological suits (the suits of Iron Man, War Machine, Ant Man, Blue Beetle) or weapons (Thor's Mjolnir, Captain America's shield, Wolverine's adamantium claws), or reality-warping powers (Scarlet Witch, Doctor Strange) challenges the ability of states to claim to be the biggest, most powerful coercive force in their territories. This limitation is evident by their reliance on superheroes to combat supervillains (or to enforce the Sokovia Accords), and it undermines sovereignty.

These issues would pose huge practical problems for states. How easy is it (for example) to corral and handcuff the Hulk, or to incarcerate him? The underwater prison known as The Raft was created to detain superpowered individuals, but despite its apparent high level of security Steve Rogers was able to break in and free Clint Barton, Wanda Maximoff, Sam Wilson, and Scott Lang . . . without incarcerating all superpowered individuals even secure facilities aren't truly "secure"! (And, excepting Scarlet Witch, none of the imprisoned are among the most powerful Avengers, such as Thor or the Hulk, who weren't in *Captain America: Civil War* . . . we don't really know if they could have even been captured or contained). That the existence of superheroes challenges state claims to sovereignty is, I think at this point, clear and well grounded. The interesting challenge, then, is to ask *what are the implications of this in a world with superheroes*? Should we abandon the concept of state sovereignty in general?

Let us first shelve this question and ask how states could hypothetically maintain sovereignty in this world. First, they could try and eliminate (kill, incarcerate, mind control, exile from Earth, etc.) all superpowered individuals from Earth. This solution has a few issues. First, as we've established, that solution would be difficult—it is precisely because states have difficulty controlling superpowered individuals that they challenge sovereignty. Such a task would far exceed the capacities of even the most powerful states. To compensate, states would need to enlist the help of *other* superpowered individuals, whose value as a state asset and compliance with such orders is uncertain, and unless states could also secure *them* they would end up with the same problem they started.

Finally, external or new threats (which exceed state authority) continually challenge the Earth—for instance external threats like the Chitauri (*Avengers*), Malekith and the Dark Elves (*Thor: The Dark World*), Ronan the Accuser and the Kree (*Guardians of the Galaxy*), or Dormammu (*Doctor Strange*). In these crises, our states have proven reactionary and useless, and it is regularly up to heroes like Thor and Doctor Strange or teams like the Guardians of the Galaxy and the Avengers to protect the Earth from destruction. Even if the elimination of superheroes is possible, state sovereignty would be threatened time and again without superheroes' efforts to stop them.

Where does this leave the discussion of state sovereignty? The first issue with the Sokovia Accords is the practical one that *states can't guarantee their enforcement* (I mean, that's clearly the crisis of the civil war within the MCU) except on the good will of the heroes involved alone. They 'play ball' because they choose to, not because they have to. And second, there may be valid reasons for superheroes to want *independence* from the international system of states, which Steve Rogers explains in the following dialogue:

> LT. COL. JAMES RHODES: Sorry, Steve, that . . . that is dangerously arrogant. This is the United Nations we're talking about. It's not the World Security Council, it's not SHIELD, it's not Hydra.
>
> STEVE ROGERS: No, but it's run by people with agendas and agendas change.
>
> TONY STARK: That's good! That's why I'm here. When I realized what my weapons were capable of in the wrong hands, I shut it down. Stopped manufacturing.
>
> STEVE ROGERS: Tony, you *chose* to do that. If we sign this, we surrender our right to choose. What if this panel sends us somewhere

we don't think we should go? What if there's somewhere we need to go and they don't let us? We may not be perfect but the safest hands are still our own.

Rogers is expressing a real concern: exclusive sovereignty in the hands of states is *also* problematic. Indeed, Captain America has seen all too well the potential dangers of states in the Nazi genocidal efforts of World War II or in the efforts of the HYDRA infiltration of SHIELD, showing that state coercive 'protection' keeps the populace safe or endangers it contingent on who 'the enemy' is defined as, and who gets to do the defining? Subordinating the superhero community to international states is not only implausible, but taking away their independence is a threat in a world where states often fail to act in the public interest.

While the existence of superheroes challenges the concept and practice of state sovereignty (the central conflict of *Captain America: Civil War*) there are really no sound options here. The superhero community is useful to save humanity from external and new threats, and full state monopoly over coercion protects the populace only insofar as the individuals in power are good natured and wise. But if unchecked superpowered individuals are a threat to sovereignty from the implications of their super powers, and unchecked state power is *also* a threat to the populace, what is to be done?

The problem stems from the uncheckable powers of *both* parties to the conflict: superheroes and states need to be able to check each other's powers, and the disempowered populace requires that dangerous balance to avoid catastrophe because of their own relative lack of coercive potential, making self-defense against these forces impossible. The Sokovia Accords don't help the everyday populace in that regard, they just try and change which dangerous power controls the superpowered community.

The better option, it seems (though not without problems), would be to avoid states and the reliance on heroes *entirely* by expanding who has powers to begin with, restore the sovereignty of the populace versus godlike individuals and overarching states. Democratize powers among the general public, and down with the Hobbesian permanent transference of sovereignty!

20

There's Only One God, Ma'am

JAMES D. HOLT

Within the Marvel universe Captain America is the embodiment of early twentieth-century American values. An important part of this identity is an acceptance of Christianity and the moral values that it teaches. This is evident in Captain America's morality that is explored both in the comics and the movies; he dislikes profanity and nudity, often acting as a foil for Tony Stark's excesses and in return being the butt of his jokes. In the *Ultimates* offshoot from the main Marvel timeline Steve Rogers leaves a movie theatre:

> THE WASP (JANET VAN DYNE PYM): Well, it wasn't as good as the Japanese version, but it was still pretty slick. You realize Gere's actually made two good movies in a row this year? Isn't that some kinda record?
>
> CAPTAIN AMERICA (STEVE ROGERS): I'll take your word for it, Jan, but what's the deal with all that potty-mouth stuff, huh? Why does every movie these days have to feel like a sailor wrote the script?
>
> WASP: It's just realistic, Steve. Even you curse sometimes.
>
> CAPTAIN AMERICA: Yeah, but I don't need to hear it every time I go to the flicks. Likewise, these dames don't need to show me everything they got just because I paid ten bucks for a ticket.
>
> WASP: Steve, c'mon. This was the safest movie doing the rounds right now. You've killed guys with your bare hands, for God's sake. Don't make us go and see the SpongeBob movie. (*The Ultimates 2 Volume 1: Gods and Monsters*, pp. 3–4)

There is a slight incongruity in this scene as he is having a conversation with the Wasp—who happens to be a married woman that he is in a relationship with!! There must be limits to his morality.

It is possible to have morality without religion, indeed in *Infinity Crusade* the reason that Captain America is chosen by the Goddess, in distinction to what we are told about the others chosen, is "because of your moral character, your honesty, your bravery." This, however, is seemingly contradicted by the Vision who notes the common characteristics of the super heroes enlisted by the Goddess:

> Now that the appropriate files have been examined I believe I have sufficient hard data to put forth that theory I mentioned earlier. I feel confident I know why these particular paranormals were abducted. All the missing share a common trait or experience . . . An event or attitude that might be categorized as religious. Many among the missing hold deeply felt moral stands or intense spiritual belief systems. (*Infinity Crusade* #1, p. 32)

All the indications are that Captain America's is underpinned by a belief in the Christian God. The religiosity of this approach to life is explored in various aspects of the comics and the movies, hence the discussion with the Black Widow:

> *Captain America puts on a parachute to follow Thor, Loki, and Iron Man.*
>
> NATASHA ROMANOFF: I'd sit this one out, Cap.
>
> STEVE ROGERS: I don't see how I can.
>
> NATASHA ROMANOFF: These guys come from legend. They're basically gods.
>
> STEVE ROGERS: There's only one God, ma'am, and I'm pretty sure he doesn't dress like that. *Captain America leaps out of the jet.*

This dismissive response to the claims of Thor to be a god is replicated in the Ultimates timeline:

> THOR: Are you okay, Rogers?
>
> CAPTAIN AMERICA (STEVE ROGERS): Fine, but some of your friends here could use a little lesson in manners . . .

THOR: Listen, I'm sorry about this. I really didn't want that to happen and I'm serious when I said I'd nothing to do with outing Banner. That said, I think I know who might have released those files.

CAPTAIN AMERICA: Who?

THOR: My evil half-brother, Loki. A messenger from Asgard came to warn me that he escaped from his bonds again and journeyed to Midgard to do everything he could to—

CAPTAIN AMERICA: Thor, please.

THOR: What?

CAPTAIN AMERICA: Just shut up.

THOR: You go to church every Sunday, Captain. What I've got to say's no stranger than that. (*The Ultimates 2 Volume 1: Gods and Monsters*, p. 17)

Thor raises an interesting point: just because Captain America's beliefs seem to be more modern or accepted by more people in society does not make them less superstitious. If, in the Marvel universe, there is the one God of Christianity how can this be reconciled with the existence of gods such as the Norse Gods, or powerful god-like beings such as Thanos? It seems so illogical for them to exist alongside one another—they can't both exist, can they?

The Biggest Kid in the Playground

Here we can draw links with the God of the Old Testament, the God of Abraham, Isaac, Jacob and more importantly at this point, Moses. As Moses spoke with God at the burning bush he essentially asked the question "What shall I tell the people when they ask, who sent me?" God replied "I am"—a name so sacred in Hebrew that it is rarely repeated by Jews. The response has suggested to some that Moses before, and perhaps after, his experience at the burning bush was a henotheist rather than a monotheist.

Henotheism is the worship of one god which does not deny the possibility of the existence of other gods. In terms of the God of Israel this deity is the supreme deity, and while other minor deities may exist they are not on a par with him, and as such are not worthy of worship. I recognize that for some from the Judeo-Christian tradition this may seem like heresy, as tradition and modern thinking may suggest that the traditional understanding of God was revealed all at once rather than one where the understanding of his monotheistic nature developed over time as "superstition" and the existence of other gods was eroded from people's understanding and practice. This recognition of other lesser gods alongside the one God may have been the transition period as people adjusted from a belief in the existence of many Gods to a belief in one God.

As an interesting aside, the name of God in Arabic and utilized in Islam is Allah—meaning *the* God. In pre-Islamic Arabia there were many gods who were worshipped, but Allah was seen to be the most powerful and the supreme deity. With the advent of Islam the existence of other gods was rejected, the Ka'ba was cleansed and the first part of the declaration of faith became "There is no god but Allah." The transition from henotheism or polytheism was quicker and more marked within Islam than within Judaism. We see this reflected in an incident in Genesis 35 where Jacob's household, having previously accepted the God of Abraham as the god whom they worshipped, were asked to put away their idols and their foreign gods. This suggests that some if not all of Jacob's family, were able to persist in the existence of other gods while recognizing a pre-eminent God. Over time, this belief in lots of gods with one as supreme, if it ever existed, developed into the belief in one God that is found throughout the Judeo-Christian religions.

This idea of henotheism could link with the idea of God in Captain America's mind and the wider Marvel universe. Within Marvel comics there is the concept of the One-above-all the supreme entity who governs the universe and is above and beyond all else. In *Thor Annual* #14 even Thor and Odin acknowledge their paling into comparison next to the Living Tribunal, who is himself only the representative ("the biggest kid in the playground") of the One-above-all:

> and 'tis said that a being, called the Living Tribunal—the final judge— hath the power to enforce his will 'pon any cosmos he doth judge! And 'tis said his power is supreme in all the Multiverse. Even I, son of one of the mightiest of all gods, find it impossible to conceive of such levels of power! And 'tis a humbling thought to consider how much greater the Creator of all Universes must be than that of all of His creations combined! (*The Mighty Thor Annual* #14, p. 42)

It is therefore possible to see the Marvel Universe as either henotheist or monotheist. If the other gods are truly gods and not just beings of immense power then it is henotheist; if on the other hand they are just beings on a different level of creation similar to a human and a mouse, then the universe is monotheist. Either way it would seem that Captain America's declaration that there is only one God is consistent with Christianity in the real world. It is slightly different to the Judeo-Christian understanding as the existence of these other beings is rejected, but within the Marvel Universe they are real.

The One-above-all shares other characteristics to the Christian God whom Captain America worships. The Living Tribunal as the representative of the One-above-all can be seen to be suggestive of the relationship of the Father and the Son, even though the majority of Christians would reject the idea of Jesus being less than the Father. This similarity with the Christian God is strengthened in *Fantastic Four* #72, where Uatu the Watcher tells Susan Storm that there is only one entity that is "all-powerful", meaning One-above-all, and Uatu identifies that "His only weapon . . . is love!" (p. 13).

The Ignorant Multitude Must First Entertain Some Groveling and Familiar Notion of Superior Powers

The nature of God and the existence of godlike beings can also be seen to fit with a Humean understanding of religious belief. David Hume was a Scottish philosopher well known for his atheistic beliefs. His interpretation of religion may also be used to explore the nature of God in the Marvel universe.

In some ways Captain America can be seen to echo Hume's views; Hume sees an acceptance of many gods as uninformed: "It seems certain, that, according to the natural progress of human thought, the ignorant multitude must first entertain some groveling and familiar notion of superior powers, before they stretch their conception to that perfect being, who bestowed order on the whole frame of nature." Hume argues, in a way that Steve Rogers does, that believing in lots of gods is in fact inferior to believing in one, and that the human race could not have started with monotheism because polytheism is a primitive belief: "if men were at first led into the belief of one Supreme

Being, by reasoning from the frame of nature; they could never possibly leave that belief, in order to embrace polytheism." When people have acquired enough knowledge they will reject the idea of lots of gods and adopt the more intellectually advanced belief in one God. This is supported in the views explained in the Marvel Universe and those of the Asgardians themselves, that they are not gods but merely from another realm.

The recognition of others as gods rather than having godlike qualities, in Hume's and Captain America's views, belongs to the realm of ignorance and a lack of understanding. The existence of the Asgardians is similar to Hume's critique of belief. "Our ancestors in Europe, before the revival of letters, believed, as we do at present, that there was one supreme god." He argues that although they believed in the Supreme Being, they also had a strong belief in the magical forces surrounding the world: "all nature was full of other invisible powers; fairies, goblins, elves, sprites; beings stronger and mightier than men, but much inferior to the celestial natures, who surround the throne of god." With a true understanding people will leave their superstitions and worship of these lesser "gods" behind. It is similar to Jacob's household burying the idols of the foreign gods, or the rejection of a god who pulls the sun across the sky in favor of a more rational belief in God that recognizes the laws of nature and science rather than mystical and superstitious explanations.

Although Hume provides a structure that can be used to explain how there could be a One-above-all in a universe with godlike beings it is necessary to highlight that while this Humean understanding supports, and leads to, Captain America being able to declare that there is only God, for Hume, this view leads to atheism. And in this sense Hume can be seen as closer to Tony Stark than to Captain America.

Hume argues that all beliefs people have in religion and deities is led by superstition:

> While they confine themselves to the notion of a perfect being, the creator of the world, they coincide, by chance, with the principles of reason and true philosophy; though they are guided to that notion, not by reason, of which they are in a great measure incapable but by the adulation and fears of the most vulgar superstition. (*Dialogues and Natural History of Religion*, p. 155)

Your Soul Remains Imprisoned in the Ice of Rationalism

While there seems to be no indication of Iron Man's religious beliefs there are Humean indications in *Infinity Crusade* that he is at least rationalist if not atheist. In response to his declaration that "I prefer fact to fantasy," the Goddess remarks that "You have no belief in anything, then. You are a hollow soulless being." He does not challenge this:

> IRON MAN: I believe that scientific method is humanity's most powerful tool and that through the will to knowledge, man can achieve his own transcendence without bowing to Gods with the manners of spoiled children.
>
> GODDESS: Your body may have been thawed, but your soul remains imprisoned in the ice of rationalism. (*Iron Man* #294, pp. 5–6)

In *Civil War II* Stark is identified as a "Futurist" and it is for this reason that he opposes Captain Marvel, in the sense that he sees possible futures based on the consequences of actions done today. As such he works towards the best possible future for humanity. This understanding of reality seems closer to Hume who rejects all belief in God as superstitious. Iron Man could be described as post-religious; someone for whom the idea of God and religion is at odds with the rational world that he finds around him—the only certainties can be seen in that which is observable.

Taking Hume's progression of belief in God to its natural conclusion it seems to be that he suggests a staged approach of human understanding of the way the world works. He suggests that the first stage is polytheism as people ascribe individual deities to control of various aspects of the natural world; they then move on to a qualified monotheism or henotheism, recognizing the existence of one God, one supreme being but also that there are other supernatural beings; and then onto an unqualified monotheism where anything other "supernatural" beings are either non-existent or just beings with powers that can't be explained yet. (Hume doesn't recognize this last superhuman being but in the Marvel Universe it needs to be acknowledged). At this point reason would take Hume to the next step that there is no rational reason to believe in a supreme being, rather he would see in the progression of humanity and religions that they become post-deity. Although not discussing futurism this seems to be a worldview that needs no god but establishes a morality.

Futurism, if it is post-God does not seem to fit in the Marvel universe however. Iron Man would find it hard to reconcile atheism with the various realms that seem to exist whether they are Asgardian in nature or the spiritual realm highlighted in Doctor Strange.

While futurism and rationalism is a possible approach to life, within Marvel there needs to be a recognition of the existence of things beyond the material. For Captain America this is a belief in one God who could be analogous to the One-above-all with a rejection of the other godlike beings as amounting to gods. For Iron Man this question seems unresolved and perhaps irrelevant to his life.

21
The Extended Fight

CHRISTOPHE POROT

Questions about the mind have perplexed philosophers and societies for centuries. What is consciousness? Does the existence of the mind reveal the existence of a soul? How does our conscious experience relate to our brain? However, one of the most fundamental questions has been ignored until recently: "Where is our mind?" The final fight between Iron Man and Captain America illustrates a curious answer. The mind extends beyond the brain, and into the world around us.

Civil War sees Steve Rogers go toe-to-toe with Tony Stark. Augmented by his Iron Man suit, Stark wins the first round. Moments later, Rogers returns to the fray with his lifelong friend, James "Bucky" Buchanan. Acting together, Captain America and the former Winter Soldier defeat Iron Man. Rather than battling as their individual selves, contained within the body, in this sequence it is the "extended mind" of the two that are pitted against each other. So, the final battle can tell us a lot about a key difference between Iron Man and the Captain: one extends his mind through technology and the other does so socially.

To make sense of such claims, we need to look at the very concept of an extended mind.

Where Is My Mind?

To grasp the extended mind, we must start by challenging a common idea that the mind only works through our brains. There are many people who tend to think of the mind as some kind of central nucleus, living inside our heads, probably based somewhere in the brain. Let's call this the "brain-bound" model of the mind. From that point "somewhere in the brain," the mind throws out all our thoughts, controls our emotions, and co-ordinates the information from each of our senses. Anything we know or remember, according to the brain-bound model, is stored in there somewhere, even though we've picked up that information from "outside."

When the brain-bound mind does its thinking, it examines all this internal storage and comes up with answers, actions or options based on what it finds there. And when there is something that the brain-bound mind wants to happen in the outside world, it sends signals to the bits of us that can get things done or find things out—our muscles, or our sense organs, or our speech capabilities. All the functions of the brain-bound mind start at this central nucleus, and radiate outwards from there.

As long as we're sticking to this brain-bound model, Iron Man's mind beats the Captain every time. Sure, Captain America has those rock-hard pecs and lightning reflexes. But Tony Stark has the mental power to think through almost any problem and to build his incredible suits. He has the intelligence to design them, the vision to constantly refine and update them, and the skills to construct the AIs (first JARVIS, then Friday) that make a partial interface between him and them.

To understand how it's possible for Cap's mind to be stronger than Stark's, we need to question the brain-bound model of the mind. What if the mind doesn't stop at the boundaries of the brain? What if things "outside" of us take part in our cognitive functioning? What if our minds really extend out into the world, making use of our bodies, or technology, or even the people around us to do their business? If we can follow through with this idea, we can see why the Captain wins his fight in *Civil War* and why Stark and Cap disagree about Bucky.

The Extended Mind

Renowned philosophers David Chalmers and Andy Clark revolutionized how we think about the mind when they introduced their theory of the Extended Mind. They argue that the cognitive processes normally associated with the mind are often executed by materials or persons outside of our heads and therefore the mind extends beyond our heads.

However, Chalmers also makes clear that he's only talking about thoughts defined as functions, processes, or beliefs that tend to be associated with roles of the brain (like memory) and that his theory does not imply that our consciousness is contained in technology or other persons.

So, for instance, when someone with Alzheimer's uses a notepad to document their day and remember various things, they are using the notepad as a surrogate for the brain. Instead of relying on the brain to execute the mental function of memory, the person's mind is using the notepad. Or, for a more relevant example, when Iron Man uses his suit to calculate what's going on in his surroundings, he's using technology to process things that would normally be processed by the brain. Even if Iron Man's brain can't process these things so quickly, he is nonetheless "extending" his mind through technology; this is true of us when we use calculators for math equations instead of relying on our brains to do "mental arithmetic."

The function normally served by the brain is off-loaded onto another material device, and sometimes this device can process material at faster speeds than our own brains. But this doesn't mean we share a consciousness with the device selected—we merely make it perform an act or role that the brain normally performs.

Once we understand this "extended" model of the mind, we can find examples of it everywhere. Remember that fight we discussed above from *Civil War*, when Friday analyzed the Captain's fight pattern for Iron Man? Tony Stark's brain-bound mind could probably do this job, eventually, "given enough time." But in the heat of the moment, he outsourced the task. Iron Man and the AI Friday form a "coupled pair," with Tony Stark's mind extended outwards to this piece of technology. Or think of the big battle with the Chitauri at the climax of *Avengers Assemble*. Just as Iron Man is about to fly the nuke into the big hole in the sky, JARVIS interrupts and suggests that he might like to give Pepper Potts a "phone call."

Of course, if his brain-bound mind were not a bit pre-occupied at the time, this is something Tony Stark would surely remember through his brain alone. But JARVIS does the work of remembering for him, before the issue even occurs to him.

This is because he's made himself smarter, in a sense, through his suits. The function of remembering, or calculating, is merely just a function. It's just a thing that is done; and it's often done by our brains. In the age of technology, Tony Stark masters the art of freeing up cognitive space by having pieces of his technology do things his brain would otherwise do.

Social Extension

We have seen that we can technologically extend the mind (with calculators, computers, iPhones, and other appliances), but a mind can be socially extended as well. For instance, spouses often depend on each other for cognitive processes, like a husband depending on his wife to remember their calendar. Since spouses' minds are completely separate and external to each other (if I remember something for you, that doesn't mean we are having a shared conscious experience), this still counts as an extension of the mind. Captain America likes to set up and guide teams, with each member allocated a special role. He is, in many ways, extending his mind through others—and, more importantly, he is very good at it. When Cap is fighting in the airport, he leans on his carefully selected team to devise the appropriate solution to the battle. Recall the following exchange:

> **CAP:** We got to go . . . I'm gonna draw all the fliers. I'll take Vision. You get to the jet.
>
> **FALCON:** No, you get to the jet! Both of you! The rest of us aren't getting out of here.
>
> **HAWK:** As much as I hate to admit it, if we're gonna win this one, some of us might have to lose it.
>
> **FALCON:** This isn't the real fight, Steve.
>
> **CAP:** Alright, Sam, what's the plan?
>
> **FALCON:** We need a diversion, something big . . .
>
> **ANT MAN:** [*Once becoming Big*] You want to get to them? You got to go through me.

What happens here is more than just teamwork: Cap goes beyond his limitations by extending his mind through other people. This is, I believe, what Cap means when he says, "I place my trust in individuals and, so far, they haven't let me down." He is not placing his trust in pure technology, nor is he placing his trust in institutions. Institutions, arguably, have a collective mind that rises above any individual. Technology lacks the ability to operate autonomously (except for Ultron, of course). However, Ultron demonstrates one of the drawbacks of the technologically extended mind—and why the technologically extended mind must work for us rather than run on its own.

Why Cap Won

Philosopher Nick Bostrom has argued that the fear we should have about AI is not that machines will want to take over the world. Instead, we should be worried about the fact that machines might be so in pursuit of the function they are designed for that they allow the world to be destroyed in the process. A machine made to collect staplers could, in theory, destroy a whole city to do so.

As we know, Ultron was willing to end humanity in order to achieve peace. He had a single purpose, a single function, and lacked the emotional and other features of the human experience that regulate the pursuit of our purposes. Most people would know that if someone asked them to get a stapler, there are limits to the request: we can't kill for it, for instance. With Ultron, limits on the request just don't make sense. Whatever his function is, this becomes his purpose, and that's why he described Stark as a "weak father" because Stark had limits preventing him from achieving the ultimate goal of peace.

By contrast, when we extend our minds socially we can trust the autonomy of our counterparts. Cap had been brutally beaten by Stark and was incapacitated when Bucky autonomously, and cleverly, stepped in. Cap gets the luxury of extending his mind through agents who he can trust to act autonomously where Stark does not. The danger of making the technologically extended mind also autonomous was thoroughly displayed through the tragedies that unfolded in the wake of Ultron.

Unlike institutions or technology, a team captained by Rogers ultimately extends his individual mind through a close knit group that surrounds him. He processes problems with and through them, but he remains the leader who takes responsibility for whatever comes of their collective processing. In the battle with Stark, the possibility of having more autonomous extensions of his mind served to give him the victory.

This sketch of the extended mind might leave some big questions: Does Cap not use his shield? Does Tony not work with others? All of this is true. The point, however, is that Captain America represents an exemplary case of socially extending a person's mind while Iron Man represents an exemplary case of technologically extending one's mind. Iron Man is famously rude and off-putting so that, after the conclusion of *Iron Man 2*, SHIELD thought he "didn't play well with others." He wasn't going to be an Avenger because his social skills were so poor, but his command over technology is absolutely masterful.

Captain America, by contrast, quickly ascends into leadership over the Avengers. He does this after merely waking up into the twenty-first century, having slept through the development of most of the technologies that make it run. He's an old man, as they say, and lacks that "next gen" knowledge. As technology or other people can become tools to a person's greatness, Iron Man and Captain America extend their minds through different tools (social and technological).

Responsibility, Extension, and Bucky

Another way of thinking about this notion of Cap and Stark operating through their extended minds is to look at the ways that they take individual responsibility for whatever is done by their extended minds.

Taking responsibility expresses their sense of ownership over their extended minds. Stark takes full responsibility for Ultron, and it cripples him. In *Civil War*, when Secretary Ross shows a slide of the damage done to Sokovia by Ultron, Stark looks down and says, "That was me." In fact, for the heroes who have technologically extended their minds, the theme of being worthy of that extended mind is often repeated. Tony Stark says, "I am the suit. Take away the suit and you are taking away a part of me." Before both Falcon and War Machine embrace their technological extensions, they are proven on the individual basis to be good and worthy human beings.

This theme is also expressed in Spider-Man's saga. In the *Spider-Man* movie Spider-Man cries out, "I am nothing without this suit." And Stark replies, "If you are nothing without the suit, then you don't deserve it." So the suits are understood to magnify the mind and morality of the person who uses them, hence there is a vetting process that displays itself in stunning magnificence and often through a stand-alone movie (like *Iron Man*). In these films we see the marriage of the man and the suit. Anything done by intellectual processing of the suit is, for Iron Man at least, done by him since he processes things through his suits and technology. They are a part of his mind.

Similarly, Rogers takes full responsibility when people who are part of his extended mind act out. Remember his profound exchange with Scarlet Witch who, trying to save Cap from Crossbones' attempted suicide bombing, accidentally moved an explosion to a nearby building, killing civilians? In the wake of this politically consequential incident (a group of Wakandans were killed in the explosion), Scarlet Witch laments that it was her fault, to which Rogers responds, "That's not true . . . I'm the leader to deal with it." As a part of the extended mind that Cap uses to make strategic decisions, Scarlet Witch's ill-fated decision is effectively Cap's own.

The fact that Cap and Iron Man have different extended minds likely explains their competing takes on whether or not Bucky is better understood as innocent or guilty. In other words, people who extend their mind socially might have a different experience and set of perspectives than people who extend their mind technologically. Sometimes we learn through experience itself, and insofar as experience is a source of moral insight, Cap's socially extended mind enables him to understand why Bucky is innocent more readily than Stark does. So, for instance, if I once cheated on a test in school then I know that cheating in school happens (I did not do this, of course). But, if I've never cheated, then I might have a more naive view about the world and what will happen in it. I might just think that nobody cheats. Something like this is happening between Stark and Cap, but to see why we must first see how they disagreed over Bucky.

According to Cap, Bucky is innocent because he "could not have done otherwise." For Iron Man, Bucky is responsible because "he still did it." This exchange reflects a very popular debate in moral philosophy, centered on a simple question: can someone be blameworthy if they could not have done otherwise? Cap's position is that this is impossible. With his understanding and appreciation for autonomy and free will he does not believe an individual can be held responsible (or blameworthy) for something, unless they had a free choice to do it.

For Iron Man, whether or not someone could have done otherwise is beside the point. His statement that Bucky "still did it" highlights the notion that you are what you do. Perhaps the clearest distinction of their competing moral assessments comes through the fiery exchange that launched the fight between Cap and Iron Man:

STARK: Did you know?

CAP: I didn't know it was him.

STARK: Don't bullshit me, Rogers! Did you know?

CAP: Yes. Get out of here! It wasn't him, Tony. Hydra had control of his mind!

STARK: Move!

CAP: It wasn't him!

Cap, so often portrayed as a champion of autonomy and free will, is brutally aware that individual autonomy can be compromised. Further, he suggests, being unable to make a choice relieves anybody of blameworthiness. Why does Cap see this while Stark remains blind to the possibility?

When an individual extends their mind through machines and tech, as Stark so easily does, the traditional division between technology as an instrument and people as, well, people is easy to preserve. However, when someone extends their mind socially, like Cap, they might be more willing to accept that people can be used as instruments. If this general idea is true in the Marvel universe, then there should be some evidence that those whose minds are predominantly extended through technology are more likely to see Bucky as guilty, while the opposite is true of those with socially extended minds.

As it turns out, characters using technology instead of people to perform cognitive capacities are, in fact, more likely to see Bucky as guilty. This is even true of Falcon, who is one of the few people on Team Cap whose minds are predominantly extended through technology. His ability to strategize is enhanced through his Redwing drone. Falcon outsources his perceptive faculties to the drone, allowing him, for example, to locate Crossbones before his attack. He is a part of Captain's socially extended mind, but he himself has a much more technologically extended mind than Cap. When Cap forgives Bucky, Falcon does not. The tension arises after Bucky is activated in *Civil War*: Cap immediately accepts Bucky once he knows he is no longer activated, but by contrast, Falcon questions the whole idea of treating Bucky kindly. Thus, he asks how "we are just supposed to be cool now?"

Cap seems to have no hesitation about seeing people as versions of technology, capable of being pushed in one or another direction. Perhaps this is precisely because Cap himself pushes people in different directions, controls individuals and then takes responsibility for what they do. Remember the Scarlet Witch exchange, in which Cap argues that he is the one who deserves blame when things go wrong—he is in charge. If Scarlet Witch is a part of Cap's socially extended mind, then Bucky might be best understood as a tool who was converted into the perfect extended mind for those with dubious intentions. Hence, the experiential difference between Stark and Tony: Tony only uses actual tools and impersonal instruments to extend his mind and takes full responsibility for all they do. Cap uses other people and takes responsibility for what they do and therefore has a deep sense (from experience) that it is possible to instrumentalize people. So he has no problem understanding Bucky's lack of agency.

Cap's words and behavior reveal his deep understanding of Bucky's condition, an understanding that is more accurate than Iron Man's. Iron Man, who only uses technology, sees individual people as responsible for whatever they do since he's never experienced what it's like to take away people's responsibility. However, neither Cap nor Iron Man vocalize the direct truth. The only character in the Marvel Cinematic Universe to describe the condition of Bucky with piercing precision is actually Black Panther. He does so at the very end of the movie. Just before Bucky removes himself from civilization, Black Panther closes the dialogue about Bucky by directly stating, as a somber fact, the reality of the Winter Soldier's condition:

CAP: You sure about this?

BUCK: I can't trust my own mind. So, until they figure out how to get this stuff out of my head I think going back under is the best thing, for everybody.

CAP: Thank you for this.

PANTHER: Your friend and my father, they are both victims.

Bucky is a victim. However, the way in which he was victimized is not as immediately obvious as the way in which Black Panther's father was. Remember, of course, that Panther's father was murdered in a devastating terrorist attack at the signing of the Sokovia Accords. By contrast, Bucky is victimized on two levels. On the first, he is wrongly accused of a crime. On the second, he is a victim insofar as he lost his agency, his ability to be free and determine his life as he sees fit.

Instead of considering whether or not to write a book, fall in love, dance, or save the world, Bucky has been forced to operate as an executor of the will of Hydra. His transformation from a person capable of making choices to an instrument of force—for a fairly evil agenda, I might add—can only be described in terms of tragedy. In fact, even when Hydra's tentacles are not wrapped around Bucky's mind, he remains unfree to choose. The mere possibility of being activated into a lethal weapon terrifies him, and so he must forfeit his waking life until a cure can be found. When the steely doors entomb him at the end of *Civil War*, his invisible prison all of a sudden becomes a tangible one. If nothing else, he confesses that he would rather be in a physical prison than the mental and moral one imposed upon him by Hydra.

Captain America is completely aware of Bucky's loss of freedom—but he ultimately links this into a loss of responsibility, rather than victimhood. This is why, in an exchange between Cap and Bucky, they fundamentally disagree about what Bucky's time as an activated weapon amounts to. Cap, in an attempt to reassure Bucky, says, "You had no choice." Bucky, however, still wrestles with the agony of knowing what has been done through him. Cap casts Bucky as incorrectly assigned responsibility for a crime, but stops short of seeing Bucky as a victim of that crime.

The problem with Cap's argument about choice is very simple: whether or not we have a choice is not the question to ask in regard to Bucky's condition. The answer to this question requires immense philosophical analysis (What would it mean to make a choice? Can we do it?). The true question is as follows: was the choice, as far as we can tell, our own? Or can we identify someone else who made the choice for us, and took command over our apparent agency? In the case of Bucky, the answer is obvious: yes, we can identify who took away his agency, and it was Hydra. Cap has the experiential knowledge to know this is possible, but he lacks the philosophical skill to fully express what he knows—he can only partially assess the situation at that level.

Here's one way to think about Cap's problem: if we have no choice, perhaps we lack a choice because everything is predetermined—our destiny is like a pre-written script that we simply live through without influencing. Philosophers call this concept "determinism." Cap's reassuring nod to Bucky relies on the idea that if you're predetermined to do something then you can't be held responsible for that thing. In other words, if you could not do otherwise then you cannot be held responsible for a crime. It would be as though, in a deterministic world, a person murdering another is morally indistinguishable from a tree branch cracking under pressure and accidentally hitting an innocent passerby.

The problem for Bucky, however, is not whether he is responsible for the crimes he committed. Cap's reassurance fails to address Bucky's status as a victim. Cap's reassurances should be aimed at Bucky's trauma as a result of being used in service of the will of another. Regardless of whether you accept determinism, Bucky is a victim just in virtue of having his right to self-determination compromised. Whether the world is determined or open to choice, someone who is stabbed is a victim of stabbing, and someone who is robbed is a victim of robbery.

While Cap argues deterministically, there is clear evidence that he does not ultimately subscribe to it. When discussing the signing of the Sokavia accords, Cap simply asserts that he "can't do it." In a sense, he is suggesting that he is determined not to sign the form and therefore committed, determined to fight against it. Cap's inability to do otherwise ultimately does nothing to undermine his sense of responsibility for what he does, and for what happens as a result of what he does. This is inconsistent with his justification for Bucky's innocence, namely that

Bucky could not do otherwise. While the justification he states is inconsistent with other points he makes, Cap is always there when Bucky is in trouble. Cap immediately forgives Bucky, and holds an affectionate attitude towards him, as though he wants to help him. When Panther calls Bucky a "victim," Cap's silence and nod indicates that he understands this truth.

Maybe the gap in understanding comes from Cap's own denial about how he uses people. By instrumentalizing Bucky and others, Cap is undermining their agency. Even though Cap works as part of a team, he is still the one calling the shots in the end. In the fight at the airport, Cap's teammates are ultimately fighting to achieve *Cap's* goals. They are instrumental in achieving the goals of a will external to their own.

Perhaps Cap is unwilling to acknowledge Bucky's victimhood because doing so would mean acknowledging the moral complexity of his own methods. Of course, his methods are not necessarily morally wrong—the man tends to do the right thing! Even a small harm might be justified by the consequences it produces, the goals it achieves, and Cap seems to routinely pursue justified goals. However, his method is to constantly extend his mind socially and rely on processing things through others. The one clear truth is that other people *choose* to work with Cap and so they choose to work with his will, this should further resolve the fear that he is using them. But he is so good at inspiring loyalty, like a charming salesman is good at inspiring a purchase, that he must address whether or not (in the end) extending his mind socially threatens the agency and autonomy of others, something he values so highly.

What Does It All Mean?

If we think of the mind as being more than the brain, then we can see how the superpowers of Tony and Cap have something to do with how they extend their minds. But how we extend our minds creates different experiences in life: Tony is intimately familiar with the lack of autonomy in cold and impersonal machines, but he has almost never taken away the autonomy of another person. Cap is oblivious to how those machines work, but he is masterful at redirecting the autonomy of others. Cap has experienced and seen how people's autonomy can be controlled from the outside, while Tony's socially stunted behavior leaves him without that experience.

So the sympathy and wisdom of Cap and the unforgiving character of Tony are borne out of different experiences related to how they extend their minds . They fight over their competing takes on Bucky's situation, and the outcome of the fight is determined by a socially extended mind vs. a technologically extended mind. Maybe, for all the fireworks and theatrics of the film, it could be recast as a deep meditation on how a new understanding of the mind can influence moral thinking and our strength in this world.[1]

---

[1] The author thanks Luis Nario-Malberg, Nica Giromini, and Jacob Browne for comments on an earlier version of this paper.

IV

The War

22
A New Civil War?

COREY HORN

In everyone's life, Peter, there's an "it" . . . your wife leaves you, or you get cancer. There's your life before "it" and your life after "it." 9/11 was an "it" of national magnitude. And Stamford . . . is going to be another one.

—IRON MAN, *Amazing Spider-Man*, Volume 1

Does liberty take a backseat to security?

The United States has been relatively secure from foreign enemies throughout history, having fought only one war on domestic soil over 250 years ago. The United States has maintained a strong infrastructure protecting its borders, as well as a strong military to keep the fight overseas, but what happens when the fight is brought to the front door?

We found out early one Tuesday morning, 9/11/2001, a date that Americans will never forget. Two planes were flown directly into the two iconic towers in the heart of New York, sending a message to the world that the United States is not as secure as once believed. As the chaos unfolded in front of the world's eyes, the United States government was faced with a glaring question: how do we prevent this event from happening again? Some turned to the aid of the United Nations. Others, however, looked to strengthen domestic security through surveillance, the basis for what would become the Patriot Act.

Marvel's *Civil War* was written shortly after 9/11/2001. This comic series explored the very issue that the response to the attacks created in American society. A social divide amongst the Marvel characters, specifically between Iron Man and

Captain America, developed as each hero chose the side they believed to be right in the battle of security versus liberty.

To choose who's more in the right, Cap or Iron Man, we must dive into the moment when they were the most divided, and where each of their values is placed on display.

The Background

Civil War opens with a band of young "heroes" attempting to make their big break in crime fighting. In the town of Stamford, Connecticut, these low-level reality TV crime fighters attempt to besiege and detain some of the highest profiled villains in the Marvel universe without any backup. The result is mass destruction as Nitro, a supervillain from the Captain Marvel universe who can transform his body into an implosion, implodes a large area of suburban territory; some of the damage includes houses, playgrounds, and several hundred innocent lives.

This catastrophe creates a division between the government, public, and members of the superhero community. The government wants to begin regulation of superhuman activity by the Registration Act: "Their powers can be as awesome as nuclear weapons . . . Shouldn't they be tested before they're allowed to work in our communities?" (*Civil War*). After the events in Stamford, people began to realize how dangerous their heroes were and what price they had to pay to keep them around.

Over the course of the next few issues, our beloved superhumans take sides. Iron Man leads the charge on the side of registration; he believes that people are imperfect, so proper training as well as checks and balances are necessary if they want to continue to fight. On the other side, against registration, Captain America stands strong and tall. He believes that the identities of the superheroes, as well as the sanctioning of their activities puts the heroes in danger and makes them pawns of forces that may misuse their abilities.

Caught in the middle, attempting to decide which is right and which is wrong, lies Spider-Man. Throughout *Civil War,* Spider-Man is pulled to one side, and then the other. He begins on the side of security, signing the Registration Act and even going as far as revealing his personal identity. Revealing his identity was a difficult decision, since it risks putting his family and friends in danger. Later, after seeing what the side of security entails—namely the risk of his own family and loved ones—Spider-Man switches to the side of liberty but he remains torn in between his decision. There are pros and cons to both sides, but is either one better than the other?

Mr. Stark or Captain Rogers?

People have a "restless desire for power . . . that ceases in death." So said Thomas Hobbes (1588–1679), who in his book, *Leviathan*, speaks about the need for security. For Hobbes, prior to any society, there was a hypothetical state of nature where life was "brutish and short." People fought over resources, land, and their right to live. "During the time men lived without a common Power to keep them all in awe, they are in a condition which is called War; and such a war, as is of every man, against every man . . ." (*Leviathan*). In other words, Hobbes claims that prior to society and formation of governments, people lived in a state where it was all against all, and through society we rose above this state of war.

How do we escape this state of nature, according to Hobbes? We seek security through the social contract, much like how Iron Man sought a political solution to the issues occurring in *Civil War*. In a state of nature there is constant war, but through a social contract we can seek to resolve that conflict by means of diplomacy. For security, we give up some liberties such as our right to punish offenders, in exchange for the ability to live in a relatively safe society.

Sacrificing our liberties is always a hard action to perform. For many philosophers, such as John Stuart Mill (1806–1873), people's liberties should come before almost all else, and government should not infringe, with few exceptions. Mill writes in his book *On Liberty*, that it is ultimately to the benefit of society to give "full freedom to human nature." For Mill, liberty occurs when people are allowed to express their views and flourish in their humanity.

Captain America sees his situation in much the same way as Mill: he believes he should have the full liberty to act when and where he pleases, and no one should be allowed to take that from him. The problem with government, as Mill sees it, is that when it is not checked it tends to overreach and to interfere with private autonomy. Like many philosophers, Mill advocates for the people to run government and be the voice of reason, rather than having government dictate to the people.

Unfortunately, receiving too much liberty can be an issue just as too much government control can lead to an upset populous. This leaves us—the people, just like Spider-Man—in the middle, between feeling secure and being free.

Caught in the Cross Fires

Because of the events that had unfolded and fighting for his identity with Captain America, Spider-Man is torn throughout the series between fighting for justice under secure guidelines and ensuring safety by acknowledging the importance of the Registration Act.

Much like Hobbes's description of our state of nature, the superheroes were running around the country (and world) destroying buildings, private property, and at times taking people's lives. Just like Hobbes, Tony Stark seeks to resolve this issue through a "society" that the Registration Act would create. The piece of legislation would place guidelines on the superheroes, allowing them to work freely within a certain set of rules. However, it would also place strict punishments for any who step out of line. This can be seen later in the comic as the heroes who refuse to register are thrown in a maximum-security prison, where they remain until they register.

Captain America, ever the patriot, refuses on principle to take this view. Captain America truly believes that liberty is the heroes' driving force. As his encounters with Iron Man show, he believes that the government should keep their hands off. He does not trust government officials with the identities of his colleagues. Monitoring the activities that heroes perform would control their everyday lives. In the 2016 *Civil War* movie, he wonders, "What if something bad is happening in another country, but they won't let us go..." His main concern is not about the security of private property, or even all the human bystanders, but he is worried about being able to "save the world" whenever he feels he is needed.

Spider-Man first sides with Tony and defends the Registration Act, but after seeing the prison his counterparts are held in, he switches and sides with Captain America, even giving up his new suit. Unfortunately, it is not as black and white for American citizens in the situation of the Patriot Act. The two arguments most commonly expressed are, "If you are innocent you have nothing to hide," and, "Freedom and the right to privacy are my American rights." These two arguments are what leaves the rest of Americans standing in the road; I want my privacy, but I have nothing to hide. Which should we choose?

Deliberative Democracy Bridges the Gap

One reason this issue manifests itself within our society is because the two sides are talking past one another. Both sides of the argument—security vs. liberty—are valid, but because each side sees themselves as correct they refuse or ignore the other side.

Jürgen Habermas (1929) is a contemporary philosopher whose primary work deals with critical and communicative theory. In other words, his work deals with ways in which there can be an honest, open dialogue among people. In *The Theory of Communicative Action*, Habermas explains that in order for communication to occur, people must come to the table with an open mind and reasons available to everyone. This is essential for the formation of fair laws and constitutions because it leaves no room for selfish bias.

In *Between Facts and Norms*, Habermas introduces the idea of deliberative democracy, which is an open dialogue including as many diverse voices as possible. For Habermas, the plurality of identity is not a problem, but what is an issue is the lack of communication that occurs across the table. This concern is recurring throughout the *Civil War* comic and movie. Iron Man exhibits the role that Habermas advocates: he continually reaches out to Captain America in order to open up a dialogue about their situation. However, Captain America refuses to speak with Tony, instead using his own presuppositions to build a wall between the two.

Are We Moving into Civil War?

Habermas would praise Iron Man for his willingness to open a dialogue with Captain America and criticize the latter for building barriers that restricted talk. Thomas Hobbes relies on society and structure for security. Security—as provided by the Registration Act—is very important to Iron Man after seeing the damage they create while working independently; the Act promotes strict guidelines that would ensure the security of the society in which they live and all those societies with which they might interact.

On the other hand, Captain America is more like John Stuart Mill. They both see liberty as more important than having a government that controls everyday life: liberty left to the individual would promote human flourishing. Captain America believes that heroes left to themselves will promote the most amount of good that is possible.

Spider-Man is left in the middle to choose between security and liberty. On the one hand, the former would ensure less damage and could possibly maximize the most potential for justice and happiness. The latter would allow him to utilize his power in whichever way he saw fit without risking being manipulated by a higher power. Unfortunately for him, because of Captain America's lack of communication, his decision remains in constant struggle.

American citizens are left in a similar limbo. The Patriot Act would ensure high-level safety and security for the country. While the NSA would be sifting through our messages, and listening to our phone calls, we would still be safer from terrorism on domestic soil. On the other hand, as American citizens we have the right to our privacy, and if the government wants the information they are collecting through means of the Patriot Act, we do reserve the right to refuse the data. Unfortunately for those on this side, the government resembles more of a Hobbesian society that would comply with the Patriot Act, but the citizens live in a country that aligns with their hands-off mentality. Just like Iron Man and Captain America, the two sides rarely speak to each other on a similar level and talk past each other often.

This leaves the American citizen stuck in the middle and left to fend off the opinions of both extreme sides. I believe that more open dialogue between the two could result in a higher position that can marry the sides rather than divorce the two.

And yet, with continuous lack of communication between the two sides, our country could devolve into another state of war against ourselves, people versus government, security versus liberty, all out CIVIL WAR.

23

How to War the Marvel Way

Louis Melançon

Comparing two heroes to determine which is better assumes that their differences make one better than the other. Heck, that's kinda the point of this entire volume.

To be fair, in some cases like Steve Roger's hair compared to Tony Stark's mid-1980s perm during the *Armor Wars* the answer is obvious. But that's low-hanging fruit, as technically, even Professor X's hair (or lack of) was superior to Tony's perm. But what about those instances where the difference shows that both really wind up with the fuzzy end of the lollipop? That's what we see in how these two approach fighting.

Right away we can see a similarity between Captain America and Iron Man. They both seem to be hard-wired to resolve problems with their fists. Yes, there are some efforts to negotiate or come up with non-violent solutions to problems, but these are pretty half-assed. Efforts to defuse situations prior to a rousing bout of fisticuffs are just a formality. So it really should not be so surprising to us that each wound up on the opposite side of the Civil War.

What's interesting here is not that they fight, but how they approach fighting. Both Captain America and Iron Man embody and become avatars for different facets of a longstanding debate about war. By analyzing the different approaches to war, we can understand how each of these heroes embodies this debate and even reflects certain American attitudes about war. Of course, an underlying theme of this volume is that with their differences, one of these heroes must be better than the other. Spoiler alert: What we're going to find out is that despite the differences, both sides of the debate are on the losing side.

A Taxing Taxonomy

I'm about to take a pretty controversial stand (not really) among comic nerds: *Civil War* is perhaps one of the greatest comic events ever, it's a compelling and interesting story done with great artwork and editing . . . But let's take a moment to look at the title itself.

The term "civil war" carries a lot of weight. In just two words, a society is imploding on itself to the point of committing organized violence on its own members. That's a pretty heavy concept. But we need to look a bit broader, so let's drop "civil," take a step back and think for a moment just about this thing called "war"—or organized violence, in a broader sense. War, by itself, sits heavily in human history, whether we're talking the four-color world or the real world. Both of our characters emerged because of war: Steve Rogers fighting the Nazis in World War II and Tony Stark trying to escape from the Viet Cong during the Vietnam conflict.

Let's look at Marvel's Civil War through the eyes of the great military historian Hans Delbrück (1848–1929). Hans, in studying warfare from the ancients up to the modern age, determined that there is a rough taxonomy to warfare: "annihilation" and "attrition" (*The Dawn of Modern Warfare*, pp. 293–95 and pp. 439–444).

In a war of annihilation, we see a state or an army seeking to destroy the military capability of their opponent. There is a desire for a large, decisive battle. If things go well, then at the end of that battle the enemy will be compelled to surrender as they have nothing left with which to fight. The ability of the opposition to generate power is gone in the whirlwind of death and destruction that is the battlefield.

A war of attrition doesn't necessarily need a decisive battle. Oh, there will be battles; there will be bloodshed, death and destruction. But one side is defeated because their ability to resist has been ground down. They can no longer generate power because either the will or capability to fight has just been bled out over time. Of course, it's highly unlikely that a given war is purely based on an attrition or annihilation strategy. Small bits of fighting may be more annihilation-based in a larger attritional conflict, and vice versa.

Socking Ol' Hitler on the Jaw!

This is a good point to bring in our heroes, and let's start with Captain America. Captain America, as mentioned earlier, was born out of World War II: infiltrating into Nazi-occupied territory to thwart plots of the Red Skull, on the first wave at Normandy, always on the front lines as the Allies advanced. What was the logical end point of this behavior? Captain America would reach Berlin and sock old Hitler on the jaw because that's the driver of Nazis.

Yes, Steve Rogers is the embodiment of annihilation war. He goes after the fighting capability of his opponent, using his shield and his fists to punch them out of the fight. This behavior didn't stop with World War II; it continues on into this day. There's an Advanced Idea Mechanics (AIM) facility? Captain America beats the hell out of the scientist guards until inevitably some safeguard fails and the facility explodes or the lava powering it gets out of control and then, the living room floor is REALLY made of lava. Those wacky AIM scientists and their doomsday plans.

Russell Weigley (1930–2004) in his seminal book, *The American Way of War*, considered that this was the predominate strategy that the United States has relied upon since, well, ever. There is the exception of the Revolutionary War, which was generally attritional with flavors of annihilation inside it (side note: "flavors of annihilation" would be the worst Doritos flavor ever). The primary argument here is that the United States, based on the temporary nature of the government, tends to be lacking in larger, enduring grand strategies.

Several historians have pointed out that there are consistent trends within the foreign policy of the US. But a trend is not a grand strategy; while it doesn't necessarily have to be something written down, there should have been conscious decisions made about what policies will be pursued. That is hard to do when there is complete turnover in leadership on a regular basis.

So when the US enters into a war, it is often without the benefit of having a long lead time to contemplate and choose the best possible strategy. Or more accurately, the US enters into conflict without the benefit of having enacted a consistent

set of actions selected to most likely generate a preferred outcome. So the US defaults to the strategy most appropriate to
immediate fighting, which would be annihilation. If you
destroy your enemy's fighting force, how can they continue to
fight? It should lead to a quick termination of conflict. This logical mechanism is buttressed by how, lacking a grand strategy
but being in a conflict, responsibility for formulating a strategy
is given to the military. Of course the military would likely
want to seek to fight its opposite number, the other military, so
that becomes the focus of the strategy. That is what they know
and understand, and an annihilation strategy gives the military the best chance of minimizing their own costs in terms of
lives and budget. Now we are in a feedback loop as the destruction of the fighting capability of the opponent becomes central
to the war effort. The strategy feeds upon itself.

Captain America embodies this type of warfare. He's reflecting, at least according to Weigly, how America behaves in war;
as a nation we don't really think about a larger strategy that
spans beyond a conflict and so just enter into a war with a
focus on stomping out any military capability that the opponent may possess. It's hitting Hydra goons until there aren't
any more Hydra goons.

Just Outspend 'Em

Tony Stark is the opposite side of the strategy coin. If we think
about it, is Iron Man's true power in the suit? Not really. Some
might say the true power is Tony's high level of intelligence as
it concerns science. (I can tell you what it definitely isn't: yes,
I'm referring back to that 1980s perm.) What I'd suggest to you
is that while his intellect is powerful, that isn't the true source
of Iron Man's power. Nor is it whatever the current model of the
suit happens to be. The true power of Iron Man is that bank
account of his. This isn't to say that Tony's intellect isn't a
strong foundational pillar of that bank account, what with all
the patents and such. But like most wealthy Americans he got
rich the old-fashioned way: he inherited it.

Of course, I'm not suggesting that Iron Man uses that power
of the purse literally. He's never grabbed Whiplash and tried to
drown him, Scrooge McDuck style, in a pool filled with money.
The true power of money for Iron Man is that he can simply

outspend his opponents. Spend the money to build that new suit. Spend the money to maintain all the other suits. Spend the money to have all suits be controlled by an AI and swamp M.O.D.O.K. under the weight of too many targets and too much metal dropping on top of him.

This is attrition. Tony Stark really fights his opponents by simply overwhelming them at a point where they can't recover. They invent a new weapon? He invents a new counter weapon and can spend the money to build a new Iron Man suit around it if he desires. Which means his opponents have to spend more money to either counter his counter or attack him in a new way. And he'll just do the same thing again. Eventually, one side's pocket books will run dry. Or at least the will to keep spending at such a rate will run out.

Though there have been some exceptions, like the "anaconda plan" proposed by General Scott at the start of the US Civil War, America doesn't really rely on this strategy in the wider sense. It happens inside annihilation strategies, like World War II's emphasis on pushing volumes of Sherman tanks into the field against stronger Nazi tanks. Seeking to destroy the Wehrmacht, the aim of the effort, and doing that through pure numbers is attrition nested within annihilation. But let's take another look at those suits and how they also reflect a unique American treatment of war.

Those Fabulous Toys

Of course, there's another argument, pushed by thinkers such as Thomas Mahnken, out there about how America wages war that doesn't push back on the attrition-annihilation taxonomy, but rather builds on it. This argument is about an American reliance on technology in war fighting. Well, reliance may be too soft of a word. Many would call it an obsession with technology, and it's an obsession based on a societal desire to avoid some of the realities of conflict. Both attrition and annihilation strategies are dirty and bloody. Destruction and death occur in vast quantities regardless of the strategy a state or actor chooses to pursue. In annihilation, the premise is that this violence should be condensed into a short, but highly active time frame. In attrition, the level of violence may not reach the same crescendo, but occurs over a long duration. This is a reality of war; it is organized violence whose currency is the blood and lives of humans and the destruction of property. But in some circles, there is always the hope that technology can take away some of that unpleasantness.

Technology has always been a key driver in warfare, because getting a better or more efficient way to deal out that death and destruction on others before they can do it to you improves your chances of at least surviving, if not winning. If my sword is longer than yours, I can stab you first. If I have a bow and arrow while you have a sword, I can stand hundreds of feet away and fill your body with arrows. But in America, especially in the final half of the twentieth and into the twenty-first centuries there has been another trend: the use of technology beyond battlefield advantage as a prophylactic from the blood and destruction of the battlefield. This has manifested itself in a variety of ways, such as news broadcasters airing videogame-like footage of camera feeds from bombs barreling into targets or drones firing missiles with the pilots sitting halfway around the world and going home to their families at the end of their shifts. Technology, it is suggested, can reduce or eliminate—at least on the American side—all that blood and dirt of warfare. It can make it "clean" and so less costly in terms of human life. This new American way of war is not so much about leaving attrition or annihilation behind, but sanitizing them on a wave of innovation and technology.

Sound like any comic book characters you may know? Really, it's both of them: the super soldier experiment is a great example of how this hope for technology is to make the annihilation fight a bit cleaner. If the serum and the vita-rays can make one soldier fight like a hundred soldiers, then with just a handful we could liberate Europe! Technology doesn't change the annihilation strategy, just offers to polish it up, make it less costly, at least in terms of American lives put at risk.

And there's also a certain weapons manufacturer: Tony really embodies the American love affair with technology in combat. Just as he essentially tries to outspend his opponents, he tries to solve the tactical problems of combat with a new suit outfitted with new and exciting weapons and technology. We can't even call technology a metaphor anymore; it's gone beyond that because when a dirty/bloody fight occurs, the suit not only protects, it isolates. If Fing Fang Foom swallows our billionaire playboy industrialist, he doesn't have to worry about space dragon digestive juices ruining his clothes, just the paint job on the suit. If the rocket boots happen to incinerate a Hydra minion as he takes off, it's no worry to Iron Man, as he's shut off from the outside world by his metal cloak. It's even better if he has a bunch of empty suits fly at and engage an opponent: they'll be overwhelmed and he's somewhere else entirely; perhaps regretting that perm from the 1980s.

If both of our heroes are pursuing this lure of technology within each of their strategies of annihilation or attrition, how can we actually figure out which strategy is superior? The obvious place to measure would be in outcome. Unfortunately, it seems that both of our heroes meet the same result: unending conflict, despite the different paths they take to get there.

The Problem with Endings

While each of our heroes prefers a different way to fight, they both have a significant problem in that they can't resolve conflict. We need to quickly make another set of distinctions between conflict terminating and conflict resolving. A conflict can be terminated, in the way Nick Fury terminated his conflict with Baron Strucker: a bullet to the head (*Secret Warriors* 27). But that doesn't mean the conflict is resolved. SHIELD and Hydra are still going at it. For a conflict to be resolved, the matter at the root of the conflict must be settled in some form or fashion. This is much harder to do.

It would be useful to put this in some concrete terms rather than just dipping about in abstraction. Before the Civil War between Captain America and Iron Man there was the American Civil War, a little thing that happened between 1861 and 1864. (Maybe you've heard of it?) The cause of the war, the root issue, was about slavery and the rights of African-Americans to not be owned by others. Yes, some push a narrative about "state's rights," but the right they were fighting for was to own people, a defense of slavery. By issuing the Emancipation Proclamation and having his generals kill thousands upon thousands of confederate soldiers, Abraham Lincoln was able to terminate the conflict and take the core root issue off the table. But I'd suggest the conflict was not fully resolved. To this day, there are several states who have incorporated the treasonous symbol that is the confederate flag into their own state flag, a reminder about how disloyal their forbearers were to American values. It's a symbol used by racist organizations and individuals as they carry out acts of hate against minorities. The core issue of the American Civil War was only partially resolved: though the American south complied with the notion of not owning other humans, the animus simply shifted to anger at African-Americans and other minorities, rather than the recognition and acknowledgment that such positions were morally wrong.

There are dozens of other cases of conflict termination without resolution: did the hard terms of Versailles in 1919 lead to the rise of Hitler? Perhaps. Did the coalition which fought the First Gulf War truly resolve the animus between Kuwait and Iraq? Not really. The point is, resolution is hard. Termination isn't necessarily easy, but it's a lot easier to determine how and when to terminate a conflict than it is to resolve a conflict.

Let's go back to Cap. The problem with the annihilation strategy is that it assumes your opponent has a fixed source of power, a source that you can engage with, eliminate, and so defeat the opponent. So for Cap to be able to defeat, say, Hydra, there would need to be a single point of power that if Cap could disrupt or somehow destroy, would mean that Hydra would no longer be able to pursue new nefarious plots. Is this source of power the hordes of Hydra foot soldiers? Cap has certainly knocked down lots of them. But let's think about their slogan, "Cut off one head, two more replace it." That's not this needed source of power. Would it be the leadership like Baron Strucker or Madame Hydra? What about Kraken or Gorgon? Seems that just like the foot soldiers, there's always someone else ready to assume organizational leadership, so that's not it either.

Iron Man's technology-loaded attrition doesn't appear to have much more success. Though the lure of technology is strong, it has never appeared to really help in the long term termination of conflicts with, say, AIM or the Mandarin. The same problems that Cap had in terminating the conflicts apply here as well: whichever strategy Iron Man takes, his opponents can yield to the pressure, move in a new direction, and continue the conflict.

Though this volume is supposed to identify a point of supe-riority between these heroes, in terms of the strategy they use to fight there is no clear victory in comparison. That's not with-out a bit of irony, as neither of them seems to be able to actu-ally successfully terminate their conflicts. Both are stuck in patterns of behavior that don't lead to true conflict resolution, even less the easier goal of conflict termination.

They're trapped in their own perpetual states of violence and war, a pretty sad condition for heroes who are supposed to represent the best of us: our ability to innovate or just do the right thing no matter the situation. More importantly, this can cause us to reflect whether this is how we want our society to interact with the rest of the world: trapped in never ending wars of our own creation, or looking for new ways to achieve actual conflict resolution.

24
Aftermath

STEPHEN FALLER

A massive explosion. A huge red fireball billowing black smoke. Concussive forces that rattle the chest and deafen the ears. And it is resounding. Time itself is fractured like shattered glass and the moment drags on forever. A wailing siren in the distance. And a mushroom cloud.

That's usually how these things begin.

The set-up for *Captain America: Civil War* is no different. The movie centers on a terrorist action with Crossbones as the mastermind. The heroes prevail, but the victory is Pyrrhic and the innocent casualties of war prove that life will never be perfectly safe, not even for our perfect heroes.

It's important to take a step back for a second and zoom out past the wide-angle lens, past the theater of battle, and past the movie theater itself. Because the movie *Civil War* is an adaptation of the 2006 comic book, and the comic starts the same way. Good guys fight bad guys, and a bad guy explodes, and innocent people die. In the comics, the response is the Superhero Registration Act. In the movies, it's the Sokovia Accords, and both mean third-party oversight of super-powered persons. A disaster happens, and responsible people have to make responsible choices.

And whether it's the Superhero Registration Act or the Sokovia Accords, both of these fictional devices point to something else, something very real: *Civil War* is how Marvel Comics decided to explore 9/11 and especially the aftermath of 9/11. Like

George Orwell and *Animal Farm*, Marvel Comics used its most popular characters to reflect the sentinel event of our time.

But Civil War isn't a disaster movie. We've had plenty of those, and it's not as simple as putting a human face on the reality of weapons of mass destruction. The story doesn't stop with Crossbones or 9/11—no, that's where it starts. It's about the aftermath, about what has happened to us, to our ideals, to our democracy, and to Captain American and to Iron Man.

The Unbreakable Shield Against the Unstoppable ARC Reactor

This is what it's all about. This movie was such a box office blockbuster because that's what people wanted to see. Like Helmut Zemo himself, moviegoers felt compelled to pit these heroes against each other. And this is why the movie never could have ended with the airport fight, because there will be no theatric satisfaction until these two titans go man to man, toe to toe.

But why? Unless we have a villainous vendetta worthy of Zemo himself, it doesn't make sense. Why do we want to see these guys slug it out? Why do we want see these heroes destroy each other? What does their fight say about who we are?

The fight between Cap and Iron Man is a visual expression of something we have felt for fifteen years, and something that had been working its way to the surface decades before.

Steve Rogers represents the idea of the Blue Dog Democrat. He's the sort of a blue-collar union guy who's also been in the military. He understands the little guy and is enough of a patriot to serve Uncle Sam. Almost conservative enough to connect with every fan. But push comes to shove, and ol' Cap leans forward and to the left. Cap's defining virtue is "The Good"—he believes in goodness and justice. There's no justice in trying to punish Bucky for things Bucky was forced to do. So Cap is going to remain loyal to his friend, and stand by what he knows is good in his heart even if it means "being outside the law on this one."

Tony Stark is a different kind of guy. He's a neoconservative type with libertarian leanings. Mom and Dad may have been Blue Blood Republicans, but Tony is not so conservative that he's above having fun himself. He's an open-minded and creative guy, but his politics are definitely right of center. It's this balance that makes him a pragmatic futurist. Iron Man's defining virtue is "Truth." Tony believes in hard truths, even the hard truth that if the Avengers have absolutely no oversight whatsoever, then these heroes run the risk of being just as destructive as the bad guys. And he wants to fix what is broken, either with a new armor or a new law like the Sokovia Accords or the Superhero Registration Act (or even Bush's Patriot Act). Republicans believe in the "rule of law."

It begins to make sense. When we see their fight, we start to recognize what has been all around us. Red versus blue, blue versus red. That's why we want to see these two fight: they are fighting the very battle that has marked and marred our cultural political landscape. You could say it's the ultimate depiction of "red" America versus "blue" America.

This is why Iron Man and Captain America have teams. Cinematic allegory, this is about something much larger than these two. This is about something that is polarizing our whole society. And here is the real reason why *Civil War* was so much more successful than *Batman v Superman*: the fight between Tony and Steve is the fight that matters to us. It's the great ideological war of our time.

Does that mean *Civil War* is about 9/11? Almost. We even hear Vision echoing many of the academic arguments we all heard about 9/11: maybe the US caused 9/11 because it was too strong as an unchallenged superpower like the Avengers and superpowered people. Rather, *Civil War* is about what 9/11 and its aftermath has revealed about us and our collective soul. For the last four presidential elections our country has held a point-of-view polarized by ideological extremism. And several of those elections were decided by a margin of victory that was smaller than the popular vote. It is between the red and the blue where we find our great civil war, our talk of secession and dualism, and our national divide.

But if this really isn't about 9/11, any more than the movie is about Crossbones' terrorism, where can we turn for philosophical understanding? We turn to Socrates.

Captain America, Iron Man, and . . . Socrates?

Why do we turn to Socrates to understand the dualism of democracy? Socrates (470–399 B.C.) was the forerunner of philosophy itself. He's usually considered as the starting point in Western thought, where philosophy was born, and people began solving things through rigorous analysis and self-examination. It's Socrates who gave us the sentiment, "The unexamined life is not worth living." But for us today, what Socrates said to a young ethicist named Euthyphro will make a lot of sense out of the *Civil War*.

What we have in the *Civil War* is a showdown between Captain America's defining virtue of "The Good" and Iron Man's defining virtue of "Truth." Greek thought celebrated many virtues, so our first question is, "Why these two?" Why isn't *Civil War* and the great American polarization about the virtues of Beauty and Charity, or Courage and Love?

This is where Socrates comes in. Socrates lived in Athens. Athens is the key, because we have one thing in common with Athens: democracy. For this reason, Athens is an even bigger clue to understand *Civil War* than Socrates himself. Scholars may argue whether Athens is the birthplace of philosophy and Socrates its father, but nobody argues that Athens is the birthplace of democracy, because it was.

What I suggest is this: it is our very democracy that creates this divide between Truth and Good. And because democracy is the very thread of our social fabric, we never, ever saw it coming.

But why does democracy shape our thinking this way? Because democracy is a high-speed intersection between consensus and process. Democracy is the self-rule of people; it's what people vote for and what people want. The consensus is around what most people will agree as being good for them. But for the consensus to work, there has to be some kind of established process to determine the consensus. Who gets to vote? How are the votes counted? How do we know the vote is fair and people don't vote twice? The process is determined by rules, and the rules are established by laws. Democracy is a climate where in a sea full of virtues, Truth and Good will always pop up to the surface, and this makes Socrates the perfect candidate to reveal to us who we are.

So there it is: the great Mason-Dixon behind our cultural civil war. Democrats are on the side of Good. Republicans are on the side of Truth. We'll split hairs later on, because there are plenty of democrats that care about Truth, and plenty of republicans that care about Good (remember Bush and the branding of "compassionate conservative?"), but this is why people on the Left didn't care if Clinton lied during the impeachment trials. Their core value is Good, and on the whole, they like the good things that Clinton was doing. This is also why the Left tends to be enamored with smart and intelligent candidates. When things get morally complicated, you have to be smart to calculate the greater good.

On the flip side, this also reveals why the first George Bush was a one-term president. "Read my lips—no new taxes." The conservative on the Right has a high value around the Truth and an outright political lie won't be tolerated. Truth doesn't require calculation, it is merely recognized.

Readers who recently voted for the first time may have a hard time testing the Truth versus Good theory against their experience. The theory does not demand that every politician and every election is able to embody these dualistic ideals. Politics is a moving target and it constantly changes. But when we look at post-9/11 partisan politics we can identify a distinctive divide. If anything, the election of 2016 was a flat out rejection of the polarized partisanship that marked the fifteen years following 9/11.

This is exactly the cultural context that Socrates was speaking into, and what is highlighted so well in his conversation with Euthyphro. Socrates's student Plato (428–328 B.C.) wrote books about Socrates called "dialogues," and Plato's dialogue *Euthyphro* demonstrates exactly how this democratic dualism operates. *Euthyphro* is one of the earliest dialogues of Plato, and with it, Plato begins to set the stage for why Socrates was executed as a result of a democratic vote. In *Euthyphro*, Socrates is on his way to the Agora, the very place where his trial will be held that will decide his fate. He has been brought up on charges of impiety to the gods and corrupting the youth of Athens with all his philosophical questions. Euthyphro is a young ethicist, a self-proclaimed expert on piety, and a master of deciding what is morally right and wrong. That's handy, figures Socrates, because if he has to go defend his life on trial on the basis of morals and what is right or wrong, what could be more useful than a refresher course in ethics from an expert? Cut to the end—it doesn't turn out so well.

It's As I Said . . . Catastrophe

These are Vision's words to the Scarlet Witch, in the throes of the battle at the airport between team Captain America and team Iron Man. This is just seconds before Vision's vision gets clouded and he accidentally shoots War Machine out of the sky with friendly fire. Rhodey falls and we begin to feel that loss and catastrophe.

But there are many losses that come out of the *Civil War*. The Avengers are divided and broken. People are injured. And we lose our innocence. (Thinking back to the allegory of 9/11, the "Raft" prison is a disguised reference to Guantanamo Bay, and the torture employed by Zemo echoes back to our political debates around waterboarding.) We've been living in a social civil war, and we all know something of Vision's catastrophe. It's the visual expression of this catastrophe that we have wanted to see, and why like Zemo himself, we have wanted to see Cap jam his shield right in the middle of Tony's armor-plated chest. Everyone has chosen sides, and the big question is, "Whose side are you on?"

But why are our political extremes so far apart? Because our social discourse can't contain this, in part, because of the way that those on the political Left and Right talk past each other. They use the same words, but they mean different things entirely—and it's maddening.

Both democrats and republicans have working definitions for Truth and Good, the capstone virtues of democracy. But the words themselves almost mean the opposite thing, depending on who's speaking. It's not like Republicans actually hold the market on Truth, or that Democrats have the patent on Good. No, in such a rigid dualism, both extremes have a concept of both extremes.

For each partisan, the subordinate virtue is defined in terms of the other. Democrats hold their truth dearly, but for them truth is divined by the good that it does. A law is a true law if it does good things for the collective greater good. Republicans hold their good dearly, but for them good is determined by its conformity to the truth and law. A law is a good law, if it abides within the terms and conditions of the greater process, the Constitution.

This *is* the catastrophe. It is for *this very reason* that our society is divided. In the ether of our democracy, we breathe

Truth and Good all day long, and we cannot imagine that those on the other side are looking at the same thing and see something different. And for this reason, when Cap and Tony go at it all day long, we can't look away. We have been in this fight ourselves, and we want to understand it.

The comics had a powerful way of depicting this catastrophe—the story ends with the assassination of Captain America. The very symbol of Americana is shackled and picked off by a sniper on his way to a trial. The death of Captain America is in many ways the death of America herself, the death of democracy.

Which reminds us of another trial—the one for Socrates where he was headed before meeting Euthyphro. Under the guise of looking for last-minute legal advice, Socrates asks Euthyphro about the nature of morality and piety. The more Euthyphro pretends to know, the more it is revealed that he knows nothing at all. Socrates has a nuclear question, kind of like a dirty biological weapon, and its structure rips open the cultural fabric of Athens, perhaps even more than Plato has intended.

In paraphrase he asks, "Are the gods good because there is a higher standard for good, to which even the gods must conform? Or, are the gods good because they are all-powerful, and they have the power to decree that whatever they do is good?" You may not feel the shockwaves, but Athens was never the same.

The conservatives of the day could not tolerate a question like this. Gods that change The Good as a matter of whim don't sound very good or godly at all. That violates the concept of a good god. Except that this is the only option available to them in Socrates's dichotomy. To say otherwise is to say that the gods are not the highest of all, because then even The Good towers above them. That violates the tautology of the gods being all-powerful. Outrage. Blasphemy. Although they are confused by what has happened, they know it doesn't look good and the conservatives are exposed for not understanding the gods as well as they thought.

The liberals fare worse. Yes, they say, the gods conform to The Good. That's an easy answer, until you think it through and hit the corollary. Who gets to decide what The Good is? The liberals do. And they, too, are exposed, but for daring to judge the gods and a significant dose of Promethean hubris.

This is what catastrophe looks like Athens-style. A question like this will get you killed. You criticize both the parties, liberals and conservatives, and democracy votes for death. And philosophy herself lies a casualty.

My Faith's in People, I Guess . . . Individuals

It's shocking that Cap actually pens these words in Tony's letter. Individualism is so often paired in derogatory fashion with "rugged" that few scholars and academics today can scarcely mouth the words. But this core belief connects Cap to Socrates more than anything else. It's Plato who wants to build the perfect government to make the world a safe place. Socrates knows that the battle for hearts and minds is fought in the trenches, even if you have to die for what you believe in. Even if you have to fight man to man.

The word individual literally means that which cannot be divided into dualism. The problem is dualism. Dualism is at the heart of *Civil War* and the answer lies in cultivating the soul of the individual. And dualism is overcome with transcendence. I explore this, a lot, in my upcoming book *Christianity and the Art of Wheelchair Maintenance*, which is a response to its namesake *Zen and the Art of Motorcycle Maintenance*.

In the comics, the path of nondualism is given to Spider-Man. Spidey's journey into the conflict matches ours. His opinions change over time as he sees both sides and he's torn by the conflict. Initially he is persuaded by Stark's arguments for safety, but he later sides with Cap. What good is safety when it destroys everything that is good? His moment of transcendence is marked by the disclosure of his secret identity to the world.

In the movies, this hero's journey is given to Black Panther. He stands above the final showdown between Steve and Tony, and he becomes aware of everything that has happened and why it has happened. He understands. The might be the most important thing about his character: he understands as we have wanted to. In that awareness, he makes a new choice and decides to transcend vengeance by saving the life of the man he has been trying to kill. He puts down hatred and personal vengeance for the sake of social justice.

In *Euthyphro*, transcendence is given a different form. Remember Socrates's explosive question? The liberals were shown be heretical, because they like to sit back and judge the gods. The conservatives were exposed to be blasphemous because they had acted like they understood the gods perfectly and they ruled that way—except it was revealed that they understood very little. All of this is underscored by the fact that the man on trial is being brought up on charges of impiety, on bad ethics. But in this courtroom full of heretics, there was only one man who was not blasphemous.

Who?

The one asking the question: Socrates, himself.

Like freedom, let philosophy ring. For only when her questions are true can we step beyond our polarized thinking. Truth and Good are real, we know this at our core and these are great things to love about Iron Man and Captain America. But dualism is no way to hold these virtues. Only by transcending this false dichotomy can we find a way to have both in our society. Only then do we transcend binary thinking and find the courage to be our most heroic.

References

Adorno, Theodor W., and Max Horkheimer. 2002. *Dialectic of Enlightenment*. Stanford University Press.

Alwan, Wes. 2012. MacIntyre and the Morality of Patriotism. <www.partiallyexaminedlife.com/2012/07/04/macintyre-and-the-morality-of-patriotism>.

Aquinas, Thomas. 1981. *The Summa Theologica of St. Thomas Aquinas*. Five volumes. Christian Classics.

Aristotle. 1999. *Nicomachean Ethics*. Hackett.

———. 2011. *The Eudemian Ethics*. Oxford University Press.

Bemporad, Jack, John Pawlikowski, and Joseph Sievers, eds. 2000. *Good and Evil After Auschwitz: Ethical Implications for Today*. Ktav.

Bodin, Jean. 2009. *On Sovereignty: Six Books of the Commonwealth*. Seven Treasures.

Camus, Albert. 1991 [1942]. *The Myth of Sisyphus and Other Essays*. Vintage.

Cicero, Marcus Tullius. 1997. *Treatises on Friendship and Old Age*. Pantianos.

Clark, Andy. 2008. *Supersizing the Mind: Embodiment, Action, and Cognitive Extension*. Oxford University Press.

Clark, Andy, and David Chalmers. 1998. The Extended Mind. *Analysis* 58.

Darwall, Stephen L. 1977. Two Kinds of Respect. *Ethics* 88:1 (October).

Delbrück, Hans. 1990. *The Dawn of Modern Warfare*. Volume 4. University of Nebraska Press.

Derrida, Jacques. 1997. Politics and Friendship. Interview transcript. University of Sussex <http://hydra.humanities.uci.edu/derrida/pol+fr.html>.

———. 2000. *The Politics of Friendship*. Verso.

Ford, Martin. 2016. *Rise of the Robots: Technology and the Threat of a Jobless Future.* Basic Books.

Greene, Richard, and Rachel Robison-Greene. 2015. *Girls and Philosophy: This Book Isn't a Metaphor for Anything.* Open Court.

Habermas, Jürgen. 1996. The European Nation State: Its Achievements and Its Limitations. On the Past and Future of Sovereignty and Citizenship. *Ratio Juris* 9:2.

———. 1998. *Between Facts and Norms: Contributions to a Discourse Theory of Law and Democracy.* MIT Press.

———. 2001. *Moral Consciousness and Communicative Action.* MIT Press.

Heidegger, Martin. 1977. *The Question Concerning Technology.* Harper and Row.

Hobbes, Thomas. 1968 [1651]. *Leviathan.* Penguin.

Hume, David. 1999. *Writings on Religion.* Open Court.

Hamilton, Alexander, James Madison, and John Jay. 2014 [1788]. *The Federalist Papers.* Dover.

Kant Immanuel. 1997. *Lectures on Ethics.* Cambridge University Press.

———. 2009 [1785]. *Groundwork for the Metaphysics of Morals.* Harper.

Kierkegaard, Søren. 1983. *Fear and Trembling.* Princeton University Press.

Lee, Stan, Jack Kirby, and Frank Giacoia. 1965. The Origin of Captain America! *Tales of Suspense* 63 (March).

Lepore, Jill. 2014. *The Secret History of Wonder Woman.* Knopf.

Locke , John. 2013 [1689]. *Second Treatise of Government.* Hackett.

Link, Godehard. 2004. *One Hundred Years of Russell's Paradox.* De Gruyter.

Logan, Robert K. 2007. *The Extended Mind: The Emergence of Language, the Human Mind, and Culture.* University of Toronto Press.

Lucretius. 1999. *On the Nature of Things.* Oxford University Press.

Mahnken, Thomas G. 2010. *Technology and the American Way of War since 1945.* Columbia University Press.

Marcuse, Herbert. 1991 [1964]. *One-Dimensional Man: Studies in the Ideology of Advanced Industrial Society.* Beacon.

McLeod, Carolyn. 2015. Trust. *Stanford Encyclopedia of Philosophy* <https://plato.stanford.edu/archives/fall2015/entries/trust>.

Michaud, Nicolas, ed. 2015. *Adventure Time and Philosophy: The Handbook for Heroes.* Open Court.

———, ed. 2016. *Batman, Superman, and Philosophy: Badass or Boyscout?* Open Court.

Mill, John Stuart. 1978 [1859]. *On Liberty.* Hackett.

Neiman, Susan. 2002. *Evil in Modern Thought: An Alternative History of Philosophy.* Princeton University Press.

————. 2011. What It All Means. *The New York Times* (January 20th).

————. 2012. Victims and Heroes. In Mark Matheson, ed., *The Tanner Lectures on Human Values*. University of Utah Press,

Nietzsche, Friedrich. 1990. *The Twilight of the Idols and the Anti-Christ*. Penguin.

————. 1996. *Human, All Too Human*. Cambridge University Press.

————. 1996. Selected Letters of Friedrich Nietzsche. Hackett.

Nussbaum, Martha C. 2001. Can Patriotism Be Compassionate? *The Nation* (November 29th).

Peperzak, Adriaan T. 2013. *Trust: Who or What Might Support Us?* Fordham University Press.

Pollefeyt, Didier. 2000. The Morality of Auschwitz? A Critical Confrontation with Peter Hass's Ethical Interpretation of the Holocaust. In Bemporad, Pawlikowski, and Sievers 2000.

Russell, Bertrand. 1993 [1919]. *Introduction to Mathematical Philosophy*. Routledge.

Schelling, T.C. 1961. Dispersal, Deterrence, and Damage. *Operations Research* 9:3 (May–June).

Scruton, Roger. 2014 [1980]. *The Meaning of Conservatism*. St. Augustine's Press.

Smith, Adam. 2003 [1776]. *The Wealth of Nations*. Bantam.

————. 2010 [1759]. *The Theory of Moral Sentiments*. Penguin.

Weigley, Russell Frank. 1977. *The American Way of War: A History of United States Military Strategy and Policy*. Indiana University Press.

West, Darrell M. 2018. *The Future of Work: Robots, AI, and Automation*. Brookings Institution Press.

White, Mark D. 2016. *A Philosopher Reads . . . Marvel Comics' Civil War: Exploring the Moral Judgment of Captain America, Iron Man, and Spider-Man*. Ockham.

Author Bios

JOHN ALTMANN is an independent scholar in philosophy who was an ethics consultant on the Super Soldier project. He told the doctors he thought the experiments violated Kant's second Categorical Imperative, but they all looked at him confused and continued working.

ADAM BARKMAN is Professor of Philosophy and Chair of the Philosophy Department at Redeemer University College. He has authored or co-edited eleven books, most recently *A Critical Companion to James Cameron* (2018). He's proud to say that in every one of his kids' bedrooms there are more than two superhero posters hanging on the wall at any given time.

FERNANDO GABRIEL PAGNONI BERNS teaches philosophy in the Facultad de Filosofia y Letras, Universidad de Buenos Aires. He has written many articles on popular culture, in such compilations as *Horrors of War: The Undead on the Battlefield* (2015), *For His Eyes Only: The Women of James Bond* (2015), *To See the Saw Movies: Essays on Torture Porn and Post-9/11 Horror* (2013), and *American Horror Story and Philosophy: Life Is But a Nightmare* (2018). He is now writing a book about the Spanish TV horror series, *Historias para no Dormir*.

NATHAN BOSMA is an independent scholar who enjoys writing about philosophy and technology. Nevertheless, he's on Team Cap.

COLE BOWMAN is a writer and independent scholar based out of Portland, Oregon. She's contributed to several other Popular Culture and Philosophy titles, including *Deadpool and Philosophy: My Common Sense Is Tingling* (2017), *The Ultimate Walking Dead and*

Philosophy: Hungry for More (2016), and *Dracula and Philosophy: Dying to Know* (2015). While writing is her day job, Cole spends her nights attempting to assemble a team of renegade superheroes, much like Captain America. Feel free to contact her if you have any leads.

MATTHEW BRAKE spends most of his time piecing together adjunct work from George Mason University, Virginia International University, and William Seymour College. When he isn't doing that, he contributes chapters to whomever he can trick into accepting his work. Past victims include *American Horror Story and Philosophy: Life Is But a Nightmare* (2018), *Mr. Robot and Philosophy: Beyond Good and Evil Corp* (2017), and *Deadpool and Philosophy: My Common Sense Is Tingling* (2017). He's also editor of the forthcoming series Theology and Pop Culture, and he writes about theology and pop culture at his blog, <www.popularcultureandtheology.com>.

GERALD BROWNING is a father (and comic book nerd) who loves to instill the values of the superheroes into his sons. He is a teacher of writing whose Herculean efforts to show the importance of the Oxford comma are in vain. He teaches at Muskegon Community College and Grace Bible College. His book *Demon in My Head* is available on Amazon (promotional plug over).

CHARLENE ELSBY is the director of the philosophy program at Purdue Fort Wayne. Her areas of expertise are ancient philosophy and phenomenology. She has co-edited *Amy Schumer and Philosophy: Brainwreck!* (2018) as well as written many chapters for Popular Culture and Philosophy volumes. She knows that Aristotle would have regarded Captain America as virtuous, whereas Tony Stark would have been just another dude trying to sell his wares in the agora.

ARON ERICSON is a graduate student in philosophy at Uppsala University. He notes that "Iron Man vs Captain America" is an anagram of "Aron vs. a cinematic man pair." He doesn't like his odds, but thinks it will be good for the boys to bond over a common enemy.

JEFFREY A. EWING is a doctoral candidate in Sociology from the University of Oregon now living in LA. He's been spending his time writing a Marxist critique of Thanos's Malthusian plan for the universe. It needs only a few extra months to be complete, and then . . . wait . . . Oh no! [*dissolves into ash and floats away*].

STEPHEN FALLER is alive and somewhere in New Jersey. By day he teaches chaplaincy and by night he's an evil genius to put Zemo to shame. Although he has written about *Beyond the Matrix, Reality TV, Iron Man and Philosophy,* and most recently *Christianity and the Art of Wheelchair Maintenance*, his most current project has mistakenly landed him in the Affinity War instead of the Infinity War, armed only with weapons of unconditional positive regard.

MAX HENDERSON-616 accidentally got his PhD in Physics while he was searching for radioactive super-spiders. After spending three years in New York, he decided to move to Philadelphia (less competition if he ever gets powers).

JAMES D. HOLT teaches Religious Education in Chester, England. He lives his life trying to emulate the characteristics of Steve Rogers—without the super strength and cool shield. His wife and four wonderful children give him all the strength that he needs.

COREY HORN is a graduate student seeking an MA in History at Eastern Washington University. He spends his time running a public philosophy coalition in Spokane, Washington, that uses popular culture to reach a wider audience. When he's not doing this, he is advocating for Tony Stark's superhero status, and attempting to show that Captain America is beneath him in the hierarchy of heros.

STEVE INSOOKS is definitely not a genius playboy billionaire philanthropist who just bought out the publisher to stop them from slandering his good name.

CHRISTOPHER KETCHAM: If you wish to speak to God press one; Christ, two. If you wish to speak to Thomas Aquinas, press three. For Iron Man, press four. For Captain America, press four. For all other calls please hold for the author . . . Chris earned his doctorate at the University of Texas at Austin. He teaches business and ethics for the University of Houston Downtown. His research interests are risk management, applied ethics, social justice, and East-West comparative philosophy. He has done recent work in the philosophical ideas of forgiveness, Emmanuel Levinas's responsibility, and Gabriel Marcel's spirit of abstraction . . . The wait time is 4,234,987,456,772 hours and thirty-seven minutes. Have a nice day. Fade to Gregorian chant mood music.

ROB LUZECKY lectures at Purdue Fort Wayne and spends his time lecturing about aesthetics and metaphysics. He co-edited *Amy Schumer and Philosophy: Brainwreck!* (2018). He thinks those who punch Nazis tend to be more heroic than those who attempt to surround the world with a suit of armor.

DANIEL MALLOY teaches philosophy at Aims Community College in Greeley, Colorado. He has published numerous chapters on the intersections of popular culture and philosophy, including contributions on Batman, Superman, Green Lantern, Spider-Man, Iron Man, and the Avengers. Cap once tried to recruit him for the Avengers, but some people are just irredeemable.

TRIP MCCROSSIN teaches in the Philosophy Department at Rutgers University, where he works on, among other things, the nature, history, and legacy of the Enlightenment. Writing about popular culture and philosophy is for him, to paraphrase Stark, "and then, and then, and then . . . you never stop . . . because the truth is you don't want to stop."

LOUIS MELANÇON thinks the Captain America/Iron Man choice is a false dilemma; he picks Doctor Strange because of that snazzy cape! Louis is a US Army officer with a variety of tactical and strategic experiences around the world, has been an Assistant Professor at the National Intelligence University, and a PhD candidate at The George Washington University.

NICOLAS MICHAUD teaches philosophy in Jacksonville, Florida. He's just like Tony Stark, except for the being a genius, billionaire, playboy, philanthropist. Well, Nick has a goatee; it's almost as cool.

CLARA NISLEY finished her MA in philosophy and began writing on pop culture. She has presented at Cons hoping to get others interested in philosophy. She's eagerly waiting for Tony Stark to show up at her next presentation, so she can tell him to go easy on Steve Rogers and recognize that they need each other to fight against the enemies of this world.

CHRISTOPHE POROT is an aspiring philosopher who received his BA from St. Olaf College and has pursued his postgraduate studies at the University of Oxford and Harvard University. He is currently a Dean's Fellow recipient at Harvard and a Managing Editor, along with Dr. Charles Taliaferro, for a series on Philosophy of Religion in the journal *Religious Studies Review*. He has edited for the the Stanford Encyclopedia of Philosophy and the *Ashgate Companion to Theism*, and has published chapters in *Mr. Robot and Philosophy*, *The Limits of Naturalism*, and *Ten Years after Donald Davidson*. His attempts to be a litigator on behalf of Iron Man have failed miserably and now he just borrows Cap's shield every once in a while to protect him from Tony's revenge.

HEIDI SAMUELSON earned a PhD in philosophy in 2012 but has since torn the velvet bands off her uniform, dropped the title of professor, and is currently a nomad writer and editor in Chicago. Her writing strays toward the socio-political and economic. Unlike Tony Stark, she would make a terrible capitalist, and she would probably side with Cap in a civil war, but only if he remained stateless.

Nicol Smith possesses the superpower of masocoffeenation—the more punishment he inflicts upon himself, the more coffee he needs. His favorite form of self-punishment is lecturing on philosophy at the University of Zululand in South Africa. He's not sure whether either team Cap or Shell-head would want him so he is pre-emptively stating that Tony Stark is clearly overcompensating for something and that Captain America needs to start wearing bigger shirts.

Craig Van Pelt teaches sociology in Eugene, Oregon. After saving New York from an alien invasion, Craig would have voted for pizza instead of shwarma. But if Tony Stark was paying then it probably wouldn't matter where the post-alien-invasion-dinner happened.

Eduardo Veteri is a student of philosophy in the Faculty of Philosophy and Letters, University of Buenos Aires. He is currently doing research on dystopian cinema and the movies of Fred Zinnemann.

Jessica Watkins is realizing, more and more, that all of our heroes are not quite perfect. She's not quite sure whether this is a good thing or a bad thing. Like Cap, she wants to be a good friend, and like Iron Man, she wants to change the world. Like them both, she sometimes misses the mark but tries like hell not to.

Index

POPULAR CULTURE AND PHILOSOPHY®
BATMAN, SUPERMAN, AND PHILOSOPHY
BADASS OR BOYSCOUT?
EDITED BY NICOLAS MICHAUD
This book has not been prepared, authorized, or endorsed by the creators or producers of the Batman or Superman comics, movies, or TV shows.

Batman, Superman, and Philosophy

Badass or Boyscout?

Volume 100 in the Open Court series,
POPULAR CULTURE AND PHILOSOPHY

EDITED BY NICOLAS MICHAUD

"Batman or Superman? Which of these shining examples shows us the better way to fight terrorism? Which one is a morally better person? Who's more rational? Who makes a better god? Who's more mentally healthy or are they both irredeemably psychotic?

 Twenty-some philosophers try to decide who wins—Superman or Batman. Some of them give it to Batman, others to Superman, and others make it a tie. They all lay out the evidence so that you can decide.

"This is fascinating stuff! Superman and Batman are the original superhero icons that gave birth to an entire genre. They're two of the most important characters not just in comics, but in all of fiction. Now you can see what makes them tick."

—RON MARZ, legendary comic writer of *Emerald Twilight*, *Green Lantern*, and *Silver Surfer*

"An intense, in-depth analysis of the Dark Knight and the Man of Steel, this book is a must for any fan!"

—MATT MACNABB, Editor of LegionsofGotham.org and author of *Batman's Arsenal: An Encyclopedic Chronicle*

ISBN 978-0-8126-9918-0

AVAILABLE FROM BOOKSTORES AND ONLINE BOOKSELLERS

For more information on Open Court books, go to
www.opencourtbooks.com.